Weather in the City

Sanda Lenzholzer

Weather in the City

How Design Shapes the Urban Climate

nai010 publishers

Table of Contents

Foreword

A city can be mapped. A map to find your way is a different map than a map to study morphology, and a cadastral map is again different from that. A map can also make you see the city in a wholly new light. Forget the space for a moment and try to 'read' the city as an organism in which many complex processes of our industrial society come together. An organism, moreover, where streams flow into, to be processed or influenced and then flow out again, in short: an organism showing all the signs of an active metabolism. The various processes and streams (energy, food, data, cargo, biota et cetera) of this metabolism are of major influence on the functioning of the city. And all of them are, from a designer's perspective, worthy of closer inspection.

Of all streams touching the city, air isn't the most tangible. It is invisible yet can be felt. When the wind plays with your hair, it can momentarily connect you to something bigger than yourself, to the outside world, to the clouds you see drifting in the sky. Every city writes the choreography for an everlasting air-ballet. An ever-changing dance of air movements, all part of what you might call the urban micro-meteorology. The stony city becomes warmer than its surroundings, in extreme cases even by ten degrees. Highway mirages above the heated asphalt are an icon of Summer in the City. The warm city air rises, and the lower air pressure this causes is balanced by the surrounding – hopefully cool – air being sucked in. The topography and shape of a city largely determine the temperature differences between the city and its surroundings. In turn, the proximity and character of these surroundings – Are they green? Is there water? – determine if the air sucked into the city will offer its inhabitants some cooling.

'Large' meteorology works exactly the same way. Air movements between high- and low-pressure areas produce winds of different speeds, from no more than a whisper to raging storms. The layout of the city directs, transforms or blocks these air movements. The city sometimes adds to the sounds of the wind. The deflected, locally blocked and sometimes sped up air can literally howl, roar and whistle in the city. The wind sweeps through the streets and shakes the treetops. The urban choreography not only determines how the air moves, but also what is allowed to dance in the air. The urban metabolism intentionally or unintentionally adds all kinds of substances and other gasses to the passing air. The vapour of cooling installations, the exhaust fumes of cars, the emissions of factories, the carbon dioxide emissions of power stations, the fine dust of all these activities – and smells, lots of smells. Just like water, the air is a medium you can add, mix or dissolve all kinds of things into; but not unlimitedly, not without consequence. City air is liberating, but you have to be able to keep breathing.

In one city, the choreography steers toward a wild, modern ballet in which people are blown off their bicycles when the wind comes from the wrong direction, or a toxic ecology of smog is brewed that is literally breath-taking. Other cities come across as sheltered places or are known for their fresh air, often a successful combination of topography and adequate environmental measures taken in the past.

That a city's topography, structure and layout write the choreography for the air-ballet opens the perspective that we can influence the dancing air and be cowriters of its score. Why wouldn't the administrators, planners and designers of the city be able to influence its use, structure and layout? Naturally, you could only determine the topography position of a city if you were to design a New Town from scratch. Can cities be designed with wind and climate as the starting points? Of course they can! The history of urban development is full of beautiful cities and towns perfectly attuned to their situation and setting in the landscape. Think of fishermen's towns built in such a way that they offer shelter from storms from the prevailing wind directions. Think of ancient China. The oldest document example known to me, from the second century BCE and relating a much older oral tradition, *The Rites of Zhou* provides precise directions on how to build a city. A square consisting of nine quadrants, dissected by nine north-south roads and nine east-west roads, with three gates in all four wind directions, the northern gates always to be closed. Ideally, mountains would protect the north side of city and a river or another water body could be found south of it. This way, an ideal configuration could be achieved for the Chi (energy) to flow optimally through the city, providing its citizens with wealth and prosperity. You can read references to the later Feng Shui into it and the important role of numerology is clear – each scale prominently features the square and the number nine – but these directions also had practical backgrounds, about the optimal layout of a city based on natural and landscape givens, in other words: considerations of what we would now call the 'urban climate'. I always have to take a moment to let it sink in that at the time the Batavians in Europe hollowed out tree trunks to float down the river Rhine, there was already a guidebook to building cities in China, which, by the way, also covered geography and agriculture, and (indeed) the spatial planning of the entire empire.

For a long time, we have neglected to integrate climate issues in our urban design. Once in a while, scale models of new city districts do get tested in wind tunnels, but this is not standard procedure. More often, it is done afterwards to diagnose and correct failings and problems, for instance when it turns out a building produces the most awful whistles. Also when it comes to heat, we will sooner see scientists monitoring large urban areas than designers paying active attention to possible mitigating measures in the planning stages. In short: we mostly do tests afterwards, but it is no longer in the mind of the designer to mitigate design failures.

We can't keep ignoring the urban climate. The size of our cities and vast urban landscapes creates urban heat island effects, which can make it almost impossible to live in a city or parts of it in the summer, and which can be dangerous to vulnerable groups such as the elderly or infants. This is a relative problem in temperate climates, but more to the south and especially in the tropics, the urban heat island effect is literally a killer. Climate change in combination with unbridled urban expansion adds another dimension to the problem. That it wouldn't be that bad in temperate cities is no reason to ignore the urban climate. And on the European latitudes, let's realize that 2.5 degrees rise in global mean temperature at the end of the century is not an implausible scenario. And that climate models point to Europe as the continent with the most sweeping rises in temperature. Not only can the city be a much more comfortable place to be, but a climatologically well-designed living environment can also be mean the difference between having to place air conditioning everywhere or not, which doesn't only guzzle energy, but also solves the indoor climate problem by exporting it to the outside environment, blowing out all that heated air.

This book is about reviving designs with a focus on the urban climate. About examples of how to do this adequately. About the instruments we have at our disposal. The ancient Chinese were on to a good thing. Feng Shui literally means 'wind' and 'water', and those are also the main elements for optimizing the urban climate. You can steer the wind by optimizing the urban layout and by modelling the shape of buildings, the dimension of squares and the profiles of streets: the shape of the public space. You can cool the warm city air through strategic placement of open areas. In the city or outside of it.

In this day and age, when everything has to be legitimized through cost-benefit analyses, we can say that we are only two handshakes away from hard, economic advantages. A good urban climate adds to the high scores of cities like Vancouver, Copenhagen and Zürich in the charts for 'most liveable cities' in the world. In conclusion: if we manage to write such a choreography for the air-ballet that the resulting urban climate produces a comfortable living climate, we will be rewarded with a thriving business and living climate.

Professor Dirk Sijmons

Acknowledgements

More than 20 years ago, I started researching the topic of urban climate adaptation and soon afterwards I also started teaching students on the topic, which was later supplemented with lifelong learning classes for professionals. A bit later, consultancy for municipalities and other stakeholders followed suit.

I would like to thank all the students, professionals and other people I've had the pleasure of working with for their enthusiasm in this topic!

All these efforts to communicate urban climate science and how to solve urban climate issues made me think that an easily comprehensible and easy-to-use handbook was missing. This nudged me to write the first version of the book, first in Dutch (2013) and not long after also in English (2015).

I would like to thank all the people and funders who made it possible to write and to publish these first editions.

After 10 years that brought new insights in urban climate science and solutions it was time to update this book and create a new edition. I am very grateful to the people and organizations who enabled the new edition of this book.

First of all, I would like to express my gratitude to the main financial contributor, Wageningen University.

I am also very grateful to my colleague Gert-Jan Steeneveld (Wageningen University) for his review of the book and his good suggestions. Last but not least, Monique Jansen, thank you so much for helping me update and prepare new imagery and graphs.

Introduction: Why this Book?

We all experience the urban climate

Have you ever been unable to fall asleep during a sweltering summer night, even though your windows were wide open? Or during a windy autumn day: has the wind ever almost swept you up on a city square? Perhaps you have even been blown off your bicycle at the foot of a tall building? This last thing happened to me when I had just moved to a coastal city in the Netherlands. I remember being very surprised; I did not know wind could be *that* strong. But I did not yet connect it to the phenomena of the weather in the city, or, in technical terms: the urban climate. The heat and strong winds at specific spots are typical phenomena of the urban climate and we all feel it, be it usually unconsciously.

Unfortunately, many of the people involved in the design of cities lacked a more 'active' awareness of the urban climate. I used to be one of those people. When I was working as an urban designer, for instance, I once designed a beautiful, open square, which was constructed precisely as planned. However, after just one 'outdoor' summer season, people started complaining about wind nuisance. Regrettably, the clients, who knew the location very well, and I had not considered the issue of the local wind climate. In the end I had to design matching windscreens for the square, but this solution 'with hindsight' interfered with the open concept of the original design. Had we all thought about the urban climate from the start, none of this would have happened!

Urban climate is becoming an important theme in urban planning and design

These experiences in practice pointed me to the urban climate theme and I soon found out that there was a lot of scientific knowledge about the urban climate. Yet, I also came to realize that those who 'make' the city paid far too little attention to the urban climate and that this significantly reduced the quality of life in cities. When the first version of this book came out in Dutch in 2013, there was a lot of attention from the public and the media; a clear sign that the urban climate theme deserves more attention. After the English version of the book had been issued in 2015, there was even more interest and the book became a 'classic' for practitioners in urban planning and design. It forms a primer for those interested in urban climate and to prepare for the more advanced scientific literature on the matter such as the celebrated book *Urban Climates* by my colleagues T. R. Oke, G. Mills, A. Christen, and J.A. Voogt, (2017).

Also, recent worldwide research on urban climate policies conducted by my 'Climatelier' group shows that this topic is seen as increasingly relevant, especially in the light of global warming. This called for a revised edition of the book that includes the latest insights about urban climate-responsive planning and design from the past ten years. The scientific literature has brought about new and more precise insights about how urban and landscape design interventions influence their microclimatic environment and I have tried to include these. Still, many more studies are needed to gain a deeper understanding of how effective urban and landscape design interventions should be shaped.

Urban climate is not the same as the climate in the countryside

Despite clear scientific evidence of the existence of the phenomena of 'urban climate' and the very rapidly growing number of new studies in the field, we still regularly see that planners, designers and policymakers ignore this body of knowledge. We have known for quite some time that the urban climate has a number of characteristics clearly distinguishing it from the climate of the surrounding landscapes. Due to the impact of buildings and streets, the daily mean air temperature in cities is at least 1 °C higher; usually the difference is even bigger, up to 12 °C at night in summer. This impact also causes the air in cities to have up to 10 per cent lower relative humidity and 30-50 per cent lower wind speeds, but much stronger winds at specific spots. The built environment clearly is of great influence on our cities' climates. Yet, as the recent worldwide study of my research group showed, there is still little awareness of the fact that every intervention in the urban tissue also means altering the urban climate; and that the urban climate is thus largely 'designed' by those who make the city.

Climate change makes urban climate problems worse

The urban climate is of course also affected by global climate change. Generally speaking, there is a clear rise in temperature, in almost all countries on Earth. For instance, the 2019 heatwaves in France, Belgium, UK, Germany and The Netherlands had record-breaking maximum temperatures (in France from previous 44.1 °C to 46.0 °C and The Netherlands from previous 38.6 °C to 40.7 °C). These heatwaves were the deadliest events in 2019 and many people in cities had problems coping with the heat. The past years showed extremely high summer temperatures again and the trend is not turning.

The International Panel for Climate Change (IPCC) observes these developments in climate change and generates different climate change scenarios up to the year 2100. In some countries, the rise in temperature will lead to more droughts, whereas other countries can expect more precipitation and downpours, and sometimes changing wind patterns as well. All these effects have different repercussions in cities in different climate zones. As many cities are situated in temperate climate zones worldwide, this book will focus on urban areas in these climate zones.

In temperate climate zones the most important influence of climate change on the urban climate is its impact on urban temperature regimes.

With temperatures rising in general, the temperatures within cities will rise as well. Global warming thus adds to the already existing urban heat effects. Heatwaves become a much bigger problem for those who live in cities than they already are. These projected effects will negatively affect people's health and productivity, and mortality rates are expected to go up even more than we have seen recently. Apart from potential public health issues due to bad quality of potable water and open water bodies (e.g., algae blooms) and the need for cooling buildings will amplify energy use. To prevent these heat-related problems, we need to act soon and introduce more climate adaptation effects in urban planning.

Renewable energy lessens air pollution

In time, another global change will influence the urban climate: the use of energy. The world's sources of fossil energy will be depleted, and renewable, clean energy sources will have to take their place. Today, the use of fossil energy causes air pollution in many cities. When we use cleaner energy sources in industry, buildings and vehicles air pollution will be reduced (although some particulate sources such as vehicle tyres and breaks will remain). The need to address air pollution issues in urban (re)design would be significantly smaller, and the solutions for air pollution can be addressed more effectively at the source, such as a factory, an individual building or car rather than through an 'end-of-pipe solution' by adjusting the urban environment. Therefore, I have not addressed the theme of air pollution in this book.

Aim of this book

I have written this book to cater for the need for basic urban climate knowledge and for understanding how to design with urban climate. I translate scientific knowledge into useful design knowledge, primarily meant for those working in temperate climate zones. Part of this knowledge comes from my own research, but most of the knowledge derives from the growing scientific body of literature about urban climate. This book has been written for a broad audience in accessible language supported by many visuals. It is structured in a way that responds to planning and design processes: from a basic understanding of the subject matter to ways to analyse cities and sites, to large-scale planning and small-scale design interventions.

Target groups

Being the ones who design the city, we have to be aware of the consequences of our designs on the way people experience the microclimate. This experience is closely related to people's health, but also to the usability and liveability of cities. So, it is important for everyone involved in urban planning and design to know about microclimates and the urban climate, especially in the light of climate change, which has become an obvious fact in the past decade. For large-scale interventions, policymakers and planners at city and regional government bodies should get to work. On smaller scales, the same goes for (future) urban designers, landscape architects and designers of the urban interior and street furniture. It also concerns those who indirectly influence the design of the urban environment, such as managers, developers, and retail and gastronomy organizations, and city branders. The differences in readers' background and knowledge might mean that some of the information shared in this book is already known to part of this broad audience.

Main topics and structure of the book

Knowledge about the urban climate and how it can be influenced through design concerns various scales ranging from small to large, as you can influence the urban climate on all these levels. But before we discuss the urban climate itself, we should clarify our perspective on it: how we humans perceive our microclimatic surroundings, in other words the concept of microclimate experience or thermal perception. This concept has three main aspects, which also determine the structure of this book: physical temperature experience, physical wind experience and psychological aspects of microclimate experience. The pages of this book are colour-coded according to these three aspects for easy navigation: red for temperature, blue for wind and yellow for psychological aspects. After discussing how these factors determine people's experience of microclimates, they can be used to analyse the urban climate. The chapters about analysis and adaptation of the urban climate are similarly structured according to these three aspects. You should always analyse the climate before you start designing for the urban climate. Therefore, this book suggests analysis methods and design solutions for different scale levels. The analyses and solutions work differently on large scales than they do on small scales. Various planning and design instruments can be of influence: from regional structural planning to detailed plans. To cover the larger scale, chapters 3 and 4 concern the planning of the entire city. To cover the small scale, chapters 5 and 6 focus on the urban design interventions, ranging from neighbourhood to details (e.g., street furniture, paving materials). For the micro level a plethora of design solutions exists. To distinguish them according to the readers' typical work fields these are subdivided into five spatial types: the direct environment of buildings, gardens and parks, squares, streets, and parking facilities. This book's structure with its focus on scale and space will be easy to use for everyone who 'makes' the city, thus facilitating the 'design of the urban climate'. The book also contains many illustrations to show how the urban climate works and especially how we can adapt it. I sincerely hope the examples appeal to the imagination of the cities' 'makers' and encourage them to adapt our cities with the urban climate in mind.

1
How We Experience the Microclimate

The microclimatic environment is vital to us human beings, because our physiology only functions well in a relatively small range of temperature and wind circumstances. Physiologists have recently discovered that humans also have special receptors for temperature sensation, so we could even say that the thermal sense is another vital sense next to the five classical senses of sight, touch, hearing, taste, and smell. The fact that temperature is so vital for us as humans requires us to create a comfortable microclimate directly around our body. With this in mind, we choose which clothes to wear and whether we stay indoors or outdoors. When we are outside, we usually opt for a certain microclimatic environment, even if we often do so unwittingly. Depending on our microclimatic need, we choose a sunny or shaded spot or route, in the wind or protected from it. The 'ambiance' also plays a role in our experience of the microclimate, so if we experience a place to be 'warm' or 'cold'. The microclimate experience helps us seek out places beneficial to our physiological and psychological well-being. We can think of these different aspects as pieces of a puzzle supplementing each other to complete the big picture of microclimate experience. For instance, imagine yourself during a warm summer day in two different places: one in the sun, exposed to the wind and one in the shade, protected from wind. You will have the same thermal experience because in the sunny, windy spot the heat impact from the sun is mitigated by the wind and in the shady, calm spot the lack of cooling from the wind mitigates the cooling by the shade. And as you can imagine, an urban designer can influence all these spatial settings where shade occurs and how wind is guided by spatial objects. But we need to know which aspects we can influence through design and which ones we cannot.

The many factors influencing the way people experience the microclimate can be categorized in three clusters (see illustration 1). The first contains the individual physical and physiological factors, such as age, metabolism and clothing. These cannot be influenced through urban design. The second cluster contains the external physical stimuli for people's sensation of temperature and wind (see illustration 2).
A combination of factors influences the temperature sensation. Air temperature and the influence of thermal (longwave) and solar (shortwave) radiation determine thermal sensation to a very large extent (see section 2.1.1). Wind sensation is also very important for the physical microclimate experience. To a lesser extent, the microclimate experience is affected by the air's relative humidity. Especially the temperature and wind sensation can be influenced through design measures. Psychological factors form the third cluster. In part, these can be manipulated through the design of the city as well.

Microclimate experience is mainly influenced by temperature perception, wind and psychological factors

We can make calculations on the physical factors through 'thermal indices'. For indoor spaces, for example, an index based on air

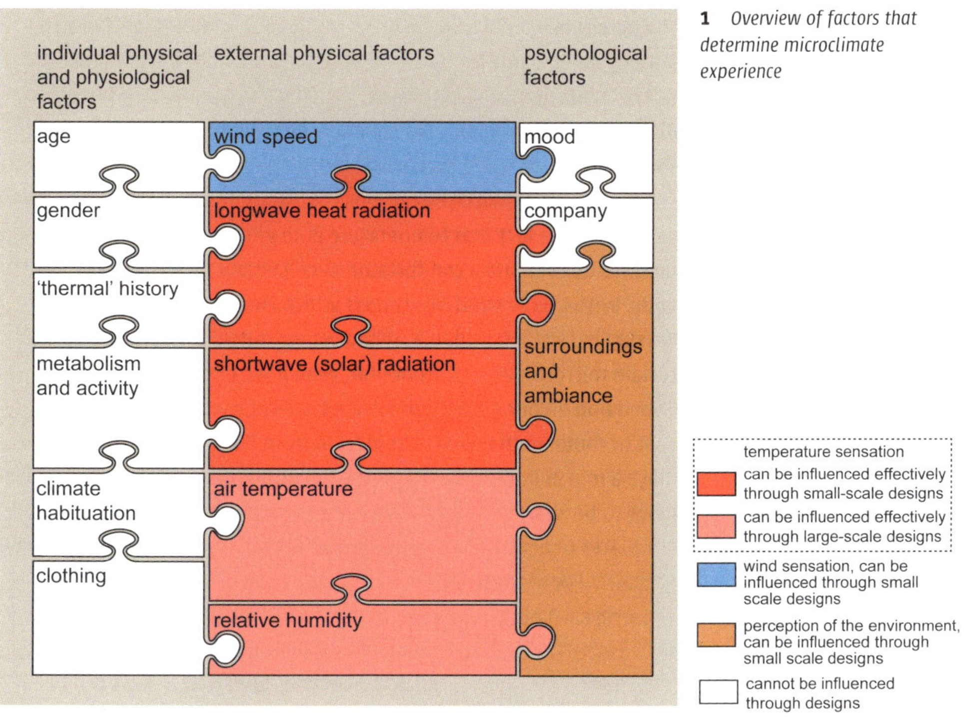

1 *Overview of factors that determine microclimate experience*

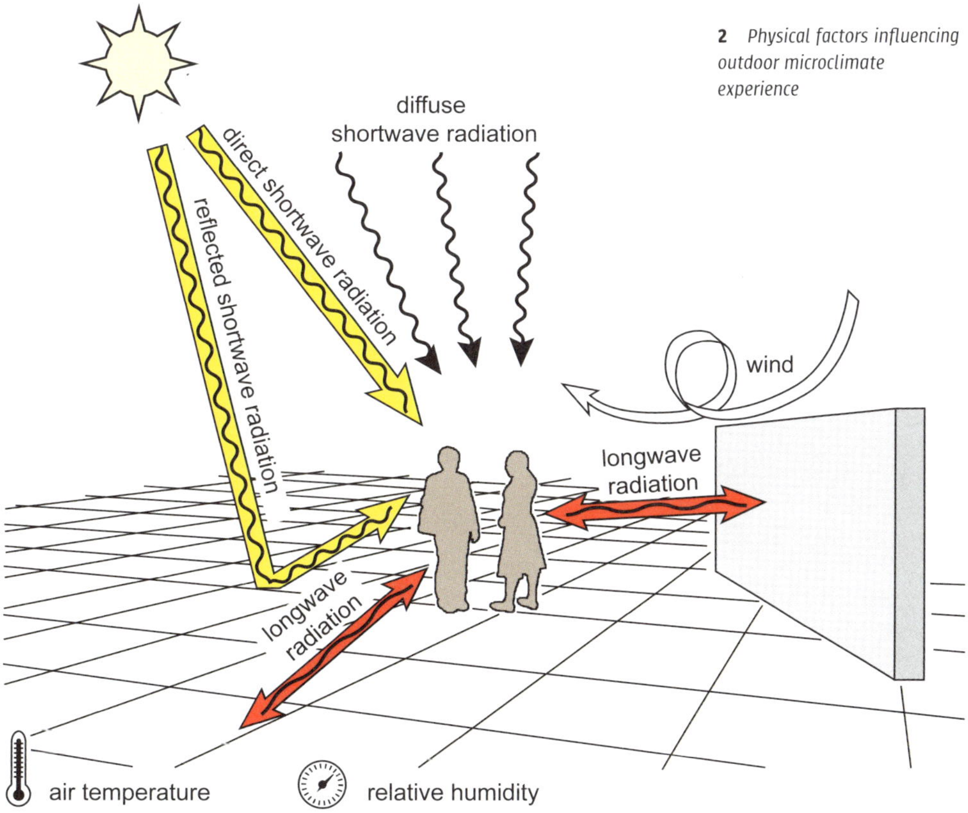

2 *Physical factors influencing outdoor microclimate experience*

temperature and radiation is often used. More complex indices also take air movement, clothing, metabolism and such into account. Two common indices that describe all these factors (air temperature, long- and shortwave radiation, the air's humidity, air movement, clothing, metabolism) are the Physiological Equivalent Temperature (PET) and the Universal Thermal Climate Index (UTCI). Both try to represent how we experience 'temperature' as an agglomeration of these different factors and would express them in common terms like 'cold' or 'warm'. Accordingly, both indices express thermal sensation as a 'temperature' in degrees that are similar to degrees centigrade so we can easily relate to it, but we should always bear in mind that they entail many more aspects than the air temperature alone.

To calculate the microclimate with these indices, you either need extensive measurements or computer simulations, and that is work for experts. To take suitable general urban design decisions, you do not need to use these indices. Those designing for the urban climate should primarily keep the combination of thermal and wind sensation in mind and know that environmental psychological factors can also come into play. The size of the boxes with the influential factors in illustration 1 gives a rough outline of the interaction between these factors (or 'puzzle pieces'), and whether or not they can be influenced through design.

This chapter describes the different factors influencing microclimate experience one by one. First the physical factors air temperature, short- and longwave radiation, relative humidity and wind are explained and subsequently the psychological factors. Urban design can have an effect on all these factors. This chapter also features factors that cannot be manipulated through design.

1.1 Physical Factors of Microclimate Experience

1.1.1 Experience of Temperature

Influence of air temperature

The first and best-known factor often chosen to express temperature sensation is the air temperature, even though more factors play a role, as we can see in illustration 2. On a scale of just a few metres, the air temperature in outdoor areas in cities only changes minimally. It does change during the day, with maximum temperatures in the afternoon and minimum temperatures at night (with a few exceptions). Of course, air temperatures change with the seasons as well. Urban design interventions can have a limited effect on air temperatures on a small scale. For instance, planting one tree in a street will have a minimal effect on the air temperature. Yet, many small measures combined *do* have a great effect, for instance when a city is planted with many new trees, air temperatures will decrease through their shade and evapotranspiration.

Another factor with a very strong influence on thermal sensation is short- and longwave radiation (see section 2.1.1), which can give people a sense of warmth. How we feel short- and longwave radiation should not be confused with the way we experience air temperatures. The differences between these types of temperature experience can clearly be felt in a number of situations. A typical example of our experience of shortwave radiation can be felt outside, when we go from a sunny place with high levels of shortwave solar radiation into the shade. On a small scale of only a few metres, the air temperature between these two spots is not different. But as we all know, the direct radiation of the sun does make the sunny spot and the shaded spot feel very different. We all have experiences with the longwave radiation emitted by materials, for instance when we sit in front of a wall after sunset that had been exposed to the sun over day. Even though the air temperature has come down, our body is warmed by the wall's thermal radiation. This example demonstrates another important aspect of this radiation: its orientation. We can clearly feel the direction the radiation is coming from and the parts of our body exposed to the radiation source are warmed as opposed to those that are not exposed. So shortwave and longwave radiation have a prominent effect on the way we experience temperatures, and spatial measures can make a real difference.

Influence of shortwave solar radiation and longwave thermal radiation

3 *People do not sit on the benches, but squeeze into small, shaded spots*

Influence of relative humidity

The relative humidity also has a slighter influence on the way we experience temperatures. For example, a very high level of atmospheric humidity on a muggy day can have a negative effect on people's microclimate experience. The air is saturated with vapour and can't take up people's sweat. Just like air temperature, relative humidity is quite uniform on small scales and can barely be influenced by spatial measures.

Heat stress

Extreme heat conditions can significantly disturb people's thermo-regulation, and this can have serious consequences. This especially applies to the impact of heat, because heat is much harder to avoid or prevent than cold is, since people can put on warmer clothes when it's cold or stay indoors. For many people heat stress does not only make them feel uncomfortable, but also negatively affects their concentration and labour productivity. We are talking about a decrease in productivity of 10 to 50 per cent for people who do physical work outdoors. This is already a very costly phenomenon for society and will increase due to climate change. Add to this the trouble people have sleeping on hot nights: it takes longer for them to fall asleep, and when they do, their sleep is shorter and not as deep.

Serious heat-related health risks and mortality

For vulnerable groups such as children, elderly people, obese people, people suffering from heart, lung or blood pressure conditions and for pregnant women, heat stress can cause various health problems. Think of heat rash, heat cramps, exhaustion, dehydration, kidney failure and breathing problems. These issues are reflected in the number of people consulting their doctor about heat-related problems or even having to be hospitalized. The heatwaves we've had after the year 2000 resulted in significantly higher mortality rates, especially among vulnerable populations and the elderly. Global average heat-related mortality per year for people older than 65 years has increased by 53.7 per cent between 2000 and 2018, with Europe being most affected (with an excess mortality of more than 104.000 deaths). A short heatwave lasting a couple of days generally leads to a higher mortality rate of 10 to 15 per cent in many countries.

1.1.2 Experience of Wind

Wind chill

The movement of the air, for example draft or wind, is important for how people experience the microclimate as well. When the air moves, it takes up more sweat and heat from the skin than it does when it is still, providing the air temperature is lower than that of the skin, which is usually the case in temperate zones. The faster the air moves, the more heat and sweat it takes up. That is why weather reports in some countries include *wind chill factor* forecasts in addition to temperature forecasts. The direction of the air movement is a factor as well. Body parts directly exposed to the wind cool faster than other parts do. But we do not only feel air movement as a decrease in temperature; we also feel

its force through kinetic energy. There are different degrees of this type of wind effect. We might be uncomfortable at wind speeds of 1 to 4 metres per second (1-3 Beaufort: Light Air – Gentle Breeze), with our hair blowing in the wind and our clothes fluttering. We speak of wind nuisance when speeds reach 4 to 15 metres per second (4-7 Beaufort: Moderate Breeze – Near Gale), because these speeds make it harder to walk or ride a bicycle. Speeds over 15 metres per second (7 and more Beaufort: Gale, Storm, et cetera) are considered dangerous; even walking is very difficult in strong winds like these. Wind speeds of over 20 metres per second will simply blow people over.

4 *How will these girls safely cross this windy square?*

Wind nuisance

1.1.3 Other Physical Factors

A number of factors that play a role in people's thermoregulation are connected to the individual person and his or her activities and behaviour. The way people dress is the first thing that comes to mind. Everyone dresses according to their own ideas – whether these clothing choices are appropriate for the weather conditions or not. Another main individual factor of microclimate experience is physical activity. When we exercise, our metabolism gets a boost and we warm up faster than when we are at rest. A person's 'thermal history' also plays a role. When we step from a hot sauna into frosty air, for example, it will take us a few minutes to feel the cold. Gender and age are also big factors when it comes to individual microclimate experience. Women are more sensitive than men and older people are more sensitive than younger persons. Habituation is yet another factor. People visiting from warmer climates, not used to the winters in northern countries, will feel cold much sooner than locals will.

1.2 Psychological Factors of Microclimate Experience: 'Ambiance'

Influence of ambiance on microclimate experience

Beside the 'hard' physical factors, how we experience our surroundings also has some influence on how we experience the microclimate. Influences such as the 'ambiance' of a place are part of this experience. American scientists did an experiment in the 1980s demonstrating that people's estimate of the temperature in a space differs depending on its ambiance. For this experiment people were placed in a climate chamber, heated to exactly 20 °C. They were asked how they experienced the climate in this room. The first subjects visited the room in its original setting, with a sterile and technical look. Then the climate chamber had a cosy makeover, with carpeting and comfortable furniture. In this setting, subject estimated the air temperature to be much higher, while in fact it was exactly the same.

Influence of expectations and mood on temperature experience

Whether someone is outside alone or with other people also has an effect on the way the microclimate is experienced. Last but not least, the mood someone is in influences this person's experience of the microclimate. These examples show that thermal comfort is not just the result of physical factors, but that much of it is 'in our heads'. So, the 'ambiance' of a place, determined by such things as size, colours and materials, is also part of people's microclimate experience. Creating different 'ambiances' through design can thus make a difference in how the microclimate is perceived.

5 *Enjoying shade and the cooling effect of water evaporation – the grotto behind a waterfall in Sonsbeek park in the Netherlands*

2
Factors Determining the Urban Climate

To design for the urban climate, you need to know about a few basic processes, because virtually every urban design intervention in the spatial layout and use of materials changes the microclimate of an environment. Think of shadow patterns created by built elements or by plants, the heat radiation of building materials, and the way buildings change wind fluxes. This makes each city, and each spot in it with its own spatial configuration, unique. The urban climate and microclimate also change constantly: per day, with each season and because of climate change. Therefore, designers and planners should keep the basic processes of the urban climate in mind and design for specific spots and their temporary climatic dynamics. These dynamics can mean that processes can be a problem in one situation, while they can be beneficial in another. Wind, for instance, can sometimes be a nuisance, while it can bring much needed ventilation in other situations. The complexity of these processes can be an exciting and inspiring planning and design challenge for the 'makers' of the city

As we know from the first chapter, two aspects are vital to the physical part of people's microclimate experience. The first is the sensation of temperature, that is based on air temperature, long- and shortwave radiation. The second aspect is the sensation of wind, based on various effects of air movement. For a considerable part, urban climatic processes determine the sensation of temperature and wind. This chapter is about these influences. Because all air movements are basically the result of differences in temperature, the processes relating to temperature are discussed before those relating to wind. The psychological influences on microclimate experience will be discussed at the end of this chapter.

The urban climate has several factors that apply to different scale levels but are inextricably connected. For example, small-scale microclimatic changes usually only have a very small local effect, like slight changes to the wind's course; but because there are so many buildings and other vertical structures in the city, these effects accumulate, and the city's wind field is ultimately changed. Another example is the addition of vegetation. A few extra trees or green facades does not result in a lower air temperature for the city as a whole, but planting many trees in many places does have such an effect. A typical characteristic of the climate is its volatility, as we can see when we look at the wind. Wind is very chaotic and small changes in the city can bring sudden changes to its course, a typical example of the so-called butterfly effect. These changes come with some uncertainties, but many reasonably predictable flow patterns do actually exist. The most predictable processes of the urban climate belong to the thermal environment: light, shadow and air temperature. You can also make pretty good predictions about the psychological factors influencing microclimate experience that are determined by the 'ambiance' of a space. Because the urban climate factors differ so much in their predictability, I will mainly discuss average conditions and only a few extreme circumstances.

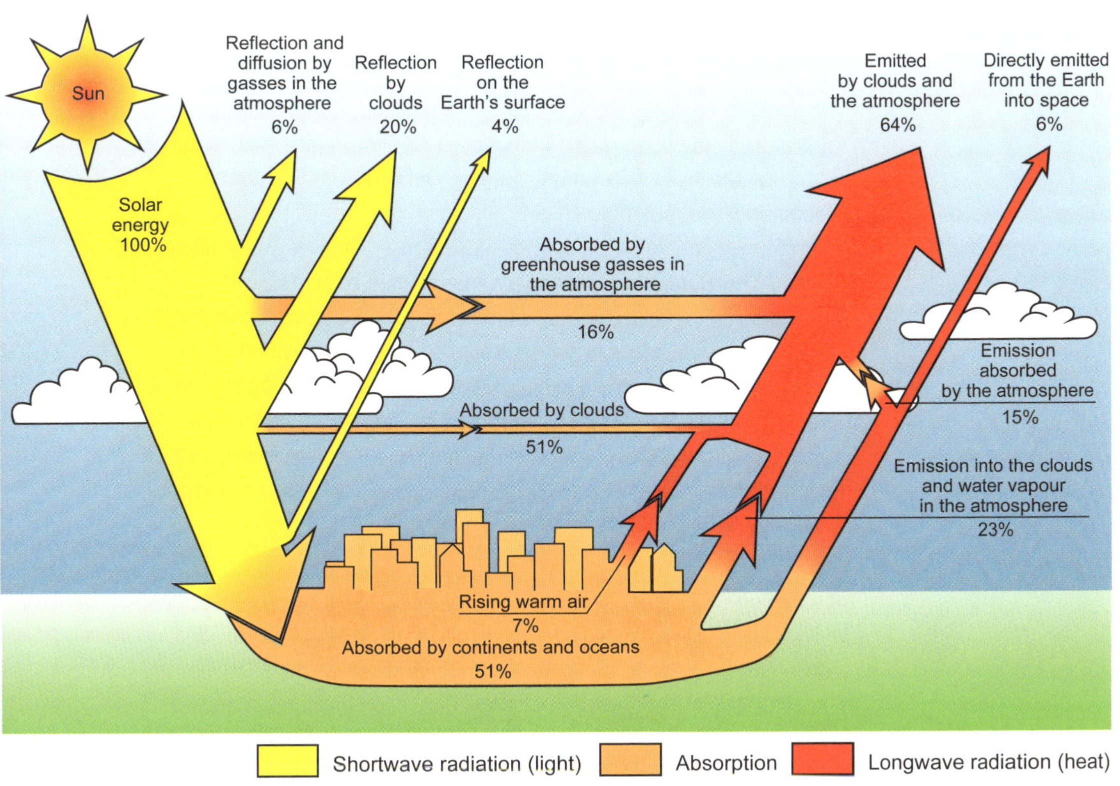

6 *Types of radiation in the atmosphere and at the Earth's surface*

2.1 Urban Structure and Temperature Regimes

The urban structure and its complexity of buildings, roads, green areas, water bodies and relief, as well as human activities such as traffic and industry have a great impact on the local thermal climate, which clearly differs from the climate in rural areas. This urban climate obviously has a significant influence on people's temperature experience. I will now explain which aspects play a role here.

2.1.1 Radiation and Heat

Shortwave solar radiation

The basis of all thermal processes on Earth is the incoming radiation from the sun (see illustration 6). This radiation can appear close to the Earth's surface in several forms, after the outer layer of the atmosphere and the clouds have reflected, scattered or absorbed part of it. As shortwave radiation, it can hit objects on the Earth's surface directly. Dust particles in the atmosphere can absorb or scatter solar radiation (making the radiation more diffuse) and different types of surfaces can reflect it. When the Earth's surfaces or materials on it absorb the shortwave radiation, part of it is usually emitted later as longwave radiation (also called thermal radiation) and this depends on the properties of different materials. Many of these radiation processes are therefore influenced by the structure of the city.

Sun and shadow

Sun and shadow have the greatest effect on the temperature regimes of objects on Earth. On a sunny, cloudless summer day in Central Europe, for example, a horizontal terrain will receive no less than 1000 Watt per square metre at noon. On cloudy days, this may be only 500 Watt per square metre and in a building's shadow a mere 100 Watt remain. So, the effect of shadow on the incoming radiation is enormous. This effect obviously depends on the characteristics of the elements casting the shadow as well. Buildings and other non-transparent objects cast deep shadows. Transparent objects and trees will offer less shade, varying with the density of the foliage.

Sun angles throughout the seasons

The altitude angle of solar rays in relation to the Earth's surface influences the strength of the incoming radiation. This solar altitude angle varies, depending on the location on Earth, the time of year and the hour of the day. Close to the poles, the sun's angle is always lower than at the equator. A lower angle means the incoming energy is spread out over a larger surface, thus creating less warmth per square metre. Illustration 7 shows the solar altitude angle close to the equator, practically at right angles to the Earth's surface. The radiation is divided over a surface at a 1:1 ratio. The solar altitude angle is lower in temperate climate zones. As the illustration shows, the incoming radiation is spread out over a surface that is 1.4 times larger. Close to the poles, the radiation is even spread out over a surface twice as large, causing it to be much colder. The time of year is also an important factor in the altitude angle. This will be explained for a location near the 52nd North latitude, a representative latitude location of many European and North American cities (see illustration 8). On the shortest day of the year in winter, the sun is at its lowest position, and therefore the altitude angle is at its smallest. The sun's path is also at its shortest. It rises more towards the southeast and sets in the southwest, whereas on the longest day, 21st of June, the sun's position is much higher, and its path is much longer. The sun then rises towards the northeast and sets in the northwest. In winter, shadow patterns are longer than in summer and cover much wider areas.

How materials reflect shortwave radiation

Part of the shortwave solar radiation reaching objects is reflected and part of it is absorbed by the object's materials. How much radiation surfaces reflect depends mostly on how light and smooth they are. The lighter and smoother the surface, the more reflection there will be and the radiation will not reach the mass underneath. Hence, the material will absorb less energy. The reflectivity is usually expressed in a percentage of the total of the incoming radiation; the term for this percentage is *albedo*. In cities, many different materials are used; so knowing about their reflectivity can help regulate incoming solar radiation (see list, illustration 9). The city's geometry with its deep street canyons also induces more reflection and absorption of radiation, resulting in a lower urban albedo (ca. 0.15) than open areas in the countryside (ca. 0.25).

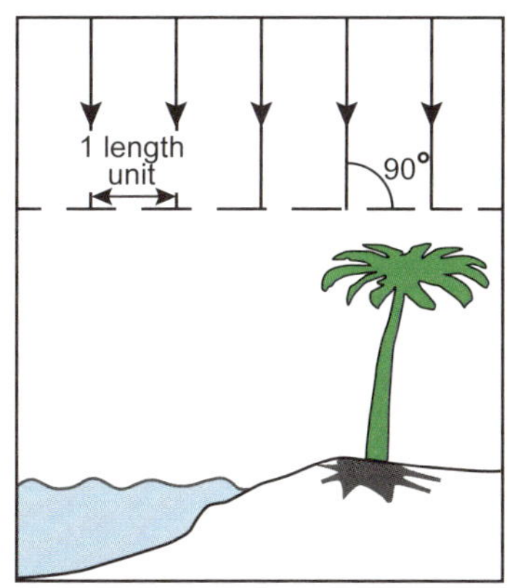

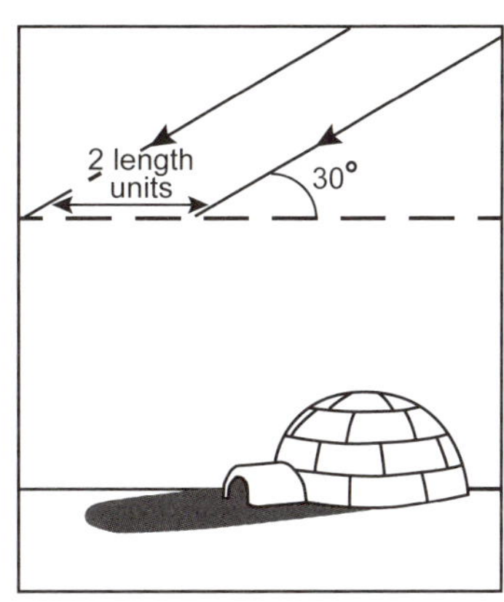

7 *Different angles of the sun in different parts of the world: summer day at noon at the equator, at mid-latitude and near the pole*

8 *The sun's path over the 52nd latitude North*

How materials store and radiate heat

All materials have different heat storage and release characteristics. Heat capacity plays an important role here. The term *heat capacity* describes the ability of materials to store energy (see list, illustration 9). Many dense building materials, for example, have a high heat capacity – they can thus store heat very well. And at some stage they will release it as warmth (longwave radiation).

When an object has a larger surface than another object at the same location, it obviously receives more shortwave radiation, stores it, and consequently can also emit more warmth. Cities have many vertical surfaces – the walls of the buildings – and thus have more surface area to receive and emit radiation than an open landscape does. But even within a city there are great differences. A very dense high-rise area has a much larger vertical surface area than a sprawling residential neighbourhood, with villas surrounded by large gardens. The high-rise area therefore stores much more radiation, emitting it as warmth later.

Material	Albedo reflected/ incoming shortwave radiation	Heat capacity C (MJ m⁻³ K⁻¹)	Thermal conductivity k (Wm⁻¹ K⁻¹)
Ground surfaces			
Rock	Depends on stone brightness	2.25	2.19
Sandy soil, dry (40% pores)	0.2-0.45	1.28	0.24
Peat soil, dry (80% pores)	0.10-0.13	0.58	0.10
Gravel paving, light	0.18-0.30	1.40-1.60	1.2
Asphalt	0.05-0.27	1.92-2.10	0.38-1.04
Deciduous plants	0.20-0.30	Depends on soil	n/a
Grass/lawn	0.16-0.25	Depends on soil	n/a
Water (high sun angle)	0.03-0.10	4.18	0.57
Water (low sun angle)	0.10-0.50	4.18	0.57
Walls/ Vertical surfaces			
Concrete, aerated	0.10-0.35	0.28	0.08
Concrete, dense	0.10-0.35	2.11	1.51
Red brick	0.20-0.60	1.37	0.83
Dark brick	0.20	1.77	0.83
Natural stone, bright	0.40-0.64	2.25	2.19
Wood, planed, light	0.22	0.45	0.09
Wood, planed, dense	0.22	1.52	0.19
White plaster	0.93	1.40	0.46
Glass	0.08	1.66	0.74
Polystyrene	Depends on material brightness	0.02	0.03
Iron	0.50-0.90	3.93	80
Roofs			
Tar paper	0.05	Depends on underground	n/a
Gravel	0.08-0.18	Depends on underground	0.86
Roof tiles, ceramic	0.10-0.35	1.77	0.8
Corrugated steel	0.10-0.16	3.93	45-50

9 *List of albedo, heat capacity and thermal conductivity of different materials*

Materials also have different levels of thermal conductivity which indicates how fast a material transports energy. This too we know from our daily experiences. A hot, metal pan (with high heat conductivity), transports the heat much faster to our skin than a piece of wood brought to the same temperature. Air does not sequester and transport much heat, that is why less dense materials containing a lot of air, such as hollow concrete blocks or polystyrene foam, but also light wood to some extent, are such good insulators.

The factors albedo, heat capacity and thermal conductivity have a great influence on thermoregulation in cities. Therefore, the choices of building materials (brick, timber, concrete, steel, et cetera) or the materials in landscape design (stone, earth, water, vegetation) are an important part of urban climate design (illustration 9).

Retaining thermal radiation in the city

The configuration of buildings is another influence on the level of longwave thermal radiation. In densely built-up areas, this radiation is (re)emitted back and forth between the buildings and cannot dissipate. As a result, these areas cool off much more slowly than open areas do (illustration 10). The closer the buildings stand together, the more the

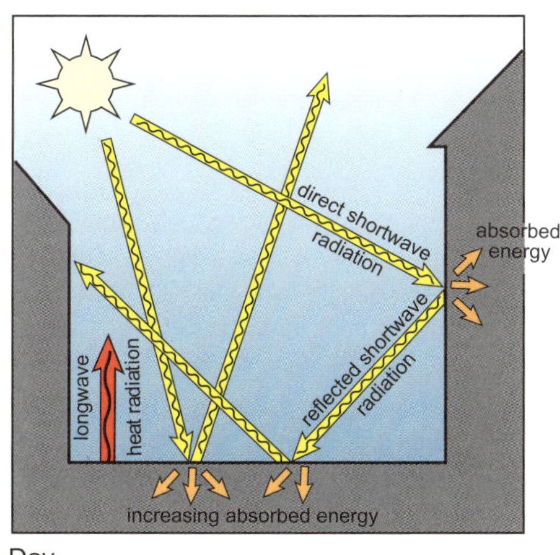

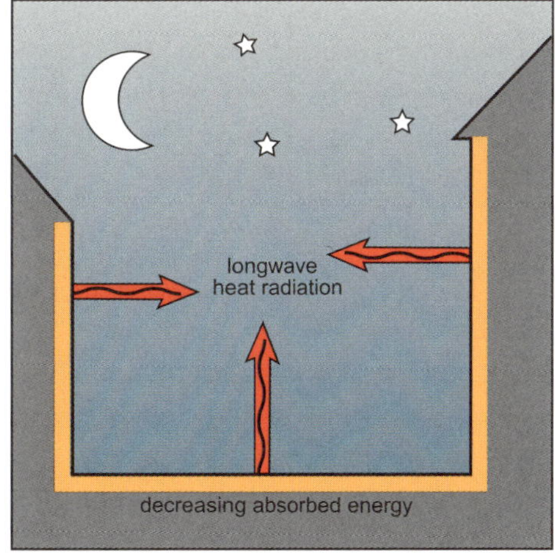

10 *Radiation flows in an urban street canyon*

upward horizon is restricted; a phenomenon termed the *sky view factor* (fraction of the sky that is seen when looking upward). Areas with a low sky view factor, such as a street with tall buildings, retain more of the thermal radiation. Eventually, this results in higher air temperatures.

2.1.2 Air Temperature

Air temperature is the best-known phenomenon of the climate. For the sake of convenience, the air temperature is called 'temperature' in weather forecasts, even though this term is not very accurate. As we saw from earlier sections, we are surrounded by many more phenomena influencing the way we experience temperature, such as short- and longwave radiation. The large-scale high- and low-pressure areas shown in the weather forecasts mainly are responsible for warm air transport from the south or cold air from the north, and determine the rural 'background' air temperature. In cities, however, thermal radiation clearly also has a role in warming the air. Besides these factors, water evaporation and anthropogenic (human-made) heat influence the air temperature in the city.

Water evaporation tempers the air temperature

The amount of water evaporating into the air affects the air temperature. Solar and thermal radiation cause water to evaporate. The evaporation process extracts energy from the air, as a result of which its temperature can't rise as fast. People often speak of the cooling effect of water vapour, but strictly speaking we should speak of a reduced warming of the air due to evaporation. The evaporation at the surface of water bodies and soils dampens the heating of the air. However, typically smaller water bodies in cities such as canals or ditches have such a small surface that they have virtually no effect on air temperature. Paving the soil and channelling waterways, thus reducing their surface area, will lead to substantially less evaporation in the city, making the air warm up faster.

At the surface of their leaves, plants evaporate a lot of water. This happens through the supply of water from the roots to the stomata of the leaves. As a result, areas with more vegetation heat up less quickly than the stony areas in the city.

Urban functions raise the air temperature

Another heat factor in the city is so-called anthropogenic heat. This involves the heat production directly resulting from human activity. Think of heat produced by heaters in buildings, escaping because of the buildings' bad insulation. But also think of air conditioners cooling houses or cars, since they give off much heat to the outside air. The production processes in commercial and industrial zones also generate extra heat. The same goes for power plants, as they often produce residual heat. Cars' engines also produce extra heat, and busy, narrow roads can heat up considerably because of this.

2.1.3 Temperature Phenomena Typical for the Urban Environment

Urban heat islands

In the previous sections many aspects were discussed that demonstrate that the city has a different climate than most natural landscapes. Especially the temperature regime of the air masses in the urban streets and just above roof level is warmer, and most prominent 2-3 hours after sunset. The urban-rural air temperature difference is called the urban heat island effect, which is thus higher at night. However, we also know that within a city, densely built-up parts with sealed surfaces and little vegetation are usually warmer than less densely built-up and greener urban areas. The higher air temperatures in the more urbanized areas are a cumulative result of retained longwave thermal radiation, anthropogenic heat and reduced evaporation. A green, loosely built-up residential area with large gardens or a park can sometimes even be cooler than the adjacent landscape. And a densely built-up and completely paved industrial zone at the edge of the city can often be warmer than a less built-up city centre. It is therefore more suitable to use the term heat archipelago to indicate that cities can contain various heat areas and that it does not concern the whole city or the central areas only (see illustration 11).

Urban heat phenomena through seasons seasons, day and night

Urban heat island effects occur both in summer and in winter. During the winter, this is mainly the result of anthropogenic heat, going on day and night. In temperate climate zones, there is much less solar radiation (the greatest source of thermal radiation) in the winter, so radiation does not heat up the air so much. During the summer, however, especially radiation is responsible for the higher air temperatures, especially at night. The radiation is mostly received and stored during the day, and it is released as longwave radiation at night. In the daytime, densely built-up areas only have slightly higher air temperatures than more open and vegetated areas. At night, however, there is a big difference in

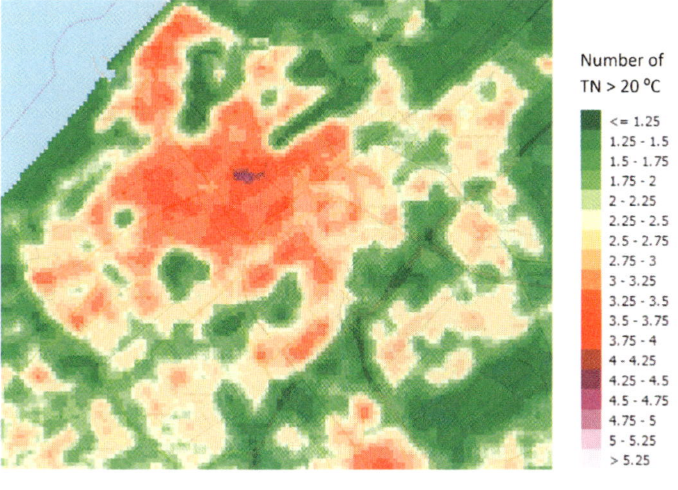

11 *Tropical night temperatures in The Hague, clearly showing the heat archipelago*

air temperature. As discussed before, this is due to the permanent release of longwave radiation by all buildings, and pavements, preventing the air from cooling off. The summer heat island effect is strongest on hot, cloudless days with little wind. Measurements have shown that the difference in air temperature between heat islands and cooler areas of the city or the surrounding land can be as much as 12 °C during such nights. Especially during heatwaves, with several hot days in a row, problems can arise because the heat can build up over the days.

Problems due to urban heat phenomena

People often say warmer cities are nice, because heating in winter can be reduced, and people have fewer problems with ice and snow, plus that these cities often have a lively outdoor urban life. In the end, though, the problems connected to urban heat are bigger. Heat stress leads to inevitable health issues (see chapter 1); food spoils faster when it's warm; insect pests such as ticks and mosquitoes thrive in hot summers; chances of legionella outbreaks are higher; and blue-green algae can grow fast in warm urban water bodies. Heat also causes problems with infrastructure: asphalt wears out and deforms; and moving parts of bridges and such can malfunction because of expansion.

2.2 Wind in the Urban Environment

How differences in temperature generate wind

It is important to get to know urban wind patterns, because urban design has a significant impact on these patterns. But first, we need to discuss a few basic principles of how wind flows are induced. Wind is caused by differences in temperature. Warm air is lighter than cold air, because there is more space between the air's molecules. The warm air rises, while the heavier cool air tends to stay closer to the Earth's surface. This rising of warm air causes low atmospheric pressure in the warmer areas, which leads to sucking in cooler air

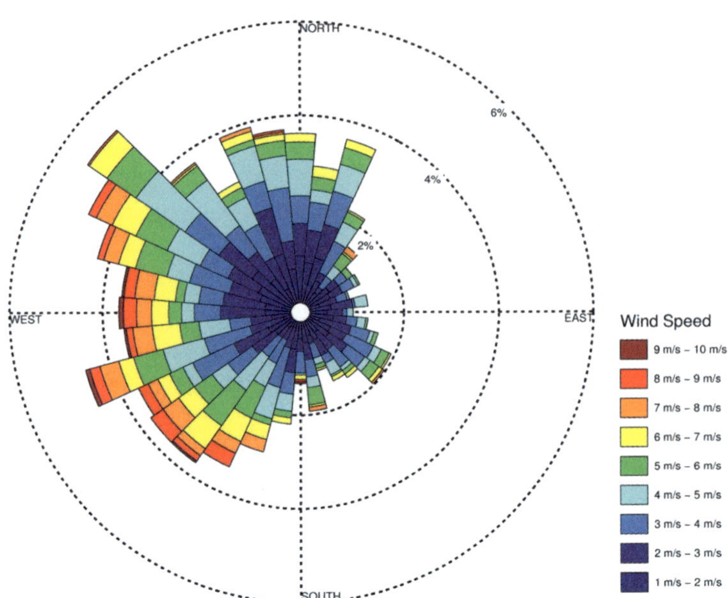

12 *Wind rose for Detroit City Airport during the autumn 2010 period*

from the surroundings. This is how air movement, or wind, comes about. On a large scale, we can see this phenomenon as wind occurring between high- and low-pressure areas, being warmer and cooler bodies of air. On this large scale, the Earth's rotation plays a role in the direction of the prevailing winds. As indicated before the focus of this book is on the temperate climate zones. In these zones, the prevailing winds on the northern hemisphere are usually south-western, and on the southern hemisphere they are usually north-western.

During many days of the year the influences of the large-scale wind systems prevail, but in some crucial circumstances such as during heatwaves the wind comes from other main directions (mainly east) and such wind systems can be used for ventilating the city. It is thus important to recognize that wind can sometimes be a solution to a problem (ventilation, generating wind energy) and sometimes it can form a problem (wind nuisance and danger).

To understand such patterns for a city you can look at typical wind data during hot days and as opposed to that, during cooler days. You can usually find these on the websites of national weather services or the local airports (see illustration 12).

Wind flows in the city are not the same as those in open landscapes

All wind flows have to change direction when they hit obstacles, including cities. Because of this, wind slows down on the leeside of objects, whereas it speeds up in narrow places, where it is compressed. These winds can be gusty and change direction abruptly. Stronger winds and bigger obstacles such as tall buildings increase the intensity of these gusts. Local topographical differences can also induce small-scale wind systems in and around cities. This can happen for instance when a city is located next to a large body of water or in a hilly area. Closely built-up areas in a city, generating heat, can also induce local airflows.

2.2.1 Local Wind Systems

As described above in broad outlines, wind results from differences in air temperature, whereby warm air rises and cooler air is sucked in. In cities, three phenomena can cause these differences in temperature: the difference in air temperature over land and over water; in hills and in valleys, warming up at different speeds; and the differences in air temperature in urban heat islands and in cooler areas. Such local wind systems can only occur during calm and warm weather when large scale wind systems do not 'overrule' the local winds.

The location and structure of the city induce small-scale wind systems

In line with these temperature differences, coastal cities deal with coastal wind systems; cities with relief have hill-valley winds; and all cities have breezes between warmer and cooler parts of the city.

Coastal wind systems

In summer, when the large-scale wind systems are weak, sea breeze systems arise in coastal cities. These are generated by the different speeds at which water and landmasses warm up. During the day, air above the water takes more time to warm up than the air over land does. So, the air over land is warmer and it starts to rise around midday. This in turn would cause a kind of 'negative pressure' but due to the conservation of mass, cooler sea air gets sucked towards the land masses. This means the wind blows from the sea towards the land. So, during the afternoon, cooler air comes into the city. At night, it is the other way around, because it takes longer for water to cool off than it does for land. Then, the water is warmer than the land is, and the wind blows from the land towards the sea (see illustration 13). The direction of the coastal wind systems is more or less perpendicular to the coastline but is also strongly influenced by the Earth's rotation direction. When it is exceptionally hot and there are no obstacles, such as mountain ranges, these sea breezes can reach almost a hundred

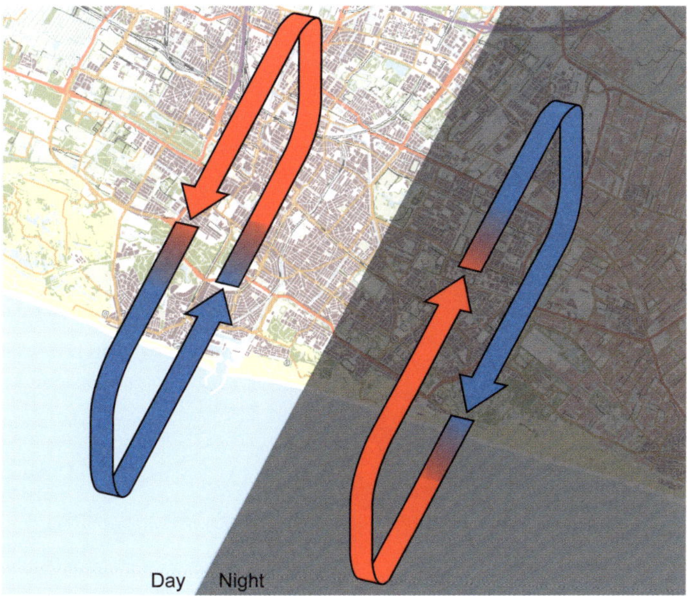

13 *Land and sea breezes during the day and at night*

kilometres inland. Such breezes can also occur in cities on the shores of large lakes. On tranquil summer days, there is usually a bit more wind along the shores than at the middle of the lake.

Valley wind systems

When a city has open hills and valleys with differences in height of over 50 metres and gradients of at least 1 per cent, valley winds can develop. The time of day and different speeds at which surfaces in the hills and valleys warm up are important for the development of these winds. The slopes warm up more quickly than the valleys do, causing the air to expand. Hence the larger volume of air no longer "fits into the valley" and it has to flow out, creating upward airflows (illustration 14, A). During the day, especially in the afternoons, an uphill breeze occurs (B). At night, this phenomenon is reversed. When the hilltops and slopes are more open than the valleys they can radiate heat more easily (C) and the air here cools off quickly. This cool air is heavier and moves to the lowest parts of the valleys. So now the airflow near the ground is downhill (D).

The opener the hilltops and slopes (for example grassland), the faster they can produce cold air through accelerated radiation and more cold air will flow downhill. This air slowly moves close to the ground, normally no more than 2 metres per second. Obstacles, such as buildings, mounds and dense planting, will obstruct these slow airflows because they do not have enough speed to pass by or over the obstacles. The obstacles block the potentially cooling valley breezes, which could have otherwise gone on to the warmer parts of the city. Therefore, it is advisable to keep these areas free from obstacles.

Urban wind systems

Urban heat areas surrounded by cooler areas can also create airflows themselves. The air over the warmer parts of the city rises, and air from a nearby cooler area is sucked in. The bigger the difference in temperature between warmer and cooler areas, the more cool air is sucked in, resulting in faster wind. The airflow between a densely built-up city

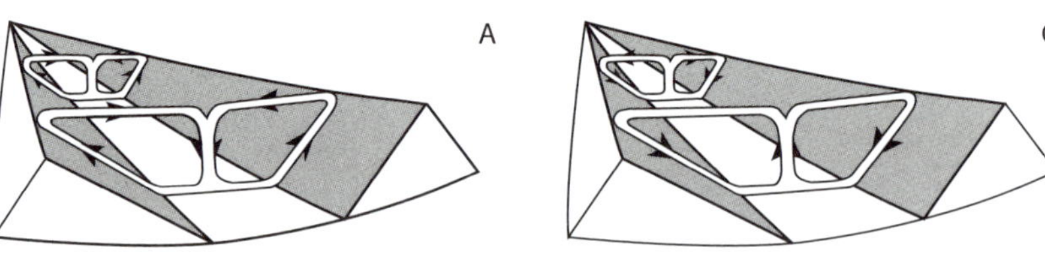

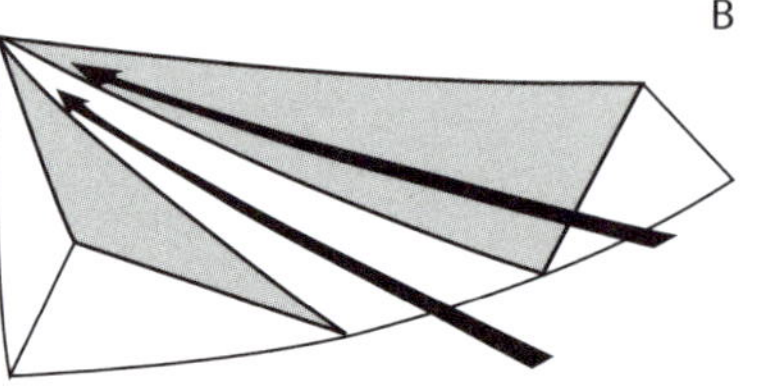

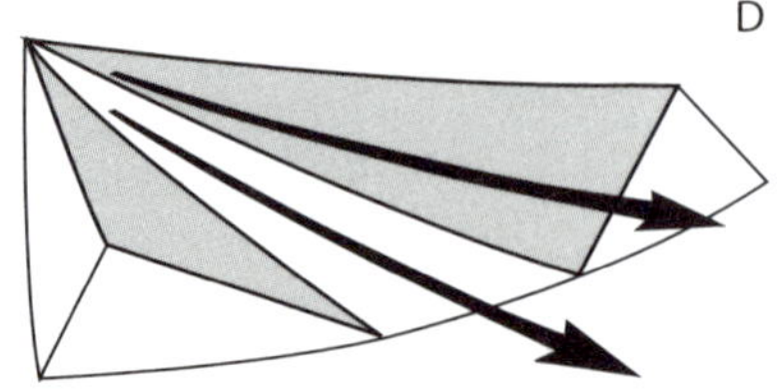

14 *Valley wind systems during the day and at night*

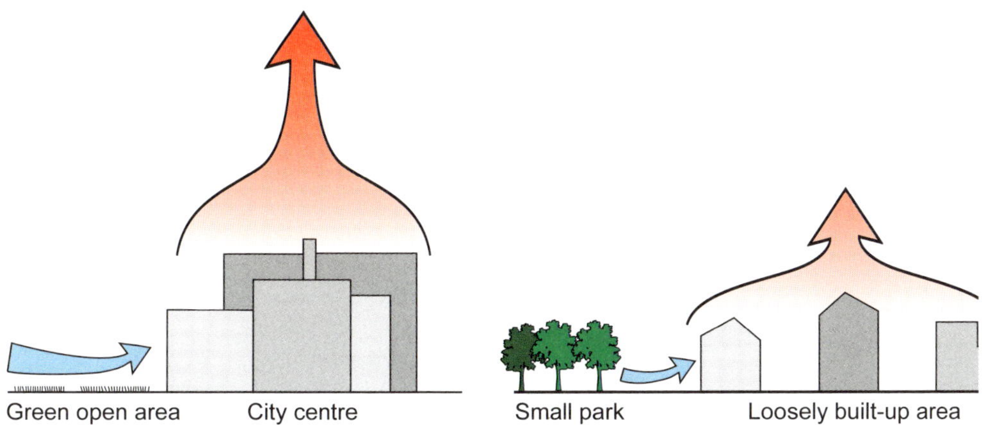

15 *Urban wind between warm and cool areas with different temperature gradients*

centre and a large, 'cool' open park, for instance, can be stronger, whereas a breeze between a small park and a loosely built-up residential area will only ever be light (see illustration 15). If cool breezes are given the space to flow, they can find their way into the warm areas of a city, thus providing ventilation. But these airflows are weak too and unable to pass higher obstacles.

All these local airflows can provide natural ventilation for the city. Their effect manifests itself especially on hot summer days and nights, so precisely when it is most wanted. To give these breezes the space they need, we should make sure the areas where the cool air originates from and the ventilation axes are kept open (more on this subject in section 4.2). On days with more unstable weather and stronger large-scale wind, this wind will force these small-scale airflows apart, so they will not be able to manifest themselves. The city does not need extra ventilation on those days anyway, because there is enough wind as it is.

2.2.2 Speed of the Large-scale Wind Around Cities

Wind speeds are different in cities and open landscapes

Close to the ground, obstacles or the so-called 'roughness' of the Earth's surface slow down the large-scale wind. Water surfaces are quite smooth, but on land, plants and relief make the surface more rugged. Similar to other spatial volumes on the Earth's surface, such as mountains and woods, cities with their buildings and tall vegetation usually form an obstacle that the wind has to flow around. A city with many tall buildings standing quite close together will be a bigger obstacle than a city with many low-rise buildings. Despite these differences, the average wind speed in urban areas is around 30-50 per cent lower than outside of the city at the same height. At densely built-up cities with high-rise buildings, large-scale wind is deflected up to a height of 500 metres over the roofs (see illustration 16). Occasionally, this can be even higher, seeing that the world's tallest skyscrapers are taller than 800 metres. Only above that the wind regains its original speed.

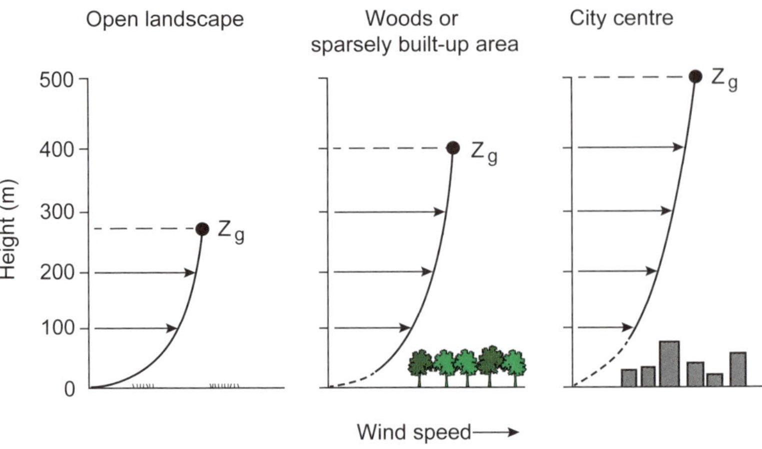

16 *Profile of large-scale wind over open landscapes, woods or sparsely built-up areas, and densely built-up cities*

From the above, one could unjustly conclude that wind is not an issue in cities, because of the lower wind speeds. But that is not the case: due to the combination of relief, buildings of various heights and openings in the urban structure, wind is deflected and the air compressed in many ways, making it very strong in certain places. Wind flows can also break off or speed up abruptly. In the city, wind is in fact much more turbulent and changeable than in an open landscape or over sea. What the flow patterns look like in the city and how strong the wind will be at certain spots, is different for each location. To get an idea of the airflow patterns on a small scale, for instance to analyse areas of wind nuisance, or where you can expect useful ventilation streams of wind, you need to carefully study the spatial volumes of each individual location.

2.2.3 Typical Wind Patterns in the Urban Environment

Wind flow patterns are different for each location, but they do have a lot in common

Although the flow patterns of wind in cities always depend on local contexts with their unique building configurations, there are some flow patterns that normally occur around certain building volumes and in certain open spaces. These patterns occur at several spots around volumes and come with either reduced or increased wind flows. The height, width and length of the volumes determine what the patterns look like. It is useful to know that, in principle, wind shows the same flow patterns on small and large scales around obstacles near the Earth's surface. That is why many patterns have no scale and are not expressed in absolute, but in relative numbers. Knowing about the patterns discussed in this section can help you predict wind patterns on a local level for many locations. Wind experts know wind patterns can be hard to predict and quantitative data on speeds can be hard to calculate.

This especially applies to combined volumes of buildings, relief or vegetation. Special simulation or wind tunnel experiments are required here (see chapter 5 as well). However, with a 'sense' for flow patterns (through observing water flows, plumes of smoke and dust, see illustration 17 as well), and knowing about flow patterns around

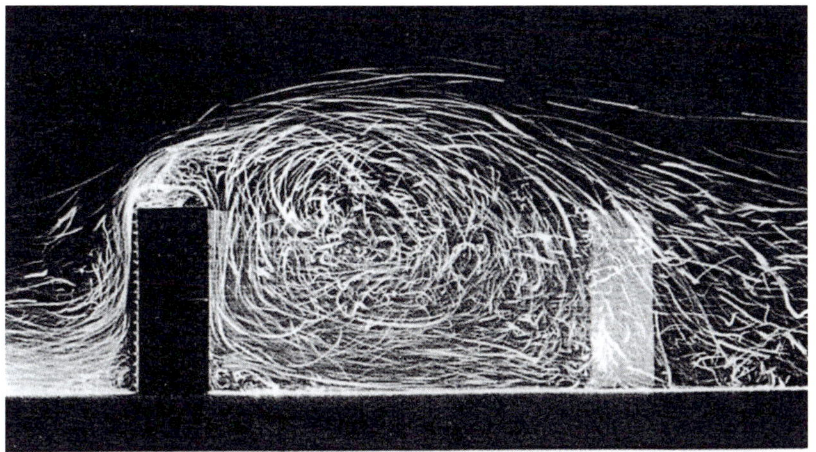

17 *In a wind tunnel, fine dust is blown around a building volume to see how the wind flows.*

freestanding buildings, you can make simple predictions about wind patterns around clusters of buildings. You could, for example, take the estimated patterns for freestanding buildings in maps or profiles, and overlap these, as it were. This can provide you with a lot of information about the interactions that are to be expected.

Developing a sense for flow patterns

First, I will sketch a number of patterns that occur around single volumes such as vegetation and buildings, then those around simple building clusters, and finally the wind patterns typical for open urban spaces, such as streets and squares. The wind in these sketches always has the same direction. In reality, this is obviously not the case, but this is not a problem when predicting these patterns. When you need to look into the flow patterns for a different direction, you simply project the patterns for this other direction. It is, however, very important to keep in mind that we are talking about some basic patterns here, and there are many possible variations. Of course, the relief of a city is also of great influence on the wind patterns in it, particularly if there are big differences in height. For example, a mountain range on the leeside of a city can deflect large-scale wind and thus decrease the wind speeds in the city itself. In a coastal city, on the other hand, the wind can be much stronger. However, also in these situations, the general small-scale flow patterns are still the same; it is only the wind speed that is lower.

Wind patterns around clusters of vegetation

Vegetation clusters as you can find in a city park come in several typical shapes, such as line-shaped in lanes or wider in tree clumps or groves. Typical wind patterns form depending on the 'depth' of such a volume of vegetation. The following phenomena occur at line-shaped shelterbelts:

1 At the windward side, there is a small sheltered area close to the ground (illustration 18, 1).
2 On the sides, wind speeds are clearly increased, forming the so-called corner streams (more on this subject under 'freestanding buildings').

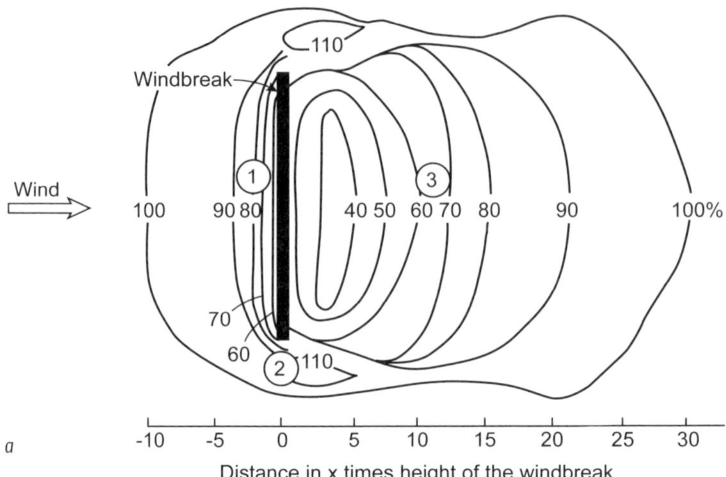

18 *Wind flows around a shelterbelt*

This is because of the compression of air flowing around the shelterbelt (illustration 18, 2).

3 On the leeside behind the shelterbelt, the air pressure is lower and there is a large sheltered area (illustration 18, 3), in which it takes the wind up to a maximum of thirty times the height of the trees to reach its original speed. In general, the length of the sheltered area at substantially lower wind speeds (less than half) is about five times the height of the trees.

Forests or broader groves have much smaller sheltered areas behind them (see illustration 19). When the trees in a grove have similar tops forming sort of a 'flat roof', the sheltered area behind the grove is smaller. When the grove has a more irregular 'roof', the sheltered area is somewhat larger. When the canopy of foliage is not very dense and the trees have high tops, the wind can flow through the top and trunk part of the grove, but the sheltered area behind it will be much longer. Around freestanding buildings of medium height at right angles to the wind, the following flow patterns arise:

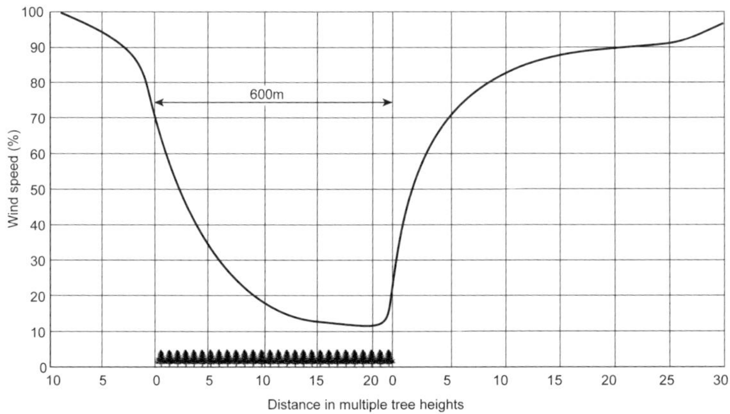

19 Wind transect over and behind a forest

20 a (left) and b (right)
Wind flows around a free-standing medium-height building, with relative speed changes compared to the original wind speed

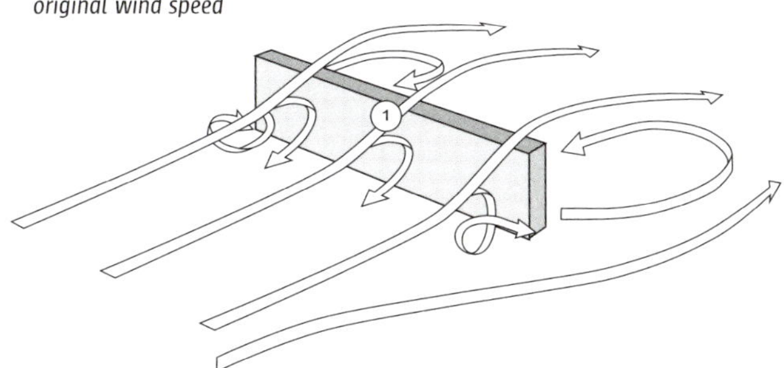

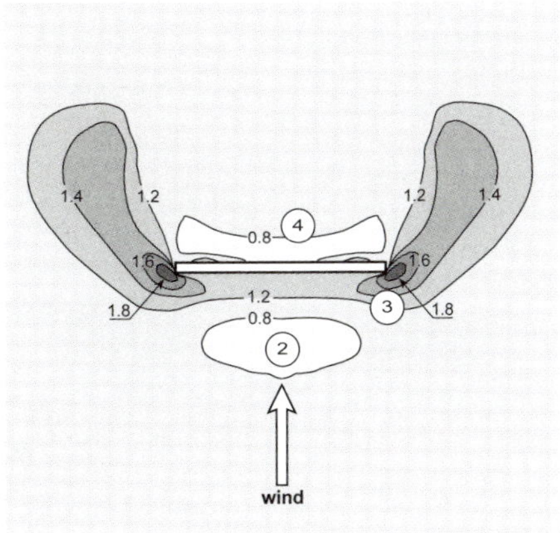

Wind patterns around freestanding buildings of medium height at right angles to the wind

1 On the windward side a little above the middle of the building front, eddies occur due a redirection of the air molecules, also called wind shear (illustration 20a, 1).
2 A way off the foot of the building, at the windward side, there is a small sheltered area, where the main flows are divided (illustration 20b, 2).
3 At the sides of the building corner, streams with higher wind speeds occur due to the compression of the air flowing around the building (illustration 20b, 3).
4 On the leeward side behind the building, the air pressure is lower, resulting in a sheltered area (illustration 20b, 4), the size of which depends on the height of the building. In general, the sheltered area with lower wind speeds is about three to five times the height of the building. But the 'depth' of the building also plays a part – as the depth increases, the sheltered area behind the building becomes smaller. Some air does flow back here, which can cause turbulence. Further away from the building, the wind speed increases again.

Wind patterns around tall buildings at right angles to the wind

Around freestanding, tall building volumes of over 20 metres, at right angles to the direction of the wind, two more phenomena occur as well:

1 Corner streams develop at the building edges (illustration 21a, 1).
2 As we know, winds blowing at rooftop level are faster and they are 'scooped' down, as it were (illustration 21a, 2) at the windward side of the building. This phenomenon is called downwash, and at the pedestrian level, it can be the cause of substantially higher and sometimes even dangerous wind speeds.

Wind patterns around passageways

When wind blows against buildings with passageways, other patterns occur (illustration 22). The wind hitting the building is forced through the small opening of the passage. This creates a compression of airflows and thus high wind speeds in the passage, which can sometimes be quite dangerous for pedestrians and cyclists.

21 a (left) and b (right)
Wind flows around a free-standing high-rise building, with relative speed changes compared to the original wind speed

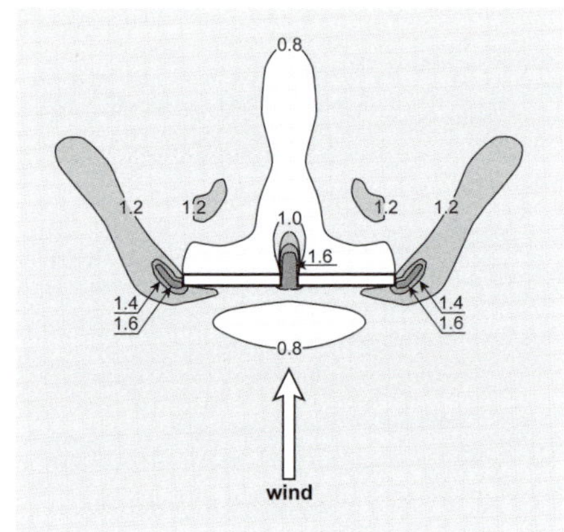

22 *Wind flows around a building with a passageway, with relative speed changes compared to the original wind speed*

Wind patterns around buildings parallel to the wind direction

When slab-shaped buildings are parallel to the direction of the wind, there is considerably less deflection (illustration 23). The air pressure at the windward side is much smaller than in a situation when the same building is perpendicular to the wind direction and there are hardly any corner streams. But the sheltered area behind the building is also much shorter than it would if the same building was perpendicular to the wind.

Wind patterns around buildings at an angle to the wind direction

When buildings are diagonal to the prevailing wind, even stronger corner stream areas develop at the windward side than around buildings that are at right angles to the wind. These corner stream areas then start to interact (illustration 24, 1). Eddies around these buildings can also be stronger.

The examples depicted here mainly represent slab-shaped buildings. For ‘deeper’ buildings, the flows are somewhat different. The chief effect of ‘deeper’ buildings is a relatively smaller sheltered area in comparison to the effect behind buildings of smaller depth (illustration 25).

23 *Wind flows around a building parallel to the wind direction, with relative speed changes compared to the original wind speed*

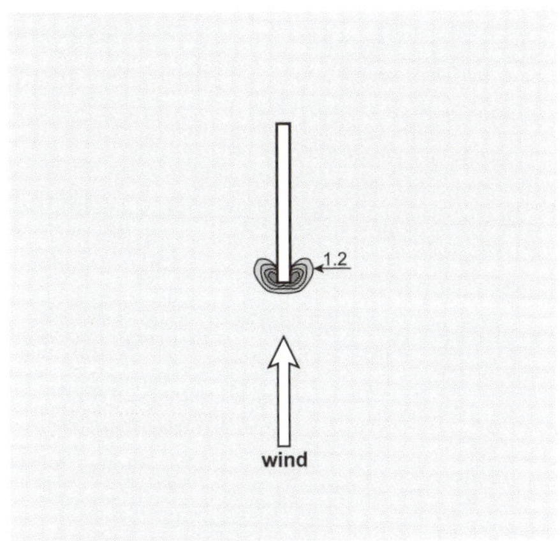

24 *Wind flows around a low-rise, freestanding building diagonal to the wind direction, with relative speed changes compared to the original wind speed*

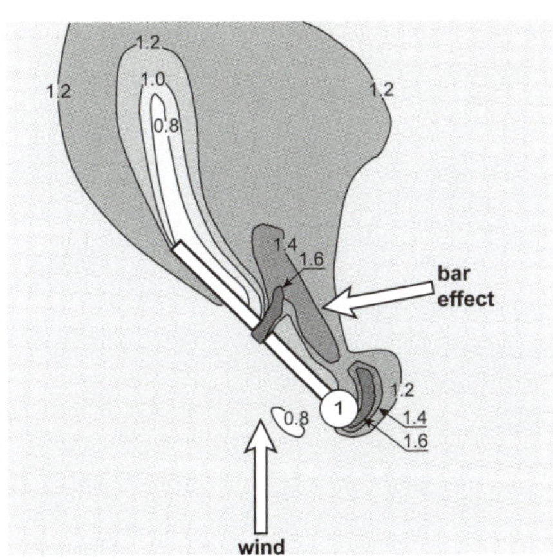

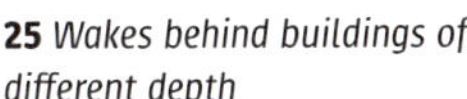

25 *Wakes behind buildings of different depth*

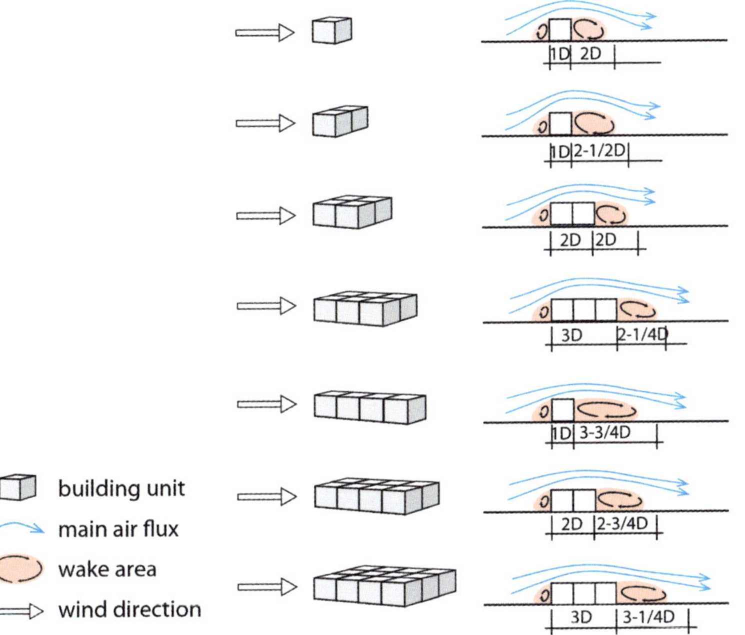

Estimating the interaction between wind patterns around groups of buildings

When buildings are grouped together, different flow patterns develop, because of the interaction between the flows around the individual buildings. These patterns are usually relatively hard to predict, but you can infer what some simple patterns will approximately look like, based on the estimated size of the corner streams. When the corner streams around freestanding buildings overlap, as it were, you can expect higher wind speeds. This also influences the wind directions around the buildings. The examples in illustrations 26 and 27 show that flow patterns around buildings lined up at short distances from each other have more interaction than those around buildings with more space between them (illustration 28).

Channelling effect of wind flows in streets and on longish squares

The wind climate in open spaces such as the streets and squares in a city is mostly influenced by the volumes of the surrounding buildings. The airflows around the individual buildings interact here as well, generating higher wind speeds and other spatial patterns. Continuous building configuration along the streets can have a channelling effect on the wind, if the street is more or less parallel to the prevailing wind direction. This effect especially occurs in streets with long, straight

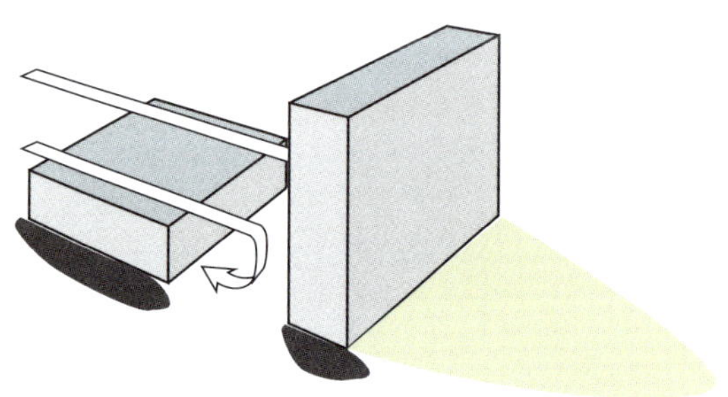

26 *Buildings with clearly interacting wind flows*

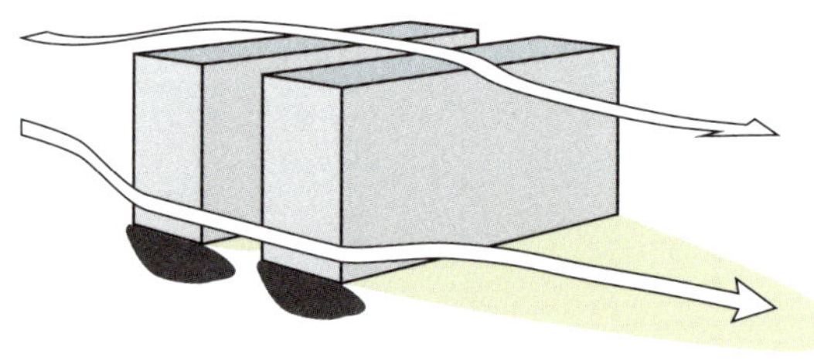

27 *Buildings with interacting wind flows and corner streams*

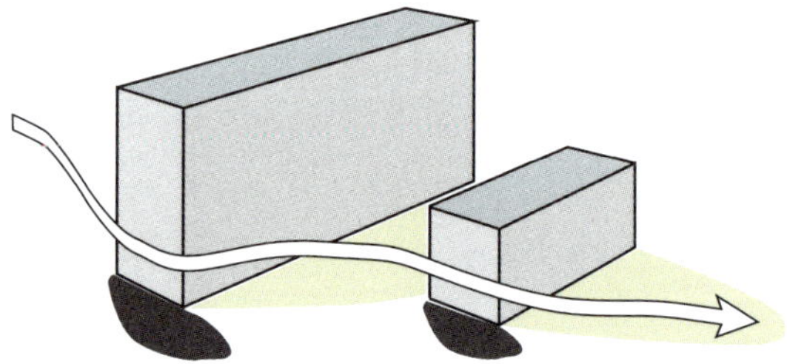

28 *Buildings at a distance from each other with slightly interacting wind flows*

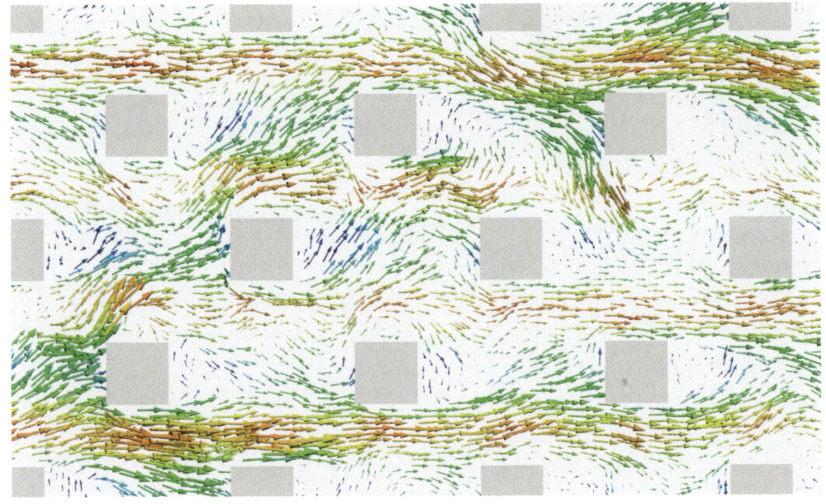

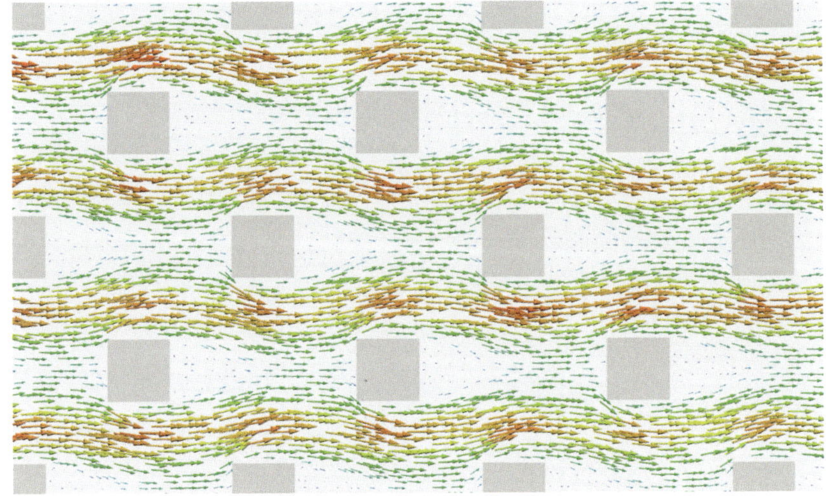

29 *Wind flows in a building configuration with wind direction parallel to building pattern (above) and oblique to building pattern (below)*

axes and smooth facades. We can also see this channelling effect when the buildings are more spaced out, but the effect is not as strong (see illustration 29). If broad streets or squares gradually become narrower, the wind is compacted and its speed increases even more.

Proportions of streets and squares and typical wind flow regimes

The proportions of open spaces such as streets and squares have a significant impact on the wind patterns. Especially the ratio between the height (H) of the buildings and the width (W) of the areas between the buildings is of influence. With the wind direction at right angles to the buildings, typical flow patterns develop for different types of proportions (see illustration 29). You will find skimming flows in relatively narrow streets. This means most of the wind flow stays above the rooftops, leaving a relatively sheltered area between the buildings. When the street or square is wider (with H/W-ratios between 0.3 and 0.7), we see wake interference flow patterns: the sheltered areas behind the buildings overlap the small sheltered areas in front. We often find

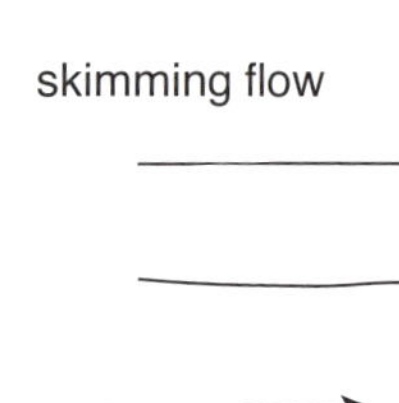

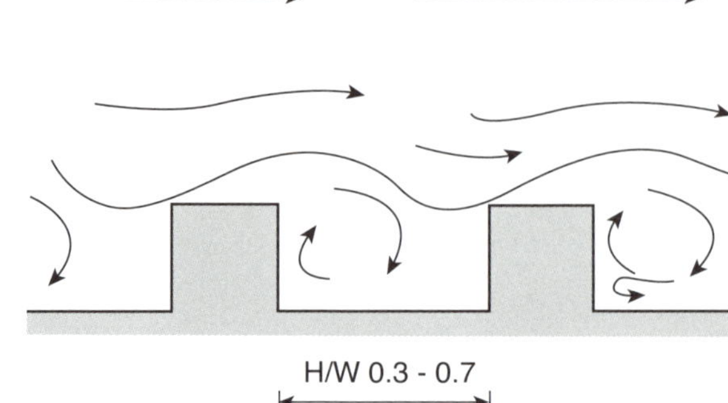

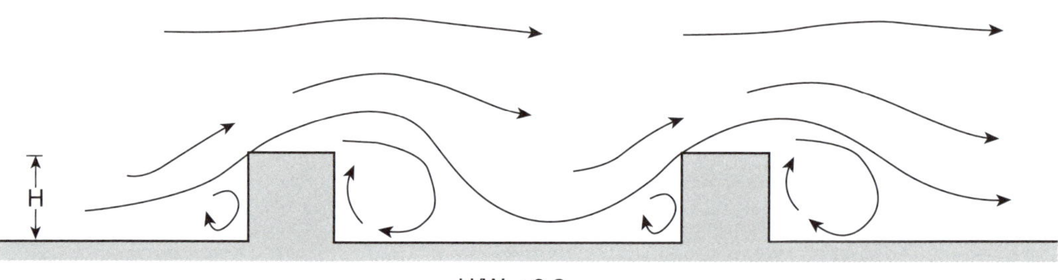

30 *Profiles of the three wind regimes: skimming flow, wake interference and isolated roughness flow*

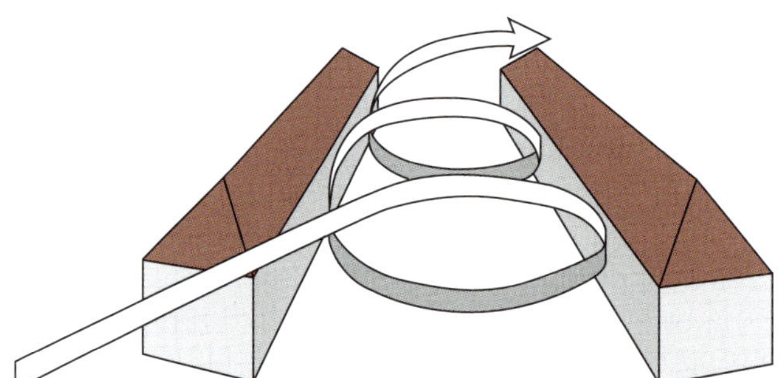

31 *A wind flow at an angle to the street's orientation spirals through the street*

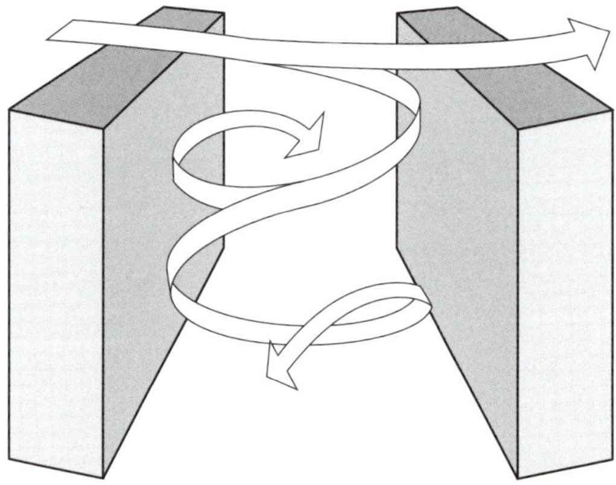

32 *Deep street canyon: two vortices running in opposite directions*

parallel eddies here, but the wind speeds are usually average. With H/W-ratios of 0.3 and smaller, the buildings are so far apart that wind can almost resume its original flow pattern and speed. This pattern is called isolated roughness flow. This type of flow regime often leads to wind nuisance on large squares or very wide streets. In deep street canyons we can even observe two vortex systems that run in opposite directions (see illustration 30).

Street length and direction with typical wind flows

The length of the street is also important for the wind climate. This works in a similar fashion as described above. Short streets with an H/W-ratio smaller than 0.3 do not have much wind flowing through them (when they are at right angles to the wind direction). Longer streets allow for the wind to quickly retain its original speed; we then see the channelling-effect we discussed before. This effect is significantly smaller when there are many trees in the street or when the facades alternate, one at least half a building depth in front of the other. When the wind comes in at an angle, you often see spiralling whirls, swirling through the streets, that part into two vortices in deep street canyons (see illustration 32).

Wind flows on squares

Squares are obviously not just 'enlarged streets'; they usually have several openings, for instance at the entrances of the surrounding streets. The larger these entrances, the easier the large-scale wind regains its original speed on pedestrian level. Also, the buildings at squares are often of different heights. On old European church squares, for example, the downwash-effect of church towers is a common phenomenon. The varied geometry of urban squares results in more complex flow patterns than those in streets, and it is impossible to generalize. However, it is possible to use estimations of corner streams and sheltered areas to gain some insight into the estimated flow patterns. Likewise, the H/W-ratios and their different wind regimes (skimming flow, wake interference and isolated roughness flow) can help you predict the wind patterns on different kinds of squares.

2.3 Ambiance and Microclimate Experience

The ambiance of cities' outdoor spaces influences the microclimate experience

Besides all physical factors, urban space also has an indirect effect on how people experience the microclimate. The ambiance of an environment plays a role here, too. A space can have a 'warm' or 'cold' ambiance even if its physical characteristics do not produce this effect. This is the effect of environmental psychology on people's experience. For example: through associations in people's minds, visual impressions can influence what they estimate the microclimate to be like, without being directly exposed to it. These 'ambiance aspects' encompass the openness of spaces, colours and materials. Some of these aspects have a clear relation to physical effects on the microclimate, and some have

33 *A square that is too spacious: Square East of La Grande Arche, Paris, La Defense*

34 *'Cold' materials in Lille Box: Perception of colours in urban outdoor spaces*

no physical effect whatsoever. You can use these 'ambiance parameters' to somewhat manipulate people's thermal experience.

Many people associate a spacious and open urban area with a low H/W-ratio (below 0.25) with wind and exposure to the elements. This perception often coincides with microclimatic circumstances typical for such spaces. In cooler climates the wind is predominant in these spacious and open areas, and in warmer climates excessive solar radiation is. The fact that people consciously think of these types of spaces as unpleasant and that the microclimate indeed often is problematic, requires adaptation measures.

The materials used in urban spaces have a big influence on the thermal experience. People especially associate the way materials feel when you touch them with 'warm' and 'cold'. People perceive materials with a low thermal conductivity, such as wood and bricks, as 'warm', and steel, glass and concrete as 'cold'. Materials with a smooth surface, such as enamel and tiles, are usually considered 'cold' as well, particularly in countries with a temperate or cool climate. This could be because these 'cold' materials, as opposed to materials with a softer surface, have no insulating layers of air, making the material feel warmer upon touch. It could also be because of the thermal conductivity

35 *The 'Ice palace' as people call it, in The Hague, the Netherlands*

of the materials. But what's clear is that people do not need to touch the materials to make this association. People often only need to see the materials (for example on higher parts of buildings' facades) to make these associations. So, for the connection to thermal experience, it does not really matter if people are in direct contact with the used materials or not.

As we all know, colours have a great influence on the 'ambiance' as well. Colours provoke mental associations in different cultures and are often described as 'warm' or 'cold/cool'. In the Western world, people often perceive colours with many yellow or red tones as 'warm' colours. These associations are the result of a symbolic connection to warm elements such as fire and the sun, which have yellow and red tones as well. Blue, white and grey, on the other hand, are usually associated with 'cool'. This is probably because of a symbolic connection to water, ice and clouds, representing cold weather situations. In other cultures, these associations are different.

Nonetheless, these colours in fact have nothing to do with the physical thermal characteristics of materials. However, how light a colour is *does* influence the albedo, and thus the reflection of light and the absorption of heat. So, whether something has a 'warm' or a 'cold' colour does not make any difference to the microclimate – but it *does* make a difference for the ambiance and whether people perceive a space as warm or cold.

3

Mapping the Urban Climate at the City Scale

Planning and design can influence the urban climate on the scale of the entire city. Before we start making concrete plans or designs for a whole city or larger parts of it, however, we need to get an overview of the current situation. Every city and every neighbourhood has a different climate, so we can't use generic solutions for all cities. The urban climate depends on the size of the city; its location, for example near the coast or in the mountains; the building morphology; and how 'green' the individual districts are. The characteristics of the urban climate for a specific city can be studied through several analysis techniques. These types of analyses as described in this chapter usually do not reflect the situation in small locations, but offer general indications about potentials and problems for the whole city with a differentiation down to the district level. These analyses are often summarized in 'urban climate map systems', which form a crucial basis for spatial policy, planning and design.

There are various ways to analyse the urban climate. These depend on what urban climate problems or potentials a certain city could have; on the available data; and on the budget for the analyses. An urban climate analysis at the city-scale normally covers the whole urban area. The surroundings of the city also have to be taken into account, because the urban climate obviously does not end at the city limits. The most precise method for an urban climate analysis would be to conduct measurements over a long period of time on very many locations, for instance in a grid of 10x10 metres and at different heights. Logistically and financially, though, this is not feasible.

In the past years predictive computational modelling of urban climate circumstances has developed rapidly and now provides a reliable basis of data that even covers resolutions of 1x1 metre. Instead of large-scale measurement campaigns, spot check measurements are nowadays conducted to calibrate the data deriving from these computational models.

Several countries have begun to analyse their cities' climates to base their policies on these analyses. These analyses are gathered in 'Urban Climate Map Systems' that often encompass temperature maps and wind maps that form the basis for policy, planning and design recommendation maps (see chapter 4). Some cities' 'Urban Climate Map' databases are also accessible to the public. Before these systems are discussed we first look into a way how you, as a non-expert, can also make quite useful urban climate maps. For the expert systems, examples from across the world will be discussed to show a broad range of urban climate analyses. For each analysis method, the specific goals are described, which aspects of the urban climate it reflects, what needs to be done in order to make the analysis, and whether specialist knowledge is required or not. This chapter ends with a discussion of vulnerability analyses that represent which people are vulnerable to the negative effects of the urban climate and at what times. These assessments are important too, since they can

indicate at which places the urban climate has to be adapted urgently and at which places this can wait.

This chapter is also set up according to the themes of 'thermal environment' and 'wind'. The environmental psychology factors are left out, since they are less relevant on this large scale of the city.

3.1 Climatope Maps as Indicators of Temperature

For relatively small cities in a fairly simple environment when it comes to relief, non-experts can make temperature maps, based on the classification of climatopes, a concept that will be described below. Experts do have to make analysis maps for very complicated urban areas, for instance when a city is located in the mountains or near the ocean. For many cities, however, the situation is not that complicated, and 'climatope maps' created by non-experts will suffice for an overview of the temperature situations.

What is a 'climatope'?

The 'climatope' concept means that different types of areas and districts in a city have typical microclimatic characteristics. This entails for example the influence of the building structure, vegetation, soil surfaces and anthropogenic heat in different areas of the city. The climatopes are mainly classified and named according to the land use, but partly also according to the building density. The maps with climatope divisions primarily tell you about the thermal behaviour of the different districts.

Determining factors for a climatope

To be able to categorize the city into climatopes, you need to integrate information about land use, building structure, vegetation and surfacing. Land use is an important factor for the thermal characteristics of a district. Human activities can have an anthropogenic heat-impact on their environment, for instance through traffic, industrial residual heat, poorly insulated buildings and air conditioners; accounting for about 10 per cent of urban thermal conditions. Such sources of heat can be found in areas with much infrastructure; with factories; or for example with buildings with many air conditioners such as shopping malls, hospitals and hotels.

The urban building structure is most important for the climatope classification. A high density and closed building structure, as you would find in city centres, results in strong heat-absorption and limited ventilation. On the other side, areas where buildings are spread out, such as garden cities, upscale residential areas and the city's periphery, have a lower heat potential.

The density and type of vegetation is of great influence on the climatope classification as well. Planting usually has a tempering effect on the temperature. The more vegetation a district has, the larger the tempering effect can be. Because of their height and thus the deeper

36 *Water climatope*

37 *'Open landscape' climatope*

38 *Forest climatope*

39 *Park climatope*

40 *Low-density climatope*

shadows they cast, trees and shrubs are more important for the tempering of temperature fluctuations than for instance allotment gardens, flowerbeds or lawns.

A final important factor is the use of materials. Materials in outdoor areas or on facades have a great effect on a city's thermoregulation, because of their different radiation characteristics and albedo. Surfacing can lead to accumulation of heat, especially if the heat gets trapped, like in narrow streets. You can use all these data to categorize the climatopes, connecting the various urban climate parameters. Below, you will find the main characteristics of the different climatopes.

Water climatopes encompass larger water bodies with a width of at least 50 metres. So, the canals and ditches that we commonly see in cities do not count here and our research has shown that they have no significant microclimate effect. Water bodies can have a tempering effect on the air temperature. The slow warming and cooling of water levels temperature peaks, both high and low. In summer, this means the temperature during the day is lower than it is in the surrounding areas, and during the night it is higher. This can lead to overheating effects during heatwaves and in late summer when the water has reached its maximum temperatures. Because of these temperature differences, land and sea breezes can develop near large water bodies, such as lakes. The atmospheric humidity near water bodies is higher, and there is more wind around large water bodies, because air can flow freely over water surfaces.

Water climatope

An 'open landscape' climatope, such as large, open arable fields or meadows, has relatively big temperature fluctuations over the course of a day. During daytime these areas have a strong impact of solar radiation and high temperatures. Because of the openness (sky view factor) of these landscapes, retained heat can radiate freely at night, quickly cooling the air. Therefore, these areas are often important 'producers' of cold airflows (see section 2.2.1). The wind is free to roam here, since there are few obstacles.

'Open landscape' climatope

Forests, but also large groves in parks, have tempered temperature fluctuations and fairly constant relative air humidity. This is caused by the shade cast by trees and by the evaporation of water during the day, the retention of heat in the trunk areas and the reduced radiation during the night, keeping the woods warmer than the open landscape. During daytime they are much cooler than open landscapes due to the shading.

Forest climatope

City parks, public gardens and sport parks with large open areas have more extreme temperature fluctuations per day than the built environment or a forest has. The bigger sky view factor in open areas allows the retained warmth to radiate at night and the air cools down. In parks with separate trees, it is a little cooler, because of the shadows and the evapotranspiration. These park-like areas are therefore often important 'producers' of lower air temperatures, which can cool the surroundings as well. Open green areas can also enhance ventilation.

Park climatope

The low-density climatope has a low building-density of up to three building layers with large gardens with trees in them. The classical 'garden cities', but also loosely built-up villages and upscale residential areas are typical for this category. The large share of open space enhances ventilation, which helps with the cooling, especially at night.

Low-density climatope

Medium-density climatope

Medium-density climatopes can have freestanding houses of up to five floors or clustered development of up to three floors, such as terraced houses or perimeter block developments with a large courtyard. They usually have a significant amount of green and typical examples are European post-war districts. The nightly cooling is limited, and the ventilation is often somewhat slowed by the buildings and the planting.

41 *Medium-density climatope*

42 *Dense urban area climatope*

43 *High-density climatope*

44 *Commercial district climatope*

45 *Industrial estate climatope*

46 *Railway yard climatope*

Dense urban area climatope

The dense urban area climatope is characterized by closed building configurations of high-rise and freestanding buildings. This climatope can often be found in historical city centres, but also many newer parts of cities. There is only limited vegetation, and thus also limited cooling through evaporation. In daytime, the area really heats up and at night, it only cools down a little bit. As a result, there is a clear heat island effect, most prominently felt at night.

High-density climatope

High-density climatopes are very densely built-up with massive and/or high-rise building volumes. You will often find this climatope in new city centres and in central business districts, such as La Defense in Paris or the Financial District in New York. There is hardly any vegetation in these areas, so evaporative cooling is strongly reduced. All this leads to strong warming during the day and very limited cooling during the night, due to the strong heat retention of all these buildings.

Commercial district climatope

The commercial district climatope has similar characteristics as the city centre climatope when it comes to heat and wind effects, but on the metal roofs of the usually very massive buildings, you do see a clear cooling during the night. The streets and parking areas, however, do stay warm. This type of climatope is also assigned to similar areas with large, massive buildings, such as logistic centres and trade fair centres.

Industrial estate climatope

The industrial estate climatope has even more intensive heat characteristics than the commercial district climatope. During the day, residual heat from the production activities heats up these areas in addition to the solar radiation. If it's an area of continuous production, this effect continues throughout the night. The roofs cool down rather quickly here too, but the streets and enclosed areas for parking and logistics remain warm for a long time.

Railway yard climatope

A railway yard climatope encompasses large, open areas of at least 50 metres width. The gravel becomes really hot during the day, but because of the large sky view factor, it cools down more quickly during the night. These areas are, however, decidedly warmer than unsurfaced, green open areas. The large, open surfaces allow the wind to stream freely, which can help provide ventilation.

You can see from this list that the different climatopes cover all larger units of the city. A comprehensive citywide climatope map can be based on it. This climatope map, in turn, often forms the basis for further conclusions about wind patterns.

Information and maps required for climatope classification

To make a climatope map of a city, you need information on land use, building structure, vegetation and surfacing. The government can oftentimes provide the required basic data. Many cities have these data in a Geographical Information System (GIS). To map the building density

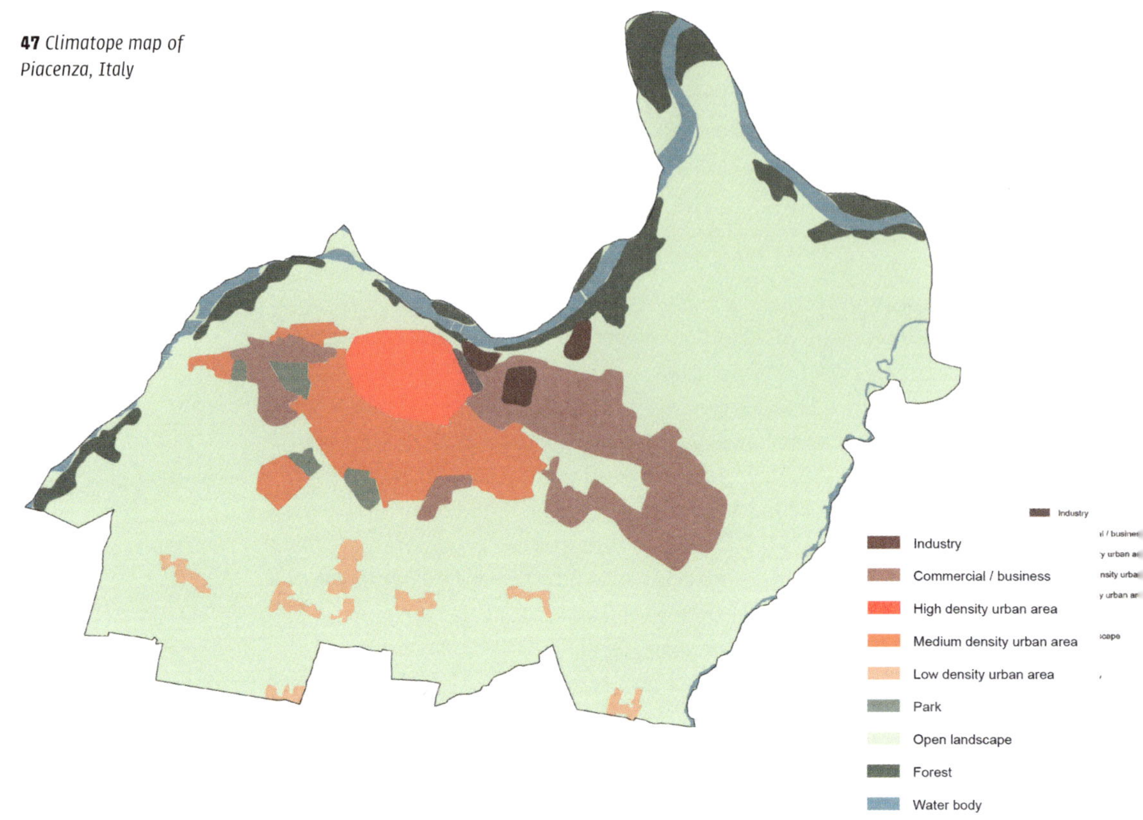

47 *Climatope map of Piacenza, Italy*

in districts, you need maps with the outlines of the buildings, but you also need to know the height of these buildings. Most municipalities have outline maps available, but not all of them have information on the building heights. Some cities have a municipal 'tree cadastre' with information about the vegetation. You can sometimes ask departments managing or planning public space for information about surfacing types. If these data are not available, you will have to use other methods (using Google Earth and Street View, asking experts, or making your own observations) to get the insights you need to make a climatope map.

If this information is not available, you can also try to find maps indicating the surface temperature to find out what locations face heat-related problems. Remote sensing infrared maps, made with satellite images or special aerial photographs can provide insight into the surface temperature (see illustration 48). These maps commonly show that some areas have a higher surface temperature than others. However, because these maps only depict the horizontal surfaces and not the vertical ones such as facades, which also retain much heat, you get a one-dimensional image. This image also does not show the air temperature. That's why these maps have only limited use, but they do sometimes suffice for a first indication of heat-related problems.

48 *Infrared photograph showing the daytime surface temperatures in Arnhem, the Netherlands*

3.2 Indicating Wind Problems and Potentials

Research into typical seasonal wind directions and speeds

Before you can formulate design recommendations and measures, you have to map the most relevant wind situations of a city. Firstly, these are the situations with stronger wind, so as to characterize periods with wind nuisance. Secondly, this regards wind situations on very warm days, to identify directions of possible cooling breezes. You can make wind roses for these two situations based on the weather data of weather stations close to the city. Within the same season, on cooler days, the wind usually has a different direction than on warm days. It will be more akin to the wind direction during cooler seasons. In many countries, the wind speeds on cool days are so high that they can lead to unpleasant situations in urban outdoor spaces. To prevent these situations, wind protection measures have to be taken. If the wind has a clear predominant direction in warm situations, it is useful to design ventilation axes to have this wind enter the urban fabric.

Localizing wind nuisance areas

Wind analysis maps of a city can show the areas with wind nuisance as well as the areas that can potentially provide ventilation. There are two typical areas with wind nuisance. Firstly, we experience wind nuisance in areas with much 'roughness', so with many buildings of strongly divergent volumes. In these areas, you can expect wind channelling, downwash and turbulence, causing the nuisance. Secondly, open areas within the city, such as large squares, very open park areas and riverfronts, often suffer from wind nuisance or danger.

To map the potential for ventilation is to analyse the locations of 'warmer' and 'cooler' areas in the city. The larger the expected temperature differences between warmer and cooler areas, the stronger

Identifying coastal wind areas

the airflows between these areas will be. These airflow potentials can come from coastal wind systems, be induced by differences in altitude or be based on temperature differences between climatopes.
Coastal wind patterns evolve on hot days without large-scale wind, when the city is already quite warm, for example during a heatwave. When there are no large obstacles like high-rise buildings or dunes in the coastal area of the city to deflect the wind, the coastal winds can provide cooling during the day. This cooling effect can fade at night, because the wind will then blow in the opposite direction. So oftentimes, a coastal wind can't provide cooling during the night. Other local airflows are usually more effective for cooling during the night, for example valley winds or local urban winds.

Identifying valley-wind areas

To predict potential cold, nightly valley winds in cities with distinct differences in altitude, you need to consult GIS or other detailed relief maps to look at these differences in altitude. Altitude differences over 50 metres mean there is a potential for these airflows to occur. For these

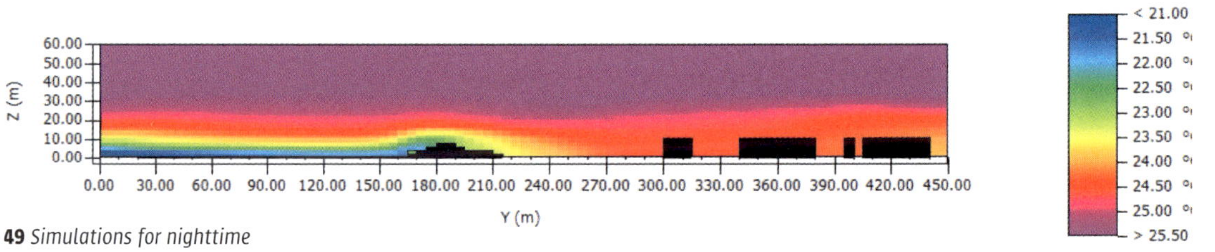

49 *Simulations for nighttime temperature differences between cool areas in floodplains and warm urban areas, separated by a dike*

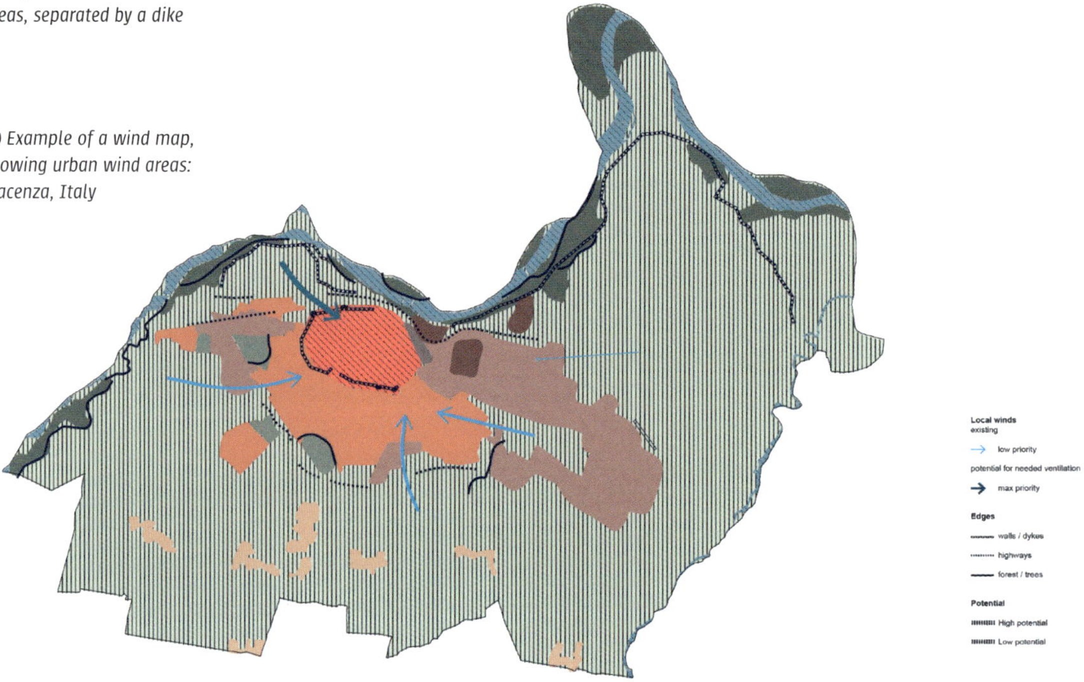

50 *Example of a wind map, showing urban wind areas: Piacenza, Italy*

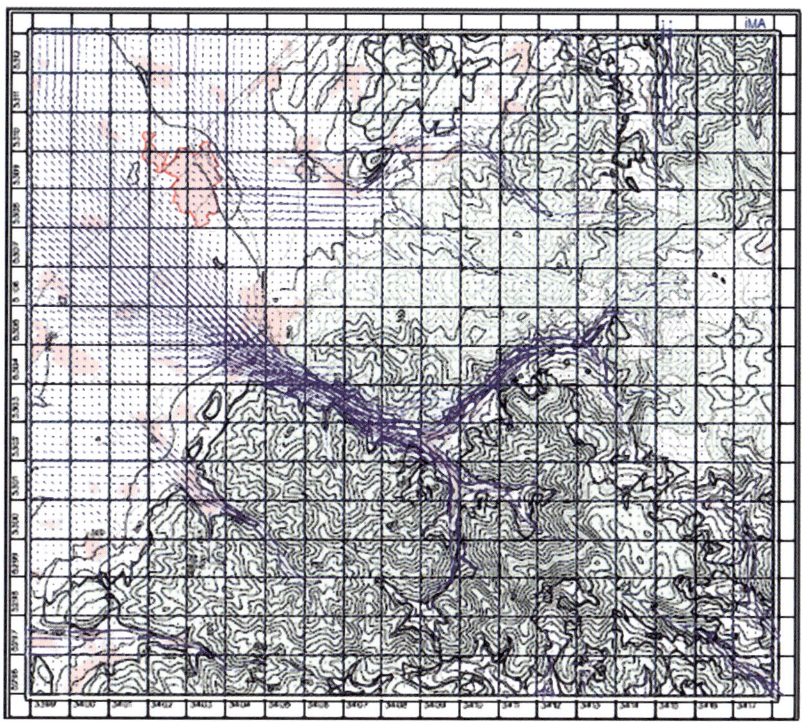

51 *Example of simulations of valley winds in Freiburg, Germany*

slow downhill air movements to flow downhill, the slopes need to be steep enough, at least 1 per cent; and there should be no obstacles such as mounds, buildings or dense vegetation.

Identifying urban wind areas

To depict the urban breezes caused by temperature gradients between warmer and cooler areas you can use the climatope map. We can expect significant temperature differences between areas with lower temperatures, such as open landscape or park, and densely built-up areas, such as city, city centre, and business and industrial estates. A breeze can form from the cooler to the warmer area – if there are no obstacles such as dikes (see an example in illustration 49), very dense vegetation or buildings at right angles to the breeze. The different wind potentials can then be mapped, with indications of the expected flow speeds. This map should also show the obstacles for such airflows, because removing such obstacles can be an important measure to improve ventilation.

Calculating local wind systems

When a city has a complex morphology, for example because of big differences in altitude and many building volumes of different sizes, experts should simulate the wind systems with airflow simulations. These can be computer-generated simulations or wind tunnel simulations. Computer simulations can be used to represent flow patterns of thermally induced local wind systems such as coastal or valley wind systems. The results of these simulations can also be used to fine-tune wind analysis maps based on climatope/local climate zone maps.

3.3 Urban Climate Maps

Urban climate maps summarize analyses

With the methods described above to analyse the thermal and the wind situation, you can make urban climate predictions for many cities. Of course, these maps only offer qualitative information, not quantitative. This usually does not pose a problem, though, since the aim of these maps is not a meticulous scientific analysis, but to create a useful basis for design measures. These urban climate maps can show the information about the temperature and the wind separately (like for the municipality of Piacenza, illustrations 47 and 50), or as overlays in one single map. Cities built on a very complex terrain, for instance with a lot of relief or along coastlines, should be analysed by experts, who will make comprehensive urban climate maps. To determine whether experts need to be brought in, city planners or designers can consult with experts in the field of urban meteorology. Together, you can arrive at a good decision on the necessity of their expert advice.

Expert systems for urban climate maps

There are several expert systems that can depict the thermal component of the urban climate. German cities have been using these analysis-map systems for the urban climate already for many decades in their urban planning practices. The city of Stuttgart has a remarkably long tradition of urban climate research, with urban meteorologists providing maps for the city. Nowadays such systems have been made for cities in various other countries such as China (with Hong Kong), Singapore, Taiwan, Japan, Australia, Vietnam, Brazil, Portugal, Spain, Switzerland, France, Sweden, the Netherlands, and the United Kingdom. Many experts base their analysis-map systems on the climatope classification (mostly automatized via GIS applications) but recent urban climate map systems now use the so-called 'Local Climate Zone' classification system that

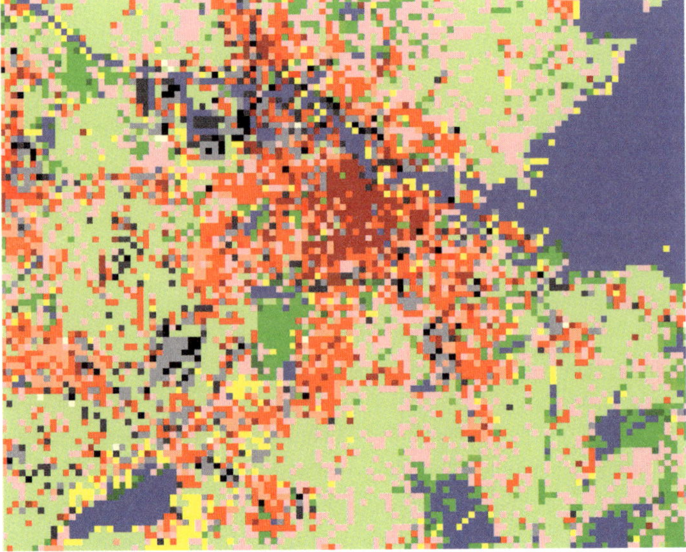

52 *Example of a local climate zone map generated with WUDAPT for Amsterdam, the Netherlands*

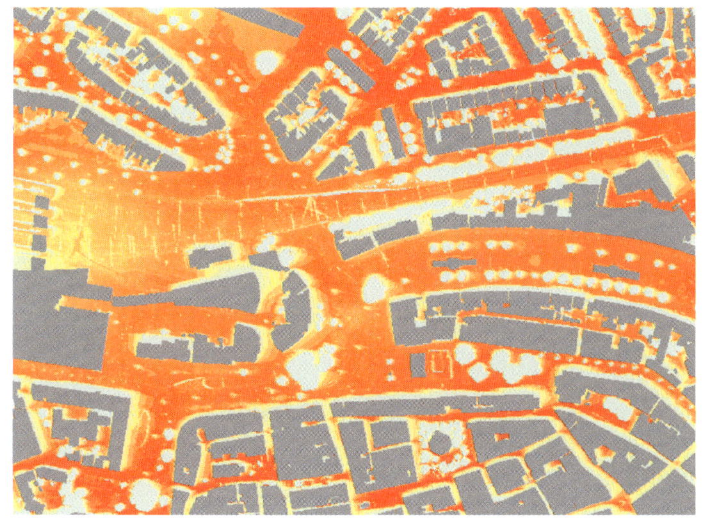

53 *PET map for a part of the city of Arnhem, with 1x1 m resolution during the afternoon of a heatwave day*

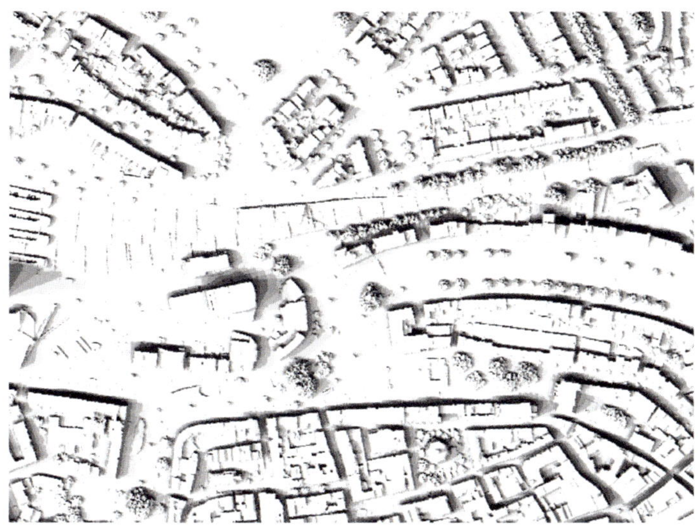

54 *shadow map for a part of the city of Arnhem, with 1x1 m resolution during a midsummer afternoon*

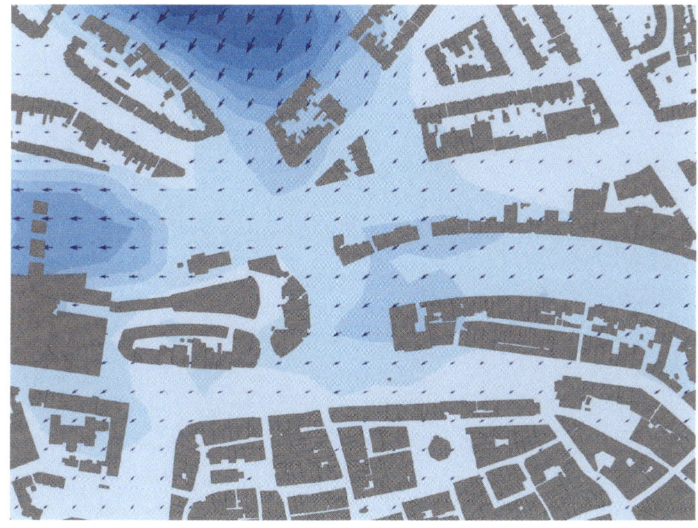

55 *Nocturnal valley wind map for a part of the city of Arnhem, hot summer night situation*

takes into account surface structure (e.g., building density and sky view factor) and surface cover, construction materials and anthropogenic heat emissions. It entails 17 standard types that are divided into 'built types' and 'land cover types' (e.g., low plants or scattered trees). In general, these 'Local Climate Zone' classes do not differ very much from the climatope systems, but they do offer a few more types when it comes to describing the 'green/landscape' parts of cities and also settlement types such as 'lightweight low-rise', which is common in informal settlements. To generate such 'Local Climate Zone' maps, the WUDAPT system is used that builds on extensive urban databases (https://www.wudapt.org/create-lcz-classification/). An example of such a 'Local Climate Zone' map for the city of Amsterdam can be found in illustration 52.

Apart from that, even more fine-grained predictions down to the scale of 1x1 m are currently derived from a combination of meteorological and geographical data in combination with indices that describe microclimate sensation, such as PET (see illustration 53). These map systems can even indicate shadow patterns for spatial objects in the city (see illustration 54) and offer new perspectives for placing shadow-casting interventions very strategically. They can also indicate the patterns of local wind systems such as valley winds occurring in the urban fabric (see illustration 55) The expert map systems always depict qualitative and nowadays also more and more quantitative information about the thermal conditions and usually also about potential ventilation situations. More often than before, these urban climate maps are openly available online (e.g., https://www.klimaateffectatlas.nl/nl/ or https://klima.geoportal.ruhr/), and they sometimes give access to the underlying data (land use, topography, building heights, et cetera).

As these maps are a 'digital twin' or representation of a reality, the map's content can also be changed to represent a new situation. For instance, land use patterns can be changed in GIS to represent a future situation, and the urban climate effects can accordingly be calculated.

The systems discussed above are evidence-based predictions of urban climate circumstances and thus only show a representation of what can be expected, but not the exact reality. The most reliable method for depicting the urban climate would be to take long-term measurements in a fine raster covering the whole city. But there are not many fixed weather stations in cities, and installing and maintaining more weather stations is difficult due to property ownership issues and it would be extremely expensive and labour-intensive. Therefore, it is not feasible to cover the entire urban area with fine-raster measurements. So urban meteorologists turn to other measuring methods, using a different way to systematically map the urban climate at important points of the city, namely mobile measurements. These follow meticulously plotted

56 *The measurement-cargo bicycles of Wageningen University*

routes, crossing the areas most essential for the urban climate. These runs are repeated a number of times, especially during the most problematic times of the year (for instance during hot summer nights). The data gathered with these measurements can give an accurate account of the microclimatic conditions along the route, sometimes down to a mere few metres. Many cities have used cars that could also measure the other factors that are very important for thermal comfort, such as radiation and wind. In several countries, specially equipped bicycles were used for these measurements. The advantage of bicycles is that they can also be used in areas inaccessible to cars, such as parks.

Measurements provide policymakers with 'hard facts'

Conducting these different measurement techniques requires a lot of expert knowledge, resources and time, but it is often worthwhile. Experience teaches us that many policymakers do not have enough confidence in the urban climate maps, because they do not offer 'hard facts and figures'. Even though such measurements often would not be necessary, because everyone with a little knowledge about the urban climate knows, for instance, that there are heat islands in every city. However, policymakers were not always convinced of the existence of urban heat effects, until the measured 'hard figures' made it abundantly clear that they do. So, one often needs extra measurements to complement and validate the other predictive analysis methods.

3.4 Vulnerability to Urban Climate Phenomena

Activities, health and age influence vulnerability

Before you start making large-scale plans and designs for the urban climate, you should also assess the vulnerability aspect to identify areas that need adaptation. In the context of microclimate experience, the vulnerability obviously pertains to how vulnerable different groups of people are to heat stress and wind danger, depending on their activities, age and health.

Vulnerability to heat

Human activities take place in different time patterns, which have to be compared with the time patterns of the urban climate. Especially keep in mind that urban heat island effects are most prominent at night. These urban heat effects occur in several climatope areas, but they differ in how far people are really affected. People living in densely built-up residential areas often have trouble sleeping during warm nights

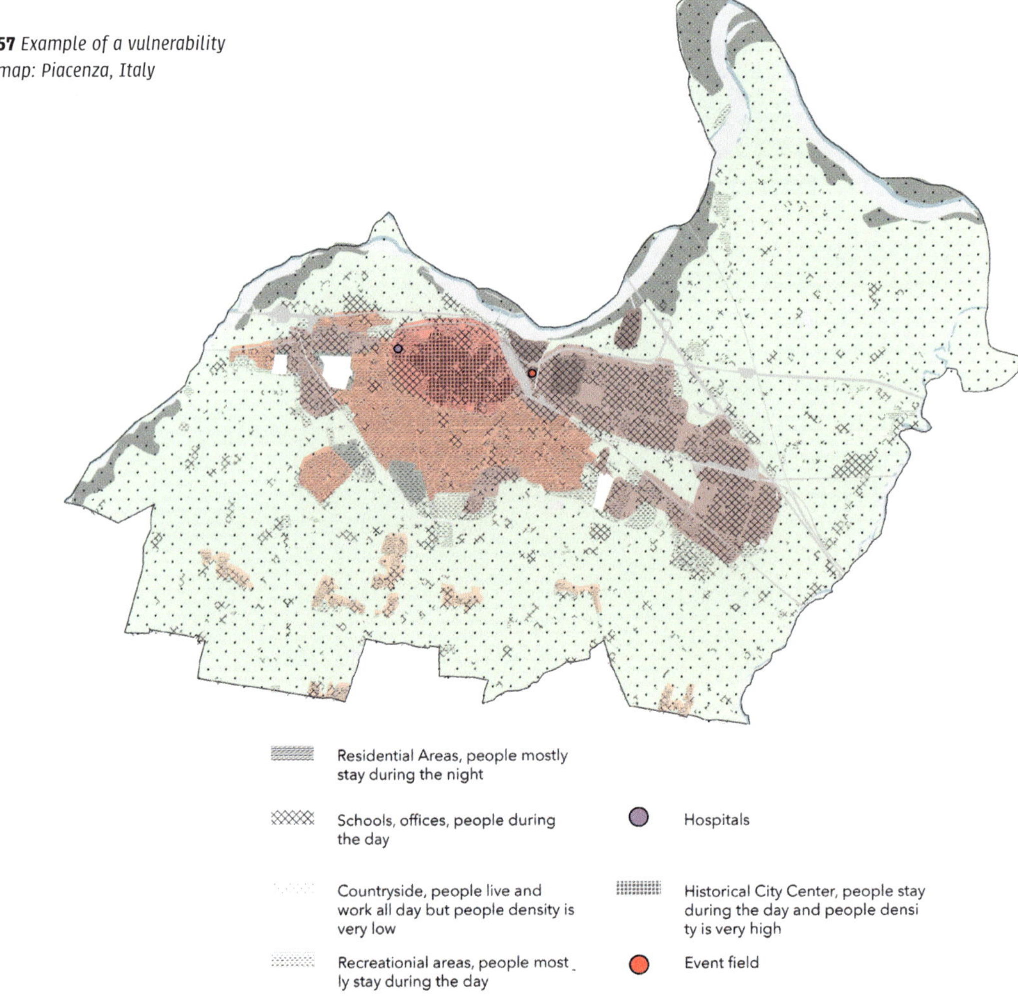

57 *Example of a vulnerability map: Piacenza, Italy*

because of the enhanced urban heat. But at a business park, also very hot at night, the heat does not bother many people. People do sometimes work nightshifts in industrial estates, but because these people work inside the buildings, which often have climate control, there is also usually less urgency for adaptation measures. There is much less urgency to adapt such areas than there is for the densely built-up urban areas with many residents.

In a densely built-up city centre, with many people coming into the area to visit to do some shopping or sightseeing, for instance, it *can* be very important to offer options for cooling during the day. The same could go for festival sites, where people can be exposed to strong heat on hot summer days.

Certain groups of people are particularly vulnerable to heat, especially young children, elderly people and people that are ill. Because these people spend a lot of their time in certain locations, such as daycare centres, schools, retirement homes or hospitals, these locations should be mapped as well, since extra heat adaptation measures might be necessary. Apart from that, groups of citizens who live in badly insulated buildings are also more prone to be affected by heat when staying indoors. Unfortunately, this frequently concerns public housing neighbourhoods in which thermal discomfort indoors and outdoors adds to other problems.

You can usually show these vulnerability aspects in one map, with different layers or symbols for the different aspects. These aspects can then easily be included in the recommendations for adaptation (see illustration 57).

Vulnerability to wind

Besides heat, wind nuisance is also a big problem in many cities. In areas where many people are outside, such as shopping streets, city squares or festival sites, it is very important to create a safe and comfortable wind climate. Therefore, areas with these activities should also be mapped and compared with the analyses of areas with wind nuisance.

4

Planning and Design for the Urban Climate at the City Scale

At the city scale, it is possible to significantly influence the urban climate, especially with measures affecting the air temperature and the ventilation patterns. The interventions concern larger parts of the city, such as making 'green wedges', 'park cool islands', and assigning functions to areas that are to be developed in the future or that should remain free of buildings. Some of the possible measures are scaled between the large and the micro scale, for instance which tree structures to use in parks, or how to keep ventilation axes open at the district level. So, there are many possibilities for adapting the urban climate on a larger scale. These have to be made explicit, to provide urban designers and policymakers with concrete suggestions about what they can do in their own city to make it more 'urban climate proof'.

All the information derived from the urban climate analyses that were described in the previous chapter has to be weighed and translated into design measures and policy. Here, the interventions to lower the temperature are often different from those providing better ventilation for the city. The scale level of the measures to lower the air temperature is very diverse. These range from realizing urban green space systems down to accumulated implementation of small-scale interventions (which will be discussed in chapter 6). The ventilation measures are usually taken at a larger scale. The first part of this chapter is about various planning and design interventions. Of course, such measures then have to be actually implemented, which often requires an adaptation to the existing policy instruments. The last section of this chapter therefore offers insights on how this implementation can be achieved.

4.1 Reducing Heat Stress

The cool air plume reaches into adjacent areas

Most of the time, interventions aimed at preventing the city from overheating mean adding 'green'. This includes preserving and enlarging existing parks; and planning more city parks, green corridors and green wedges between urbanized areas and surrounding landscapes. Several studies have demonstrated the cooling effect of green structures like parks, large gardens or natural urban areas. The name for these green structures is very befitting: park cool islands. These park cool islands can be observed within the parks and also in the surroundings of parks. The general magnitude of the park cooling ranges between 0.5-3.5 °C between a park and the temperature in more urbanized parts of the city in temperate climate zones. This effect mostly depends on the composition of vegetated open areas and tree cover, and to a smaller extent the size of the parks or gardens.
But parks also provide cooling to their surroundings in many circumstances. Swedish scientists measured a cooling effect up to 1 km

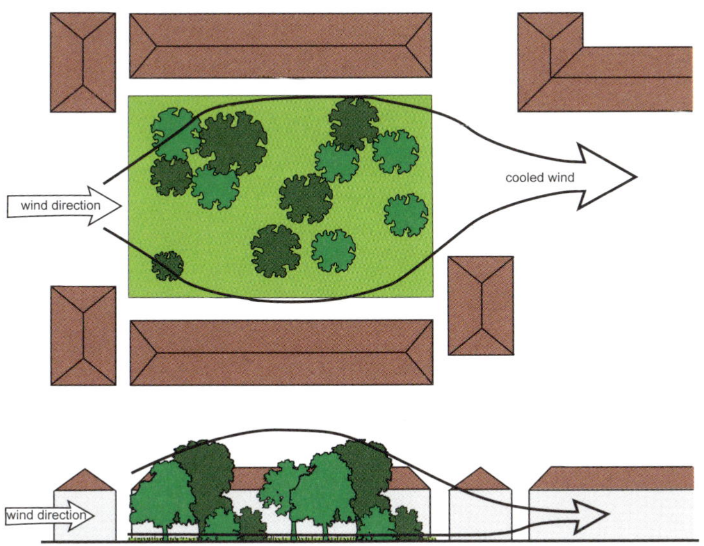

58 *Cool air plume on the lee side of a neighbourhood park entering an open ventilation corridor*

from a large park in Gothenburg (150 hectares), but this is exceptional. A Canadian study indicated a cooling effect up to a hundred metres from neighbourhood parks on their leeside, in places where the wind could carry the cool air into adjacent streets. Even light wind can transport the cool park air like a 'plume of cool air' into the surrounding area, especially on the leeward side of the park. From this study, as well as from others, we can see how important it is not to over-build or -plant the ventilation areas for the cool air at the park edges.

How to distribute green areas over the city?

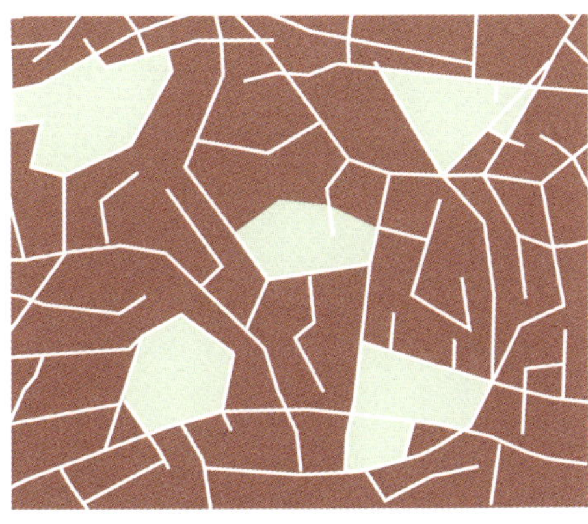

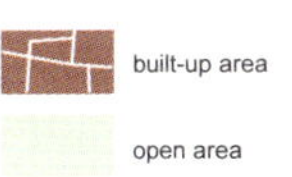

59 *Optimal distribution of green areas in a city*

Some scientists have also looked at the optimal size of parks and their distribution over the city, but these studies are still scarce. It is better to distribute several smaller or linear parks over the densely built-up areas of a city than it is to create one large park (see illustration 59). The cooling effect of such smaller parks on their environment is strongly influenced by the surrounding urban morphology and its street grid orientation. In general, the smaller parks should have a size of at least one hectare and should be equipped with ample open (street) space

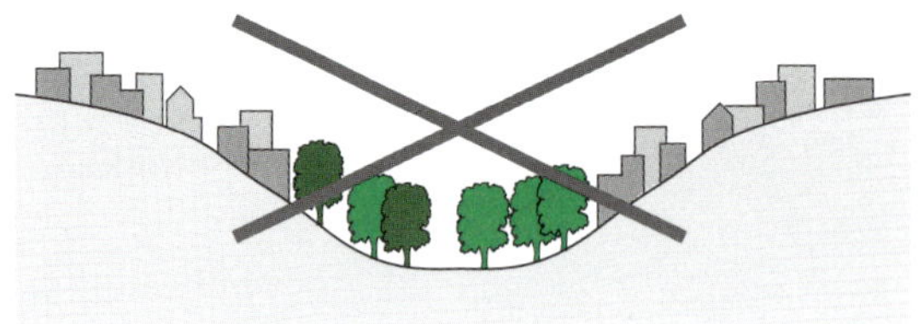

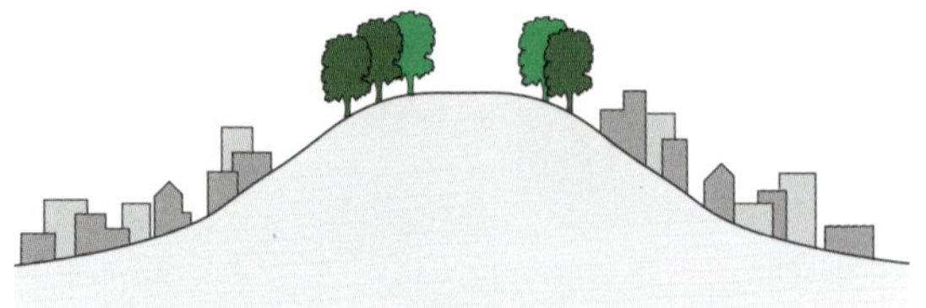

60 *Optimal distribution of green areas in a hilly urban terrain*

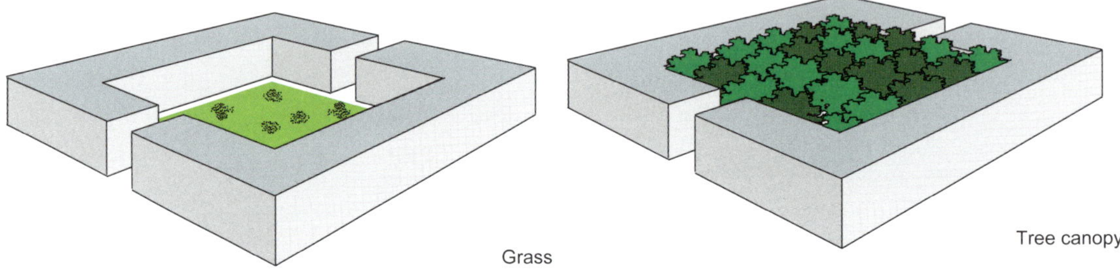

61 *Parks with open lawns cool at night and parks with trees cool during the daya*

around to allow cooler air to penetrate into the adjacent blocks. The cooling within a park itself very much depends on the spatial distribution of trees and open patches in the parks or other green spaces. A heavily wooded park will provide less cooling at night (being a 'forest' climatope) than a park with a mix of open areas and tree clumps (being a 'park' climatope) and much less than a large open park (being an 'open landscape' climatope). When designing parks, we should bear in mind that people's outdoor thermal sensation during the day is strongly influenced by the presence or absence of shade. Therefore, it is beneficial to create cool spots that offer sufficient shade. When the main aim of a park or garden is to provide sufficient local shading by trees and not a significant lowering of the air temperature, a pocket park of at least 200 m^2 would suffice for this purpose as well.

The location of open green areas in the relief of the city also makes a difference. If the green area is in a lower area than its surroundings, the heavier, cool park air cannot get away and creates a 'cool air pond'; but if it is at a higher elevation than its surroundings, the cool air can flow downhill into the urban fabric (see illustration 60).

Do we need parks for cooling during the day or at night?

In light of the fact that parks with different vegetation also have different temperature patterns, it is important to look at these vegetation types in relation to the surrounding functions. If, for example, there are many people in the surroundings of a park during the day, as in city centres or office areas, cooling is more important at that time than it is at night. During the day, parks with more trees offering shade provide better cooling than open parks with big lawns. It is therefore preferable in these locations to plant many trees in the parks.

In a residential area, on the other hand, nightly cooling is very important. Open, green surfaces with a bigger sky view factor are more effective, because these areas cool down quickly at night and thus cool the surroundings. In an area with mixed functions, it is best to alternate open lawns and trees in a park. When the trees have high crowns and the cool air is free to flow around the trunks, a nice cooling effect can be expected. To ensure enough sunlight in all parks at wintertime, deciduous trees are always preferred.

Cooling a city with green areas, especially lawns, however, can face one 'bottleneck situation'. If there is not enough water available in the soil for the plants during a heatwave, the plants' evapotranspiration will be limited, and consequently also their contribution to cooling. So especially during heatwaves, you must provide sufficient irrigation.

Swamps with dense plants can also provide cooling

Also areas that are more than sufficiently irrigated, such as swampy areas, can have a cooling function. As mentioned earlier, water bodies are not very effective for cooling their surroundings, because they absorb much solar radiation during the day, which they give off during the night in the form of heat. But when they are densely grown with plants whose shade keeps the water cooler, and which evaporate extra water through their stomata, these areas cool the air. Studies in Japan on the impact of rice paddies have shown these effects. We can expect the same effect for other combinations of water and plants, such as reed lands, alluvial forests and swamp forests.

Green and water recreation areas as 'heat refuges'

It can also help to create areas that are cool during the day in easy reach from the most heat-prone areas for people to escape the heat. These areas should offer extra cooling with trees offering shade, possibly the use of local wind systems for cooling breezes, and if available, water to swim in or just cool the limbs. Recent research has indicated that such 'cool spots' should be at about 300 metres walking distance and that they should be easy to reach via shaded paths ('cool routes'). On a larger scale, it is also desirable to create entire networks of such cool routes and provide larger 'heat refuge' areas that are well connected by public transport and shaded bicycle routes.

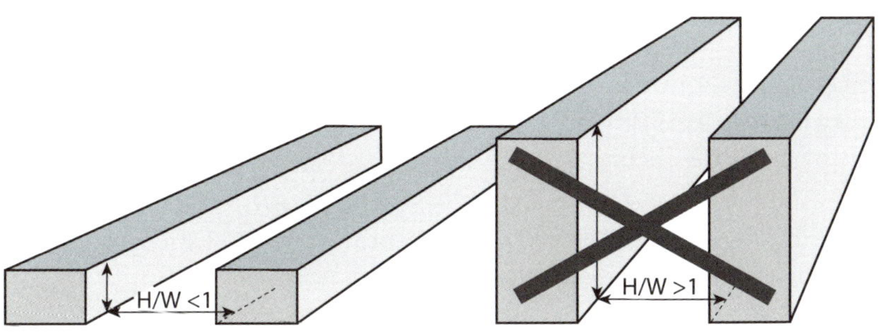

62 *Effects of streets' H/W-ratio on preventing heat accumulation*

Modifying the building and street structures to prevent warming

Besides the 'green' interventions for heat adaptation, there are also many adaptation possibilities in the built urban structure. For example, when parts of densely built-up areas are abandoned, they should not be built up anymore and be carefully replanted. New residential urban areas should be built with a lower building density to prevent heat accumulation by designing a more spacious H/W-ratio for streets or squares, so the heat can get away more easily. The street H/W proportions and their orientation should be examined carefully, so you do not unintentionally get wind nuisance (see section 2.2.3). In general, one can say that a height-width-ratio of 1:1, or narrower, retains much radiation at night and is not recommended. Moreover, the shadows of the buildings which are quite large in mid-latitude areas during most days of the year, often dominate for too many hours of the day in such narrow spaces, limiting the daylight intrusion of the buildings.

Changing the functions of areas to cooler climatope types

Changes in the functions of areas can also help solve heat problems, by changing these from a 'warm' into a 'cooler' climatope type. Many heat-producing industrial estates, for example, might be converted into area types that produce less heat, such as commercial districts or parklike campuses. Especially for abandoned industrial estates and brownfields, the latter is a very useful change in function. Where possible, large-scale traffic infrastructure can be reduced or at least de-paved wherever possible. Alternatively, governments could implement more traffic control, like they do in London and Madrid, allowing fewer cars into the city and thus producing less anthropogenic heat.

4.2 Creating Ventilation Between and Within Districts

As discussed earlier, wind can sometimes be a problem, but it can also offer a potential for ventilation. Therefore, wind-based urban design has two sides: on the one hand averting wind in areas prone to nuisance, and on the other hand inviting breezes to ventilate areas with heat problems. The areas in the city with wind nuisance are usually relatively small-scaled. For the ventilation of the city, however, large-scale interventions are often more effective. These include a number of typical interventions, serving different purposes.

Depending on a city's topography, coastal wind systems might be used for daytime ventilation in cities. At night, the coastal wind often brings warmer air into the city, which is not desirable in hot situations. If there are dunes between a coastal city and the coast itself, the soft coastal breeze usually can't reach the city. Experts should look into the exact interaction for each city. Generally speaking, though, the potential for coastal wind systems in temperate climate zones is relatively small.

Valley wind systems that can transport cool air into the city at night should be facilitated. To do so, the higher altitude areas generating the cool air and the downstream airflow lines should be kept open. This means the areas at higher altitudes ideally are not surfaced, built-on or forested. Otherwise, nighttime radiative cooling cannot reach its maximum, and less cool air is produced or even none at all. Suitable land use types for these areas are arable land, pasture, heathland or similar landscape types. The areas through which the cool air flows down to the cities are usually steeper slopes and the bottom of the valley, because cold air flows downhill (also see illustration 51 with cold airflows in Freiburg, Germany), yet the air's flow speed is much lower than that of streaming water, and these slow, cool airflows are easily blocked. Because these airflows are so weak and the areas through which they stream are so small, these open areas allowing the airflow are very vulnerable. So, these areas have to be protected in case they are still open. If these areas are already forested, built-on or blocked by other obstacles, removing these obstacles should be taken into consideration. When it is not possible to clear an airflow's entire path, the situation can be improved by arranging building or planting structures parallel to the direction of the flow, instead of at right angles to it (see illustration 63).

Ventilation axes in valleys should be kept open

Ventilation areas between open landscapes and cities should be kept open

63 *Avoiding barriers along contour lines in hilly cities to allow for ventilation and preferable building configuration on the slopes*

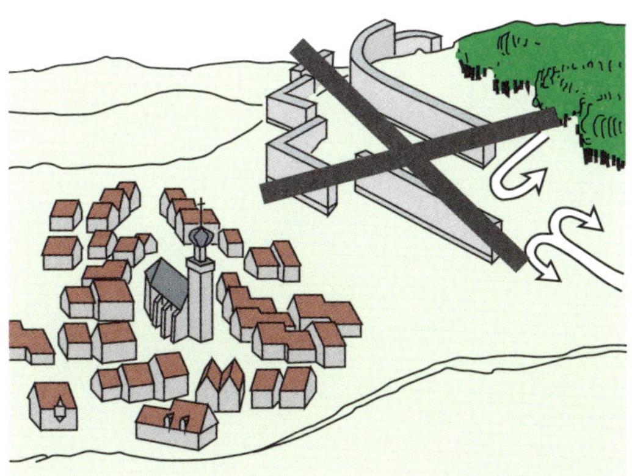

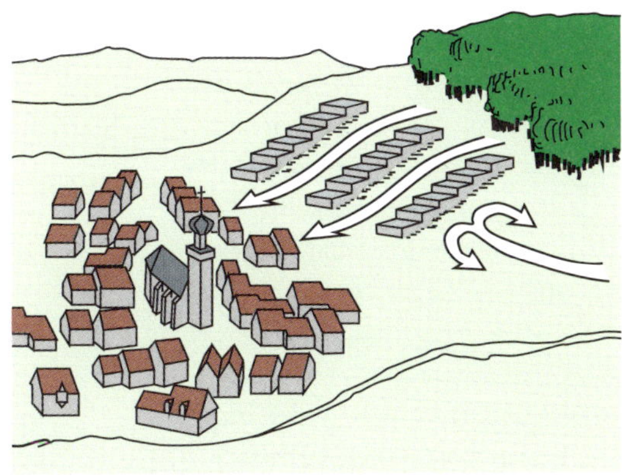

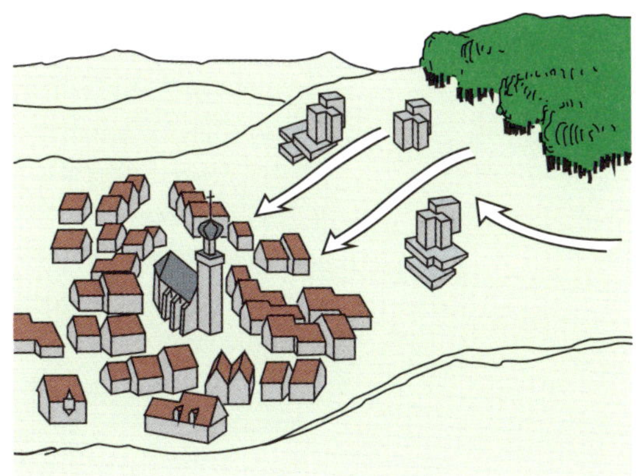

Creating longer gradient lines between open landscapes and cities

Local urban wind systems, occurring between rather cool climatopes, such as 'open landscape' (or at night: 'railway yard'), and climatopes retaining much heat, such as 'high density', or additionally generating much anthropogenic heat, such as 'commercial district' and 'industrial estate' climatopes, can also be used for ventilation. Like the valley breezes, these airflows are relatively slow and vulnerable to interception. Therefore, the possible ventilation courses between these areas should ideally be kept free of obstacles such as earthen walls, buildings or many trees and shrubs.

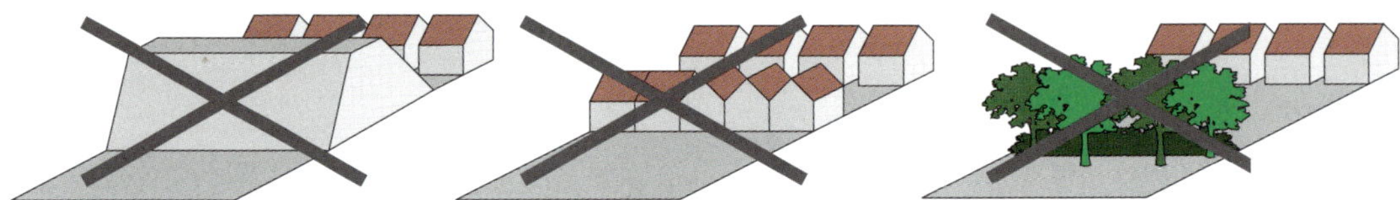

64 *Avoiding barriers for urban wind between 'cooler' and 'warmer' climatopes*

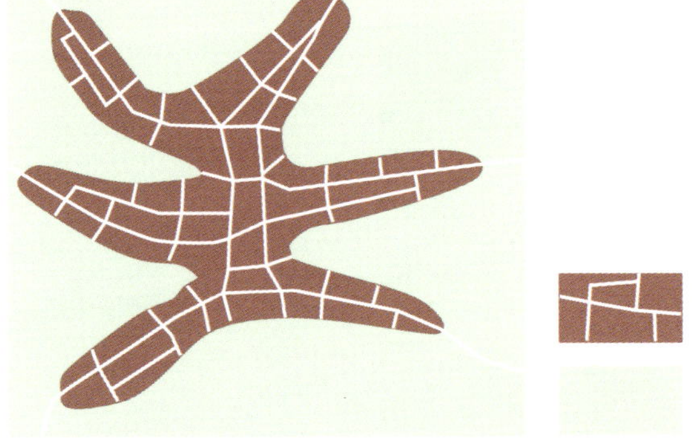

65 *Long gradients between cooler open 'landscape fingers' and the densely built-up city offer much potential for ventilation*

Cool open areas next to warm, high density / anthropogenic heat producing areas can also produce local wind fluxes

To make optimal use of the effect of the temperature gradient between cooler and warmer climatopes, the gradient line between climatopes should be elongated. This can mean 'open landscape fingers' or large green areas in a densely built-up city, ideally penetrating deep into the 'hot climatopes'. Few cities have such 'fingers' yet, but Copenhagen is a good example. To be able to realize such elongated interfaces, cities should strategically open up these 'landscape fingers' when areas are restructured. These days, we have a promising opportunity to insert 'landscape finger systems' into areas with largely empty factory, business and office buildings at urban peripheries. Part of the surfaced parking lots and such can become unpaved. The same can be done in abandoned terrains at the edges of 'hot climatopes'.

In these 'de-paved' areas, new functions such as urban agriculture have great potential. It is important, however, to keep these areas relatively open, so as not to weaken their ventilation function. For planned urban expansions, it is recommendable to plan 'landscape fingers' penetrating the city from the onset (see illustration 65). This is the only way to ensure that ventilation axes are actually realized in the future urban structure.

4.3 Implementation in Planning Practice

The 'recommendations maps' for urban planning

It is possible to implement these recommendations for urban planning and design on the larger scale in various ways. To do so, a 'recommendations map' is usually made (see example in illustration 66). It is based on the urban climate analyses maps or on climatope maps, with due consideration for areas with inhabitants who are extra vulnerable to heat stress. A recommendations map localizes diverse measures for urban climate adaptation. These recommendations cover different scale levels: opening up or preserving large ventilation corridors for urban winds between open and built-up areas, or on hill tops and slopes for downhill cold air systems. For other areas, general recommendations

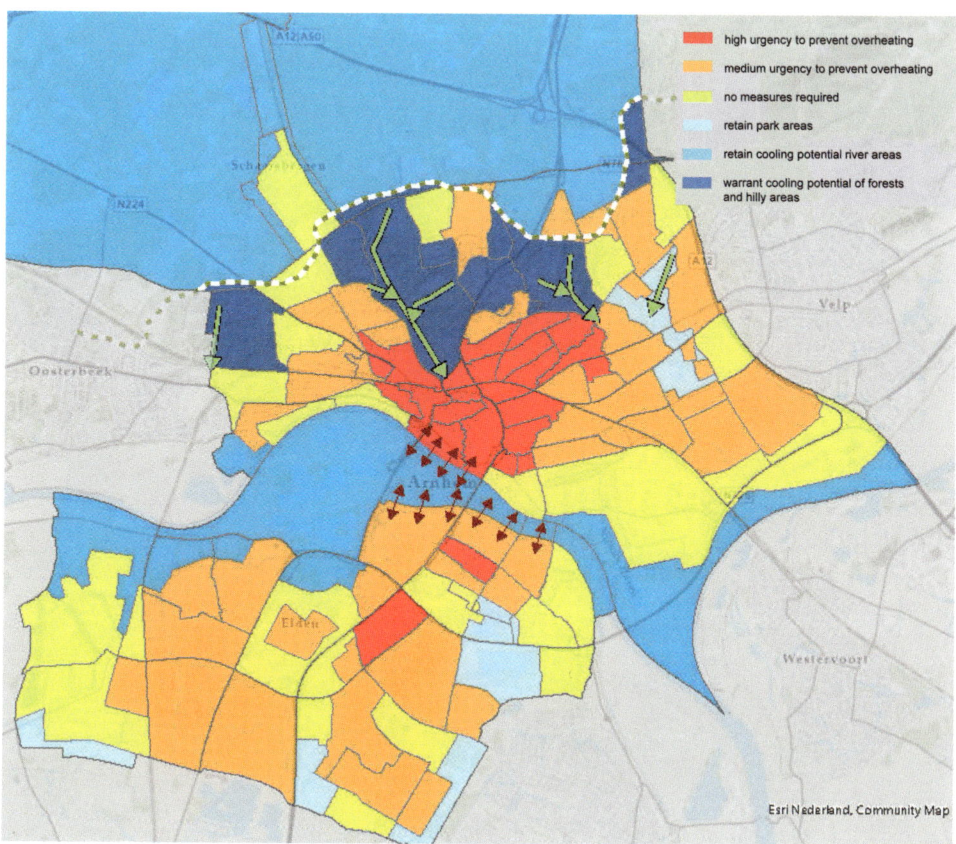

66 *Planning recommendations map Arnhem, the Netherlands*

67 *Analysis and recommendation maps for valley winds, forming a basis for zoning plans, Stuttgart, Germany*

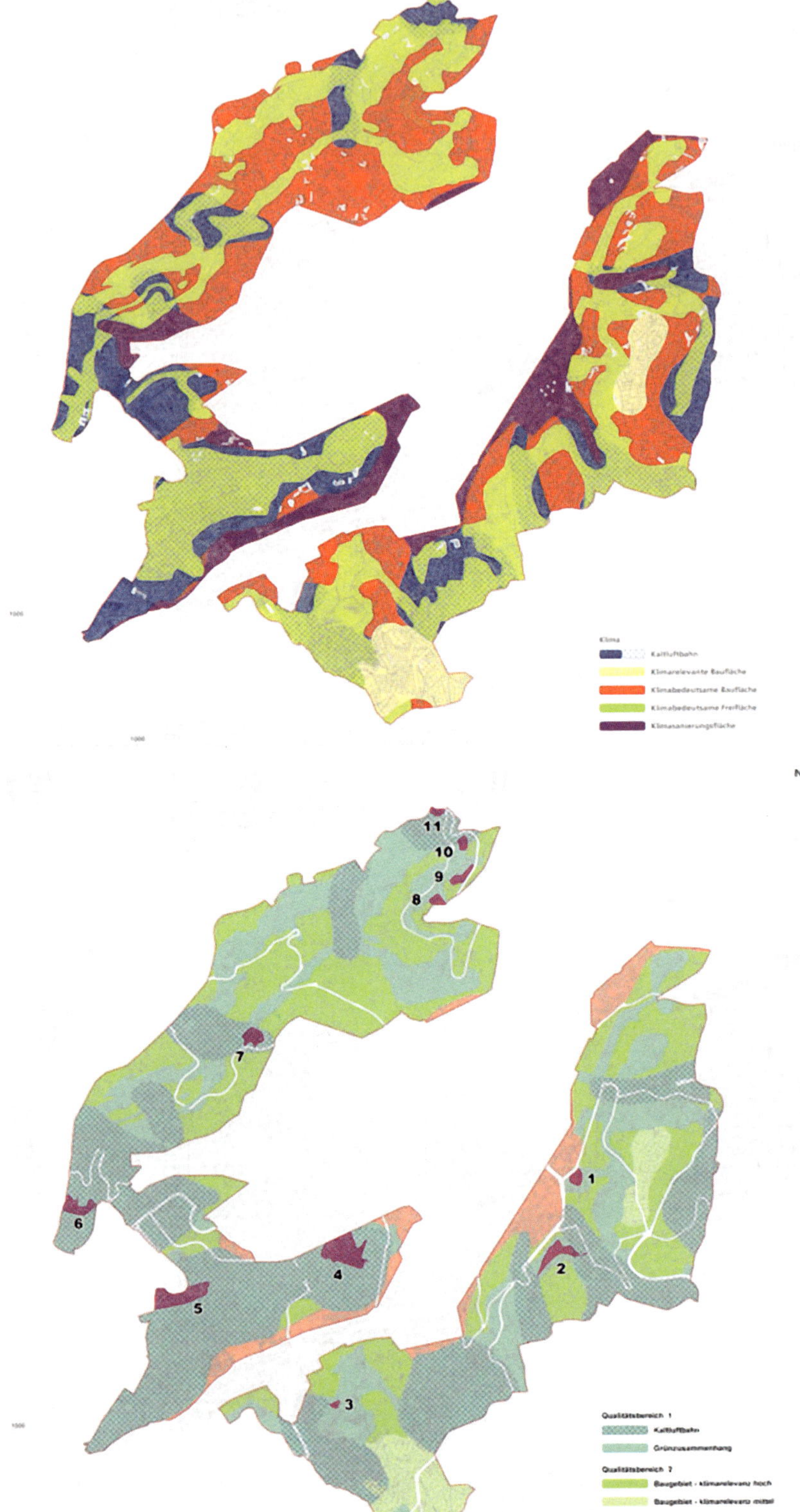

are made (strong need for cooling, no action required, et cetera), and are elucidated by suggestions for possible small-scale interventions, such as green facades, trees and reflecting materials (see chapter 6) in the accompanying texts to these maps.

Some recommendations maps are still 'paper' maps, but we see a growing number of digital and interactive systems as well that are usually combined with the urban climate analysis maps in digital repositories (e.g., the Ruhr area, city of Stuttgart in Germany, the Dutch 'Klimaateffectatlas' (Climate Impact Atlas). Generally, these data are available to everyone through a website where the user can zoom into special themes and areas or can consult the underlying databases.
How the contents of these recommendations maps eventually get implemented in different countries varies a lot but generally is still in its infancy. Our recent international research shows that many countries have not yet started to implement the knowledge into planning, some have started to experiment and only very few cities do implement the recommendations. For instance, Japan has quite strict rules for implementation now, such as compulsory heat stress tests for all new building projects.

In Germany, the information is sometimes translated on a large scale into a legally binding 'Flächennutzungsplan', an urban master plan defining the function of different areas. On a smaller scale, the information can be translated into the 'Bebauungsplan', a zoning plan. Illustration 67 gives an example of local climate and recommendation maps for parts of the city of Stuttgart, indicating that the important ventilation zones into the city centre should be kept open or even that these should be cleared. Based on these maps, changes in existing zoning plans were made. For San Francisco, United States and Toronto, Canada, urban climate analyses were made for the central districts, and these were translated into zoning plans, but these are exceptions. Hong Kong uses the information from the urban climate maps in its urban planning for problematic areas. In the Netherlands, the information is partly used for the non-binding urban master plans ('omgevingsvisies'), and partly to test how 'urban climate proof' new projects are. In the US, the need for adaptation only comes into view sporadically and adaptation guidelines are developed for these specific spots. Sometimes, also special projects are realized to set an example for good adaptation practice. So, in these latter countries, projects do get tested, partly also through environmental assessments, and, usually small-scale, adjustments are made. This is not necessarily the most effective way to improve the urban climate. Larger interventions and legally binding implementation instruments have proven more effective as our recent research on implementation of urban climate measures shows.
However, many countries do not have such instruments in place as they run against their political culture that relies more on bottom-up approaches or on negotiation. In other countries the apparatus needed for enforcement is not present.

As we can see, the ways in which the recommendations for the urban climate are used are very diverse, and they depend on a country's planning culture. Most countries in the world do not act on their urban climate issues yet, and for these countries, the example German city planning sets can be inspiring. We also know of successful implementation of urban climate measures in some front-runner cities in Switzerland and Austria (especially Vienna) and hopefully others will follow their exemplary planning soon.

Other implementation options can be imagined

Here is an overview of implementation measures that can work within many urban planning systems, and the accompanying plans on different scale levels. These recommendations are based on the German implementation practice.

Green fingers/wedges and large parks	Legally binding urban master plan
City and neighbourhood parks	Legally binding urban master plan
Changing functions of large, heat-generating areas	Legally binding urban master plan
Lower building densities	Zoning plan
Lower H/W-ratio streets	Zoning plan
Orientation buildings to keep airflow paths clear	Zoning plan
Length of streets to prevent wind nuisance	Zoning plan

For large-scale interventions to improve the urban climate involving several municipalities in a (urban) region, the municipalities should make solid agreements. The impact of a spatial intervention at the edge of one city, for instance building an industrial estate, can have a big impact on the heat climate of a neighbouring municipality. We should always keep in mind that the urban climate does not end at the city limits.

5
Mapping the Microclimate

SAMSUNG
SAMSUNG

Adapting the microclimate sometimes means generally applicable 'no regret' interventions such as green facades, but for the most part these are site-specific measures playing into the local microclimate of an urban place or a neighbourhood. On this small scale, analyses of the different characteristics of the local climate are therefore needed first, to understand the sun exposures of different places and wind patterns around objects. If you do not map the microclimate before you start working on adaptation measures, you might choose the wrong solutions. For small-scale designs, solutions need to be tested during the design process often, and for this you need to know which analysis techniques are the most appropriate. The analyses entail diverse methods, partly pertaining to the physical aspects of the microclimate and partly to the psychological ones, but also combinations of both. Because the climate changes with the seasons, analyses usually have to be made for different times of the year. The patterns of use in different parts of outdoors space often also play a role, and therefore these should be analysed as well. The analyses are generally depicted in maps, profiles and three-dimensional drawings, so they can be directly used for spatial design.

Depending on what is considered the most prominent problem for the microclimate at a certain location, a suitable analysis method should be selected. If, for example, a large-scale urban climate analysis (see chapter 3) indicates that wind and/or heat problems are to be expected, the local analysis can address this. But sometimes users' complaints about an uncomfortable microclimate can also give rise to a smaller scaled study, taking in the psychological factors as well. The following sections are about the different analysis methods; explaining for which issues these can be used, which data they will provide, how they work, what kind of expertise is needed and what you can expect in terms of manpower and expertise to conduct the analyses. The physical factors come first, again subdivided into temperature and wind factors. It is also possible to map these physical factors integrally, with computer simulations and/or measurements. The analyses of the psychological aspects are next, and this chapter ends with a discussion of which analysis methods can complement each other in which situations.

5.1 Analyses of Physical Microclimate Experience

Analyses include microclimatic and spatial information

There are many ways to map the physical circumstances determining the microclimate experience in urban outdoor areas. In all cases, this means connecting urban climatic data with geographical data, in order to get a spatial representation of the urban climate aspects. People with a background in urban design and additional knowledge about the urban climate can carry out certain analysis methods. In part, these analyses are 'educated guesses'. The analyses are of a largely qualitative nature and 'rules of thumb', but in part, they can also be used to make quantitative estimations. For example, you can make approximate predictions about many wind patterns around objects or in open areas. Such general knowledge about the microclimate is often sufficient to make designs bearing in mind that many factors have to be taken into account during the design process, and it is often unnecessary or even impossible to focus designs down to the smallest detail on the microclimate alone.

This chapter also features short descriptions of the expert analysis techniques to provide some insight into the different methods. This is geared at readers who act as commissioners for urban climate analyses. As a commissioner, you can then use this basic knowledge to discuss with urban meteorology experts which analysis method is best suited for a certain project.

5.1.1 Shadow Simulations as Indicators of Temperature Experience

For mapping the thermal sensation, for example to indicate the optimal locations of sojourn places, the long- and shortwave radiation and the air temperature are most important. However, because the shortwave radiation in light and shadow has the largest impact on thermal sensation in our parts of the world, it usually suffices to simulate sun and shadow patterns, for instance with common 3D-software such as AutoCAD or SketchUp (see Illustration 68). Beforehand, you have to carefully consider which shadow situation you are analysing: is it a place used in winter (when shadows are very long) or in summer (when shadow patterns are much shorter), and what kind of use are you designing for? The shadow simulation then has to take those situations

With shadow simulations, make accurate maps about solar radiation 'hotspots'

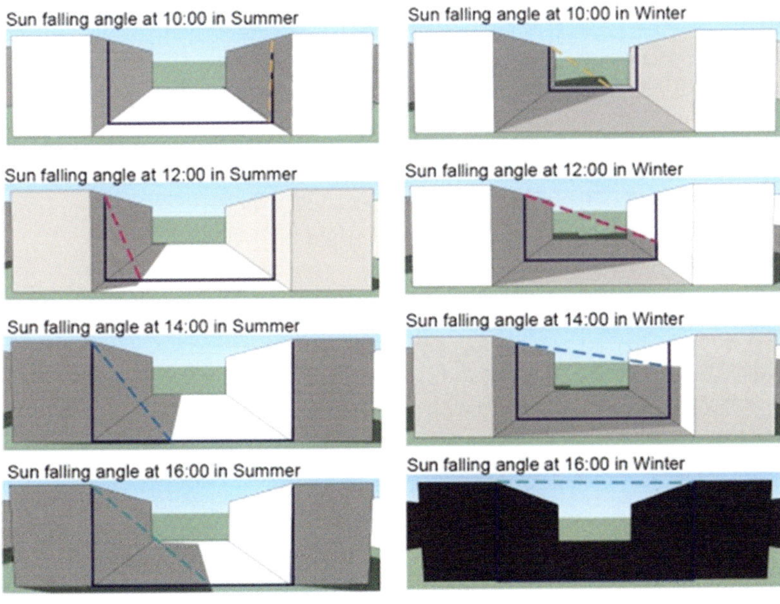

68 *Series of shadow patterns for summer and winter season in an east-west oriented street profile*

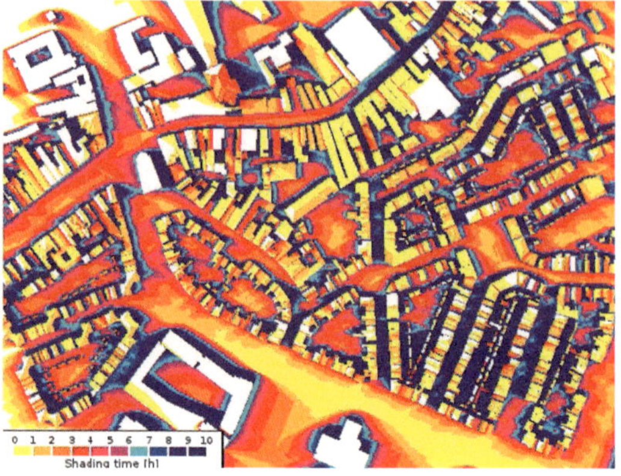

69 *Shadow patterns in different seasons, Fellenoord, Breda, the Netherlands, for spring (left) and summer (right), generated with the SketchUp Shadow Analysis Plugin*

into account. When you want to create a space that receives ample solar radiation in a certain season, you can generate so-called 'solar envelope' 3D drawings in which you can see the areas and volumes that should not be built-up or planted so as to allow maximum radiation. This can be done in common 3D software, many of which have special plugins for this purpose.

When you want to know where the levels of solar radiation are too high and require measures, you can also use 3D software. You can create images of the shadow patterns for certain shorter or longer periods of time, say over the course of a whole year. This can be done with special plug-ins in 3D software (e.g., Shadow Analysis for the Sketchup Plugin, see example Illustration 69) and in 3D GIS applications.
In case you do not have access to such plugins, you can also generate these shadow maps yourself. If you do this for a whole year you have to simulate the shadow patterns of 21 June and 22 December in your 3D software. These two dates are the longest and the shortest day of the year, depending on the location on either the Northern or the Southern Hemisphere. Because these are the extremes, they also cover all patterns in between. Using these, you can make a more in-depth analysis. Of course, you can also select shorter periods and create simulations for the longest and shortest day in those periods.

In the 3D software you can select crucial points in time (e.g., morning, noon, evening, or hourly) simulate shading, and take screenshots. You can then easily make a graphical representation by projecting the shadow pattern screenshots for different seasons or times of the day on top of each other, using a programme such as Photoshop. The overlap of shaded areas in the images indicates if a certain location has much shade (darker grey) or little shade (lighter grey). With this, you can make a rough estimation of the heat absorption, and thus indirectly also the possible radiation. When heat problems are to be expected at such places, specific measures can be taken. For example: if street profiles need to be 'cooler', it is helpful to make such an analysis for these streets. In the example (illustration 71) you can see which shadow

70 *Shadow patterns in different seasons, Grote Markt, Groningen, the Netherlands, generated with Photoshop overlay*

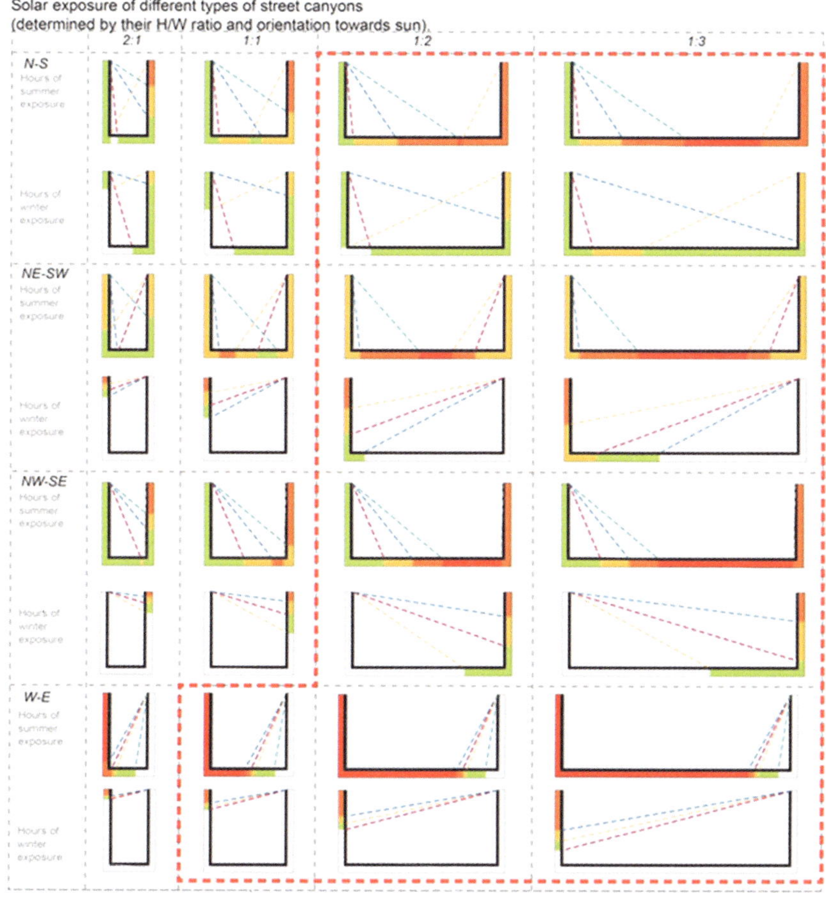

71 *Matrix of shadow simulations with sunshine percentages for different street profiles with varying orientations, plus indications of heat problem locations (red dotted line)*

patterns occur in streets with different H/W-ratios, showing a north-south and an east-west orientation. The lines in these profiles show which places receive too much sun, thus where to expect heat problems.

Pros and cons of shadow simulations

Such shadow simulations can usually be made quickly, because in many design projects, the geometrical information is already generated in a three-dimensional design programme. Then it's very straightforward to make the simulations for different points of time in your 3D software. You do not need to know very much about the urban climate, and you do not need to consult any experts. On the other hand, the simulations do not offer precise information about albedos and emissivity of materials.

5.1.2 Educated Guesses about Wind Patterns

To understand local wind patterns, for example to allocate pedestrian or bicycle routes, or locations for recreation, rough estimations of wind patterns can be helpful. Especially during the design process itself it is practical to have such estimations at your disposal to make quick decisions about design alternatives. This requires a study of the region's wind data. You can often download the data from the nearest weather station from the websites of meteorological institutes. Sometimes you get wind roses and sometimes you get the numerical data for further analysis in a spreadsheet.

The main questions in the wind-climate situation concern the problems and potentials of an area. To estimate where possible problems may occur, we should know which wind from which direction is the strongest (with wind speeds of over 5 metre per second). Does this wind occur often? This wind is usually not pleasant and has to be slowed down. For the potentials of wind to ventilate hot areas, the questions are different: which wind directions and speeds prevail on the warmest days? Is this wind strong enough (at least 2 metres per second)

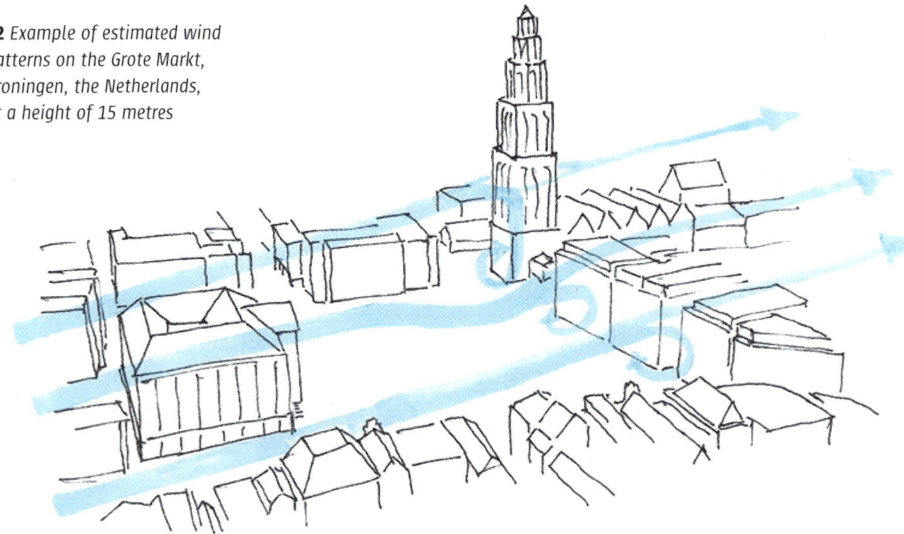

72 *Example of estimated wind patterns on the Grote Markt, Groningen, the Netherlands, at a height of 15 metres*

73 *Example square of 100 x 100 metres with wind protection hedges and sheltered areas*

to offer ventilation? If not, what are the potentials for ventilation with local breezes (coastal, valley or local wind)?

With this information in mind, we can start to identify the specific wind patterns in various spots within an area.

With the knowledge from section 2.2.3 you can draw many conclusions about the wind situation. The effects of design interventions can also be assessed. It is possible to analyse, for example, the wind flow patterns around the buildings, by plotting these in a map, profile or perspective drawing (see illustration 72). It is also possible to indicate the places with higher wind speeds caused by corner streams and their size for an existing situation or for a design proposal.

Besides sketching areas with high wind speeds, you can also make approximate projections for areas sheltered from the wind, based on the patterns discussed in chapter 2. The example in illustration 73 shows a pattern of high hedges, projected as wind protection on a square of 100 x 100 metres, with the hedges being distributed in such a way that virtually the entire square is protected from the wind.

Such educated guesses about wind patterns do not necessarily have to be made by urban meteorologists, since a good basic knowledge of wind dynamics will often suffice for simpler design assignments. Besides, it is much cheaper and faster than hiring specialists. The potential of these educated guesses is often underestimated, especially their important role in the beginning of the design process when many rough estimates about all sorts of effects of a design have to be made

and weighed against each other. On the other hand, educated guesses are obviously less reliable and accurate than the work of specialists described above. In some cases, you do need experts, such as meteorologists or urban physicists to make more accurate analyses based on physical or computer simulations and measurements.
Last but not least, you can also build a little experimental setup to understand where you can expect higher or lower windspeeds on a horizontal surface, such as a street. To do this you can build scale model of a three-dimensional environment (perhaps just use Lego blocks?) and evenly dust the surface with fine kitchen salt (see illustration 74). Once a contiguous thin layer of salt has been applied you can start experimenting to simulate wind. Determine carefully which wind direction you want to mimic, and from that angle you can then start blowing air onto the model, using a strong hair blower or a similar device, from a fixed point. After a short while you can see that the salt is moved from the areas with high wind speeds to areas with low speeds where it can settle. Eventually, typical eddy patterns may be observed on the surfaces, too.

74 *Experimenting with kitchen salt in scale models; left: applying the salt on the scale model, right: scale model after the wind blowing simulation*

75 A model of a city in the wind tunnel

76 Smoke simulations in the wind tunnel of consultancy agency Peutz, Mook, the Netherlands

5.1.3 Wind Tunnel Tests

Wind flow tests in wind tunnels are done when accurate predictions on future wind patterns are required, or to simulate an existing micro-climate situation for a location where you can't make measurements. Wind tunnel experiments are often used in projects requiring an assessment of the impact of one or more high-rise buildings. One of the important impacts is that tall buildings affect wind patterns, which can lead to wind nuisance and even dangerous situations. But these wind tunnel tests are also sometimes done when designers, municipalities or property developers expect wind problems at the pedestrian level. Some countries use technical standards to address and assess wind nuisance in outdoor spaces, for instance the Dutch NEN8100 standard. A wind tunnel test can also be part of an environmental impact assessment for large new buildings. Some municipalities have developed specific

When do we use wind tunnel tests?

guidelines that prescribe when wind danger testing must be done. The Dutch municipality of Rotterdam for example, has a rule that wind tests are obligatory for new buildings taller than 70 metres and highly recommended for new buildings that are taller than 30 metres, twice as tall as their environment or very exposed to the prevailing, strong wind direction. But many countries simply do not have these kinds of regulations. Then it comes down to a municipality or builder to have wind tunnel tests done, for example to prevent future damage claims.

What happens in a wind tunnel?

In a wind tunnel, turbulent airflows are generated and directed to scale models of areas or buildings in controlled circumstances. This way, one can determine the effect of the wind on the area or on objects, and, vice versa, that of the area on the redistribution of airflows. These wind experiments can simulate all kinds of wind situations. In the wind tunnel, you can set different wind directions, ideally representing the most important wind situations. You can also simulate different wind speeds and in some wind tunnels even gusts. This way, wind effects on buildings and people can be determined. A model for a wind tunnel experiment always represents a larger area than the area studied. This is to make sure you include the considerable influence of surrounding volumes.

In wind tunnel tests, what is measured where?

The wind speeds on relevant spots of the model (for instance where many people recreate outdoors, or where many pedestrians or cyclists pass) are then shown in different ways for a few important wind directions and wind speeds. This can be done in several ways. The most common method is to install small, electronic or mechanical measurement modules on or close to the scale model, especially in places of crucial interest for the study, for instance at the pedestrian level where wind danger can be expected or at locations where people will repose. Alternatively, lightweight threads can be glued to the surface of the object. The movement of the threads fluttering in the wind highlights local wind speed differences and eddies. Alternatively, smoke can be injected in the airflow on certain spots, so you can see the eddies around urban objects.

Pros and cons of wind tunnel tests

The predictions made with wind tunnel experiments are very reliable. The experiments have the advantage that they are independent of outdoor weather situations, because they take place under completely controlled circumstances and many different situations can be simulated. Just as with outdoor measurement points, wind tunnel measuring points cannot be installed in all places of a scale model, so there will always be 'gaps' in the spatial distribution of measurement points. But the density of measuring points in wind tunnels can always be higher than that of measurements actually done outside in the cities themselves.

Wind tunnel experiments are very specialist work and there are not many wind tunnels. Some of the wind tunnels and experts can be found in universities and some at private consultancies. Therefore, wind tunnel tests are usually quite costly.

5.1.4 Computational Wind Simulations

Computational wind simulations can essentially be used for the same purposes as wind tunnel tests, so these computer simulations are used as an alternative for the wind tunnel tests for impact assessments and such.

When do we use wind simulations?

Wind simulations can usually depict the wind flows in a relatively high resolution. These computer simulations calculate the wind's flow patterns and its speed and represent it in four dimensions: the three spatial dimensions plus time. In jargon these analyses are called 'Computational Fluid Dynamics' (CFD) simulations and they're also used for other flow-related calculations, such as water flows. There are several CFD-simulations programmes, and it is preferable to leave the appropriate software choice up to the experts. The grid sizes of these simulations can be very diverse, depending on the expected size of flow patterns. The grid resolution is interrelated with the computing power available: a very dense grid requires much more computing power than a less dense one. So, you should always consider the size of the area you want to do calculations on, the desired mesh width of the grid in relation to the available computing power.

How do computer wind simulations work?

It is best to include a large part of the surroundings in the simulations, since the surroundings are of great influence on the wind patterns.

The simulation results usually show both the wind's direction and its speed on different locations. The wind direction is generally indicated with arrows, and the wind speed through the thickness of these arrows or by colour coding. Some software can show these patterns in videos, but that requires powerful computer processors.

77 *CFD-wind simulations for a project in The Hague, the Netherlands*

Pros and cons of computer wind simulations

Computational wind simulations provide a lot of flexibility and can represent many different situations, but there are many bottlenecks. Firstly, the CFD-simulations are less accurate than wind tunnel tests. Secondly, there are sometimes problems with how much time computer processors need. When, for example, you need a very detailed simulation of a larger area (thus with a fine grid), many data have to be calculated, often too many for most computers. You then either have to buy computers with fast processors and a lot of memory, or pay for the use of external supercomputers. Both solutions are rather expensive. Add to this that you need experienced specialists to work with the software. So, it is a somewhat costly analysis method.

5.1.5 Computer Simulations for Combined Microclimate Phenomena

When to use integrated computer simulations for microclimate phenomena?

Computer simulations integrally showing all microclimate phenomena are required when it is not possible to make measurements, or when a design has to be tested on its microclimate performance before it is built. Computer simulations can represent long time sequences of, for instance, several weeks. On many 'real' locations, such longitudinal measurement campaigns are not an option. Therefore, many different simulation tools have been developed recently or older ones have been upgraded significantly. Because computer processors' power can easily become a limiting factor, you should consider carefully which time sequences have to be simulated for which locations. Apart from that, it is worth considering the high energy consumption of high-end computers for running simulations and storing all the data. For larger-scale simulations, some GIS tools have been developed recently but that scale is a bit beyond the scope of this book, which focuses more on the smaller-scale interventions. At the moment, there are two types of computer modelling software packages that simulate all physical factors of microclimate experience on that smaller scale: Envi-met® and Palm-4U. Envi-met® is a well-established commercial product. Palm-4U is a newer freely available product, but it also uses more precise predictions and computational power (and hence consumes more energy). Both models work with a three-dimensional grid, in which a spatial situation is 'built'. The user can set the mesh of that grid, so it can show larger contiguous areas. These computer simulations depict the physical variables of microclimate experience in four dimensions: the three spatial dimensions plus time. These types of software are also used to compare different simulations and map the differences. These packages require firm background knowledge in urban climate science from its users and can only be used by non-experts after intensive training.

How do integrated simulations work?

I will illustrate the use of such software with examples of Envi-met®-simulations we made of the Nieuwe Mark in Breda in the Netherlands. For reference, the existing situation was simulated first. Subsequently,

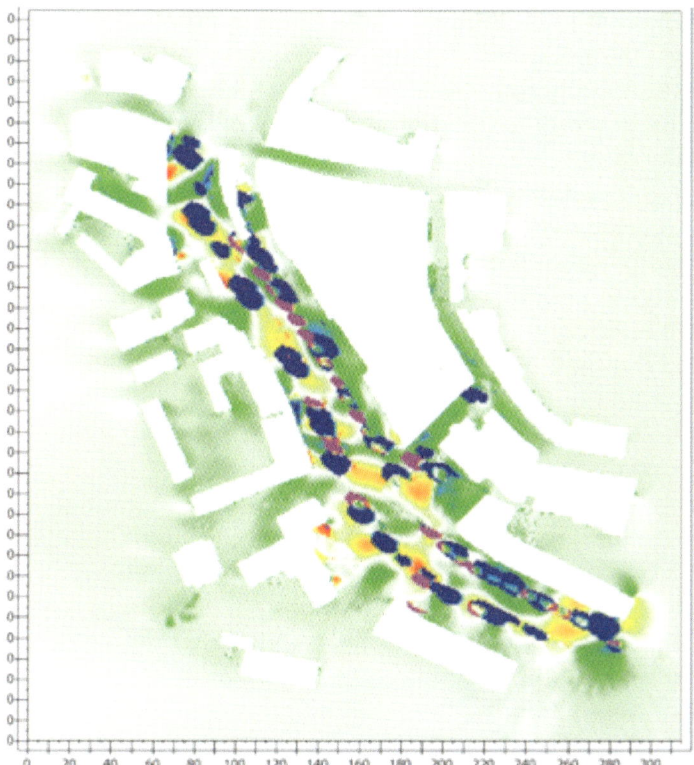

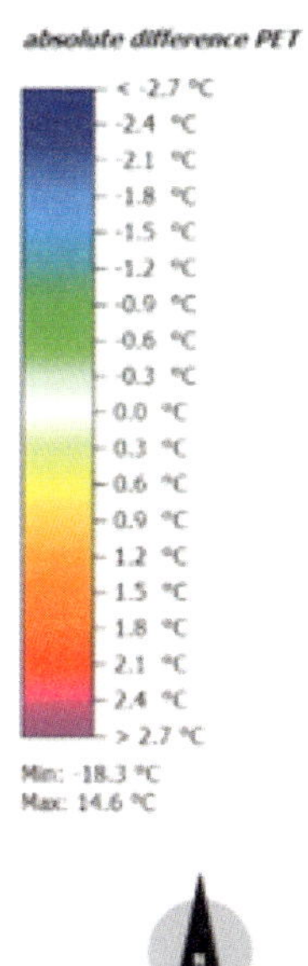

78 *Envi-met®-simulation for the Nieuwe Mark, Breda, the Netherlands, comparison of the existing PET situation with a design*

we made simulations of several design alternatives to improve the microclimate. To determine which alternative was best, we compared the simulations of the existing situation with those of the design alternatives, both for a cool autumn day, when most microclimatic problems were expected. We then looked at the improvement or deterioration of the microclimate in the new situation, using the 'difference' function. The comparative map (illustration 78) shows many green areas, which means that the design interventions will improve the microclimate in these areas.

Pros and cons of integrated computer simulations

Because such computer simulations can be used to predict the microclimate independent of external circumstances, they are very flexible. Contrary to in situ measurements, where you can only make measurements in a limited number of places, computer simulations can reflect on the microclimate of a much larger area. Moreover, these simulations can be used to estimate what non-existent microclimatic situations will be like. Consequently, the role of these integrated simulations in spatial design processes is very valuable.

But whether or not simulations can be used in design processes calls for careful consideration, because there are a few bottlenecks. The first one is the mesh or resolution of the software. For example: if you need a very detailed simulation (so with a fine resolution) of a larger area, exponentially more data have to be calculated, and computing power can limit possibilities. To prevent this, you have to invest in computers with a fast processor and a lot of memory. This will drive up the costs of the project. Another problem of these software packages is that not all model components are fully developed and validated. This means that the results of the simulations have not been sufficiently compared to real situations, so these results are partly hypothetical. Only experienced experts can assess the predictive value of these simulation results. These experts and the required computing power make the production of good simulations relatively expensive.

The long computing time can slow down design processes. Design alternatives first have to be 'calculated' before new steps can be taken. This can be disruptive for the progress of projects.

For the future, we can expect fewer computing capacity issues, because computers keep getting faster (which unfortunately often goes hand in hand with more energy consumption). In the nearer future we can also expect new ways of visualizing these data with virtual reality tools. Increasingly more often, data are visualized within 'immersive environments' and VR goggles, allowing the spectator a more direct experience. Such tools are also very interesting in participatory design processes, to test the experience of future environments by different stakeholders.

5.1.6 Measurements of all Microclimate Phenomena

In which cases do you use measurements?

Measurements are a very precise and reliable way to analyse the urban climate. In some cases, measurements provide the 'hard facts' that politicians often ask for, as reliable evidence to support adaptation measures. Logistically, however, measurements can often be complicated, so they have to be planned and prepared carefully. The main question before you start commissioning series of measurements to urban meteorologists: what situation should the measurements reflect? Does it concern, for example, an area where you can expect many heat-related problems in summer? Then the measurements should be conducted when the heat problems are at their worst. Or does it concern an area of public space with wind nuisance? Or do you want to know what the microclimate is like throughout the year? Then it is important to do measurements in different seasons. In all cases, it is crucial that measurements are conducted on several days and at different times of the day. One single measurement does not tell you much, because it can only give you a random indication of the situation at that moment in time and is very probably not representative of the general situation or the situation you want to study. Longitudinal studies are the most reliable.

What is measured where?

Ideally, series of measurements include all physical parameters of microclimate experience: air temperature, relative humidity, short- and longwave radiation, wind speed and wind direction. From these, thermal comfort indices such as PET or UTCI can be derived (see chapter 1). If you only want to map heat problems, measurements should be conducted on hot days and especially at night, when the urban heat island effect is most prominent. In some countries, where warm or problematic situations often come with a typical wind (such as the Chinook and the Föhn wind), such wind flows should also be considered. If in certain places valley or urban winds are to be expected, it is also advisable to measure the wind in these places. To show wind problems, it can be sufficient to only measure wind speed and direction. But because people's thermal comfort usually depends on other parameters next to wind, it is better to include radiation and air temperature as well. The spots for measurements should be chosen strategically, so they reflect typical microclimate situations at different points in time. When measurements are taken in a street, this ideally should be done on both sides of the street (the sunny side and the shaded side), but also on the corners (because of the different wind patterns). In a garden or a square, spots that are typically sunny or shaded should also be included, as well as the windy spots and the sheltered ones. For measurements on facades, the sun's orientation and the wind exposure should be kept in mind. So, there are many different types of measurements. Here are some examples to clarify these.

Examples of measurements on Dutch squares

Some of my own research dealt with microclimate experience on squares in several cities. The focus was on mapping possible heat and wind problems on these squares. In order to do so, I made daytime measurements several times a day during the course of the outdoor seasons spring through autumn. On a number of fixed spots on the squares, I measured the air temperature, humidity, radiation, wind speed and direction (see illustration 79). These spots were mainly chosen based on the sun and shadow situation and the wind patterns. The spots had to represent the relevant different microclimate situations: very sunny spots and spots with much shadow; spots that were very exposed to the wind and spots that were sheltered from it most of the time. This was to ensure we did not get a biased view of the general microclimate situation. The data were presented in GIS.

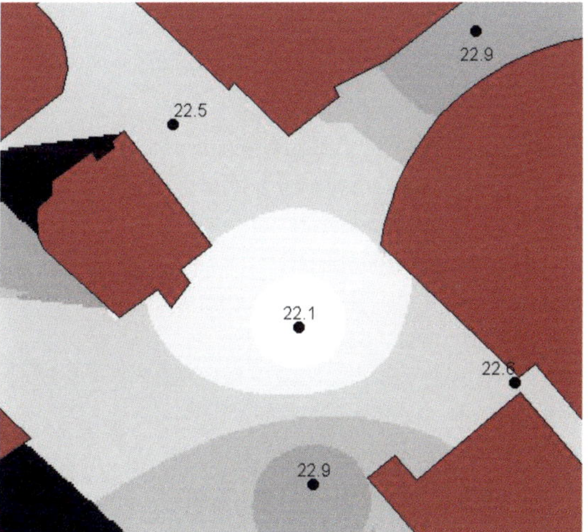

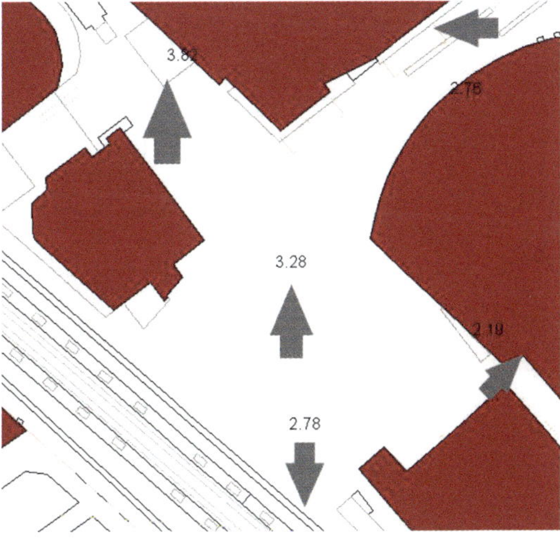

79 *GIS-maps with data of the Spuiplein in The Hague, including air temperature (in degrees Celcius), wind speed (in m/s) and directions (arrows).*

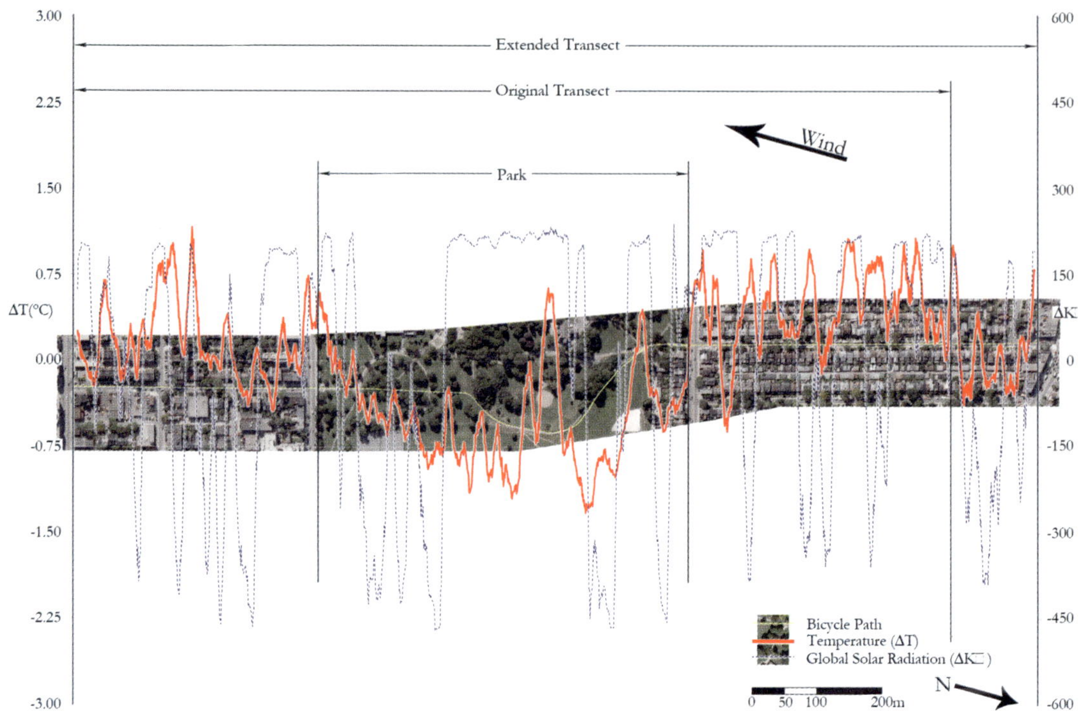

80 Measurement transects in Toronto with differences in air temperature (red) and solar radiation (blue)

Example of measurements in neighbourhood parks in Toronto, Canada

In Toronto, scientists focussed a series of measurements on the heat aspect in residential areas and on the question of how small parks can help cool these neighbourhoods. The aim was to gain a better insight into the cooling impact of the neighbourhood parks, and especially in how far the parks' cooler air reached into the surrounding residential areas. They used a specially equipped bicycle to ride through the parks and the surrounding neighbourhoods. To make a 'temperature profile' reflecting the differences between the parks and the neighbourhoods, the scientists chose routes crossing these areas in transects.

Pros and cons of measurements

Measurements result in reliable data and 'hard facts'. This is supportive in decision-making processes regarding urban climate adaptation interventions. On the other hand, series of measurements require a lot of expensive expert manpower and equipment not only in the city, but often also outside the city to determine reference temperatures for measurements. Fixed measuring equipment has to be placed in safe spots, and it has to be vandalism proof. It also is not possible to place the equipment everywhere you would like, due to ownership or inaccessibility of places or objects, so you often cannot collect data in the desired spatial distribution. Moreover, it takes a lot of time to do measurements, and they also depend on the unpredictability of the weather. In the unlucky event that a whole year passes without the relevant climate phenomena you want to measure, you have no choice but to extend the measuring period. This makes it hard to plan series of measurements. Another disadvantage is that measurements only reflect existing situations; they do not offer insights for future climate situations as sketched by the IPCC or for future planning or design interventions. And this type of information is crucial for design proposals that take into account climate change. In that case, simulations are needed to predict non-existent future situations.

5.2 Mapping Psychological Aspects of Microclimate Experience

The analysis of the physical microclimate does not cover all aspects of microclimate experience. As we know, psychological aspects are important as well. People associate certain colours and materials with 'warm' or 'cool' microclimates, even if these do not necessarily have any influence on the physical microclimate. People also associate certain spatial configurations with a typical microclimate, even if they don't know much about the laws of physics behind them. Therefore, an environmental psychological approach can be part of microclimate analyses. The results offer relevant information for spatial designers. Finally, spatial designs are largely aimed at people's experience of a place, and not just the physical reality of it. All methods mapping the psychological aspects of microclimate experience can be used to study existing spatial situations, and in the case of small redevelopments that do not have too much impact on the spatial structure. These methods are not suitable for projects in which completely new urban environments are developed.

5.2.1 Mental Maps

When do you use mental map methods?

When you need to link several aspects of microclimate experience directly to certain spaces, a mental map method can be useful. Such a mental map can reveal on which locations in an area people perceive certain microclimates. The results of mental mapping methods can be useful when smaller urban areas are refurbished, and especially when the aim is to improve microclimate perceptions.

How do you make mental maps for the microclimate?

To make mental maps, you conduct interviews with users of urban outdoor spaces. Respondents indicate what their long-term experience is with for example sun and shadow, wind and rain, and at which specific locations they experienced these conditions. With this information, you can make an individual mental map (see illustration 81). Preferably, these interviews are done on location, so the respondents can point out the areas they link to certain microclimate characteristics. Individual people usually don't know every spot in the study area, for example because their daily routines only cover certain routes. So

81 *Example of an individual mental map of the Neckerspoel area in the Dutch city of Eindhoven. Red = uncomfortable, green = comfortable*

82 *Example of collective mental maps for sun/shade (left) and wind (right), Neckerspoel, Eindhoven*

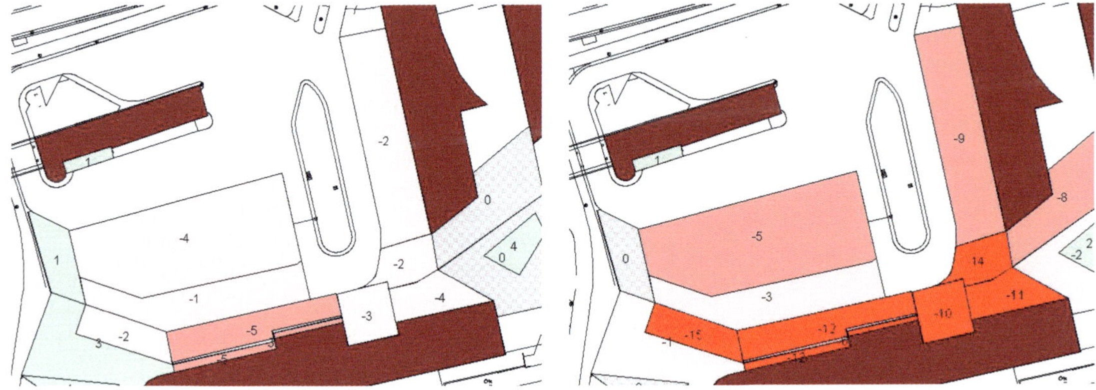

individual mental maps often do have white spots. But if you ask a sufficient number of people about their mental maps, you usually do obtain a complete image.

The results of all individual mental maps are then aggregated in GIS. The result is a 'collective' mental map of the microclimate (see illustration 82). In these maps you can use colours or numbers to indicate how many people labelled certain spots with certain microclimate characteristics.

Pros and cons of mental maps

In my own research I have found the information from the collective mental maps often tally well with the measured reality. So, it is a reasonably reliable analysis method. You can make these mental maps without much knowledge of urban meteorology. You do need to have some interview and GIS experience. If you don't have this experience yourself, you can consult with social geography or environmental psychology specialists. Since the subject of analysis is people's long-term experience, independent of the current situation, you can use this mental map method any time you like.

Moreover, several interviewers can interview people about their experience simultaneously. This method is thus relatively fast and inexpensive. The data-analysis does take some time, but certainly less than extensive measurements or simulations, which are more costly as well. Yet, these mental maps are based on non-expert knowledge, which might be coloured by other factors. Sometimes, places get a certain 'microclimate label' because they are avoided for social reasons, or because they are loved for their cosy ambiance, even though these labels have nothing to do with the micro-weather in the city. Therefore, we do have to be careful when interpreting the results.

5.2.2 Interviews

When do you use interviews for analysis?

When you want to know about people's general microclimate experience in a city's outdoor area, interviews can offer relevant information. The need for systematic interviews may arise, for example, when people express vague complaints about the ambiance and/or microclimate of an area, as we often see on social media. Interviewing users can reveal the problems behind these complaints. Interviews usually do not depend on a certain time, so you can basically use this method throughout the year.

What information can you get from interviews?

The main questions concern the relationship of microclimate experience and all factors you can influence through urban design, such as size, scale, openness, proportions, colours and materials used. It is advisable to ask about these aspects in interviews. You can also analyse which specific user groups have certain experiences or customs. People from different generations or cultural backgrounds, for example, experience the microclimate differently. Interview results can offer valuable information about target groups of a spatial design for the microclimate. A conclusion from such interviews could be that you should create more places with a very mild microclimate for elderly people to enjoy. Or such an analysis might show the need for more shaded places for picnickers. Many other results are possible, of course.

Pros and cons of interviews

Because urban design is essentially aimed at people and their experiential and behavioural patterns, these interview results yield relevant knowledge for designers, especially if this information can be translated into spatial information. In quite a short time, interview studies can gather a wealth of information, so this is a relatively inexpensive and fast way to collect reliable basic information. People with some experience in interview techniques can conduct these interviews. If you don't have interview experience yourself, you can also hire experience research specialists.

Keep in mind, however, that people's experiences do not always match with a measurable micrometeorological reality. This can sometimes lead to quite dangerous situations when people misjudge their microclimatic surroundings. For example: people often don't realize that in some places, gusts can be so strong that they can cause accidents. Also, when it comes to heat and sun, people don't always notice the threat of serious dehydration or damaging ultraviolet radiation, as you can see from the number of people with very unhealthy sunbathing habits. In cases where you can expect these types of serious microclimate problems, it is better to also use physical analysis methods. This way, you can place people's subjective estimations in a more 'objective' context.

5.2.3 Observations

When do you use observations as an analysis method?

Sometimes people can't talk about their experiences, because they are not aware of them or because they can't express themselves very well verbally (think of children or people with certain disabilities). You can then use observations as an analysis method. This can be a useful option when, for example, small interventions are needed to improve the microclimate in urban spaces. For precise localization of interventions, observations can indicate where you will find many people and subsequently if they either seek out or avoid certain microclimatic circumstances. The design interventions can then address these specific circumstances and locations.

Making observations and mapping them

Observing people's behaviour can offer information about local microclimate experiences without people having to talk about it explicitly. You make these observations on location at different times or in different seasons to map behavioural patterns. There are several indicators for behavioural changes related to the microclimate. When people experience certain situations as either comfortable or uncomfortable, they first change the way they dress, for example by taking off their coat or by putting it on. If this is not enough, people change locations. They find a place in the sun or in the shade, out of the wind or one that is nice and breezy when it's hot. The spatial configurations of places that people seek out in these cases can subsequently be categorized according to the typical microclimatic

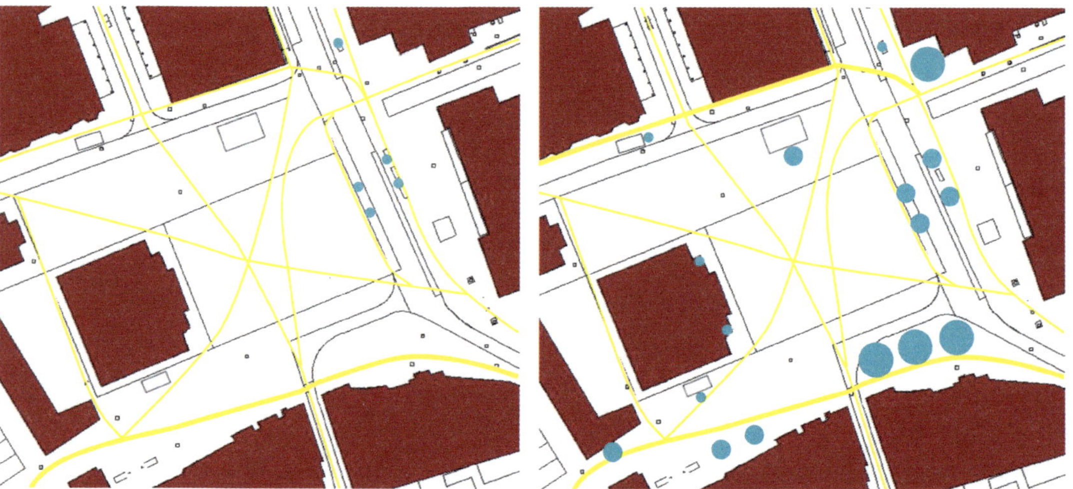

84 *Crowd state parameters map derived from mobile phone location data*

characteristics. These microclimatic characteristics can then be adapted through design interventions if need be. To make an observations map with sufficient informational value, you have to observe a larger area in its totality, such as an entire square or street. Otherwise, you can't get a good view of people's spatial movement patterns. To be able to compare results, you need an overview of the complete spatial patterns of rest and movement at the same points in time. Therefore, it works best when observers choose a spot in the middle of a space or another strategic place from where they can have a good overview. If this is not possible, more people can make observations from different spots onsite. The observations maps can represent the places where people are stationary and where they move (see illustration 83 for the city of Groningen).

Alternatively, openly accessible data from mobile phones that indicate people's location can be used (see illustration 84) to map people's movement patterns.

Pros and cons of observations

You do always not have to be an expert to make these observations. Making observations and mapping them is often a relatively simple method to analyse the way people react to the microclimate. Since this does not normally require specialists, it is also a relatively inexpensive method. Getting the information you need, can sometimes take a long time, because you have to make observations in different seasons, or you have to wait for specific weather circumstances. Moreover, people's spatial behavioural patterns depend on many other factors besides the microclimate. Oftentimes the fact that someone is at a certain location or takes a certain route for a purely functional reason, such as an appointment or taking the shortest route, is much more important than consciously choosing to be in a specific microclimate. The results of these observations can therefore only be reliable in combination with other analysis methods, such as simulations.

83 *Observations maps with stationary people (green/blue) and movement of people (yellow) patterns, Grote Markt, Groningen, the Netherlands*

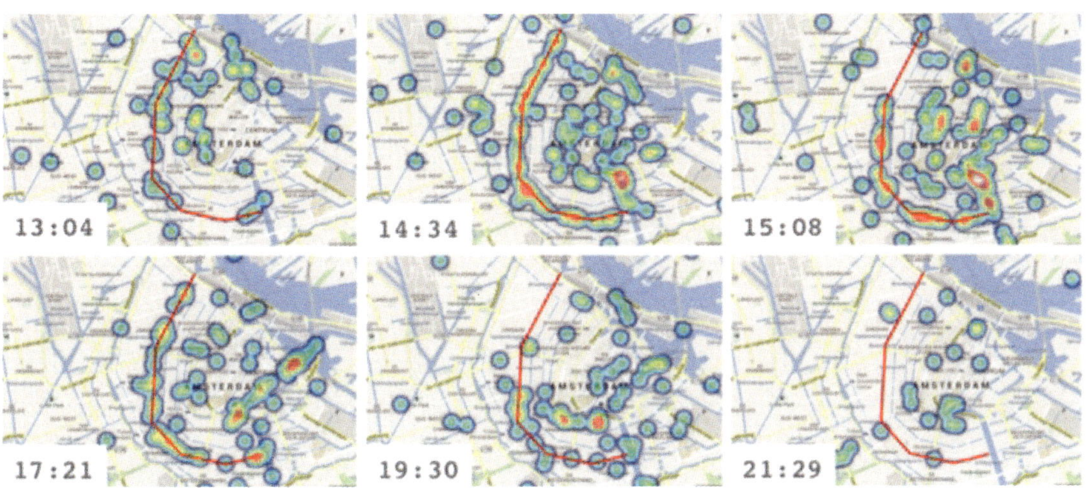

5.3 Combinations of Analysis Techniques

Use simulations and wind tunnel tests for new development projects

As we have seen before, it is sometimes best to combine analysis methods. Depending on the aim of the analyses, certain analysis combinations make more sense than others. An important question is: are the analyses used to support a completely new development project or are they intended for small interventions in an existing space? In the first case you can only use simulation methods, since these can also reflect a non-existing or a future situation. If you need to know about wind, a combination of wind simulations and wind tunnel tests is ideal. The wind simulations can then be compared to the wind tunnel results, thus adding to the reliability of the results. There are more options when projects involve smaller interventions in existing situations, for example new surfacing, street furniture or extra trees. You can then use all described analysis techniques.

Use mixed analysis techniques for redevelopment projects

In general, it is advisable to combine simulations or measurements with experience/behaviour research. In this way you make sure that you map the physical and the psychological aspects of spatial microclimate experience. These methods do, however, often require lengthy in situ studies. The measurements and simulations are often costly, as they involve much specialist work.

If these extensive and expensive analyses are not an option, then combining simulations with mental maps and/or interviews can be an alternative. The simulations generate a model of the physical circumstances. These can then be compared to the results from the mental maps or the interviews. This combination of analyses is less time-consuming and more flexible when it comes to the time in which the study is conducted.

6
Designing for Microclimate Experience

To make the urban climate more comfortable, many adjustments are needed, especially on the small scale – because many small interventions can have cumulative effects. There is a plethora of small-scale design solutions to improve all aspects of microclimate experience. Think of 'green' landscape architecture interventions; urban design solutions such as configuring buildings and open spaces; and finally, solutions in the field of public design – the refurbishment of public space. There are many traditional solutions that used to be applied in cities, landscapes and gardens, but that have since been forgotten. I will put these in the spotlight once again. But there are many new solutions as well, as will be illustrated with examples from various countries in the temperate climate zone. When it comes to multifunctional adaptation measures, inspiring examples will show there is much room for innovation. We can use all these small-scale interventions to improve the local microclimate. This will lead to authentic, location-specific designs for spaces and neighbourhoods.

After you have made suitable analyses of a microclimatic environment and identified problems and potentials, you can make location-specific designs. This chapter offers a broad overview of various small-scale adaptation interventions in a fact-sheet catalogue at the end of this chapter. You will also find a complete overview on the back flap of this book. Again, the design measures in this chapter are described in the same order as elsewhere in this book: temperature experience first, wind experience second and psychological aspects last. Protection from rain in outdoor areas is an extra theme in this chapter. Furthermore, multifunctional solutions that influence several factors of the microclimate are addressed. Many of the solutions discussed here have one main purpose. A canopy, for example, only blocks solar radiation. Measures against wind or for ventilation usually also have that one main purpose. Other measures, especially the 'green interventions', often have multiple microclimate functions, as you can see in the overview on the back flap.

The solutions are also categorized according to their spatial embedding: interventions directly connected to buildings, in parks and gardens, on squares, in streets or parking areas. Small icons represent these spatial types and can be found both in the catalogue and in the overview on the book flap. This overview is also organized according to these spatial types. For most types of interventions, the fact-sheet catalogue includes information on their effectiveness and extra advantages and/or disadvantages. When the pros clearly outweigh the cons, I conclude that you can consider these as *no regret* interventions. The catalogue also offers information about the construction and maintenance of several measures, as well as a relative indication of their costs. When it comes to wind measures, we can't speak of general pros and cons. Wind can form both a problem and a potential, so the measures for wind adaptation strongly depend on the conditions at a

specific location or of a project. Also, wind patterns exist on many different and sliding scales, so it is difficult to make statements about, for example, the costs of an intervention, since that depends on the scale of that particular intervention. The psychological aspects are also more generally applicable, so their description is different as well.

Before the detailed list of all measures described in the fact-sheet catalogue, this chapter offers a short, general discussion of the different aspects of influencing temperature and wind experience, rain protection and the psychological aspects. This includes a summary of the way the different types of solutions work (in close relation to chapter 2), and which aspects you should keep in mind when implementing these types of interventions.

6.1 Designing for Physical Temperature Experience

I would like to emphasize again the importance of sun/shade, thermal radiation of materials and the air temperature on people's temperature experience. You can adapt all these aspects with small-scale solutions. Some of these solutions are very effective, and some of them less so. On a small-scale level, you can influence sun and shadow patterns very effectively. The interventions to temper the air temperature through evaporation on a small-scale level have a spatially limited effect only. To realize a greater effect, you have to implement these interventions to lower the air temperature on the scale of at least an entire district, and ideally combine them with shade functions. Trees offer an ideal combination of shade and evapotranspiration.

One theme is left out of this chapter: the reduction of anthropogenic heat. It is impossible for an urban designer to reduce excess heat from factories or cars, for instance. Solutions for this problem are to be found more in the design of machines, processes and vehicles themselves. In the future, most cars will be electric, so we can expect that source of heat to disappear. We can, however, stop the extra warming caused by badly insulated buildings and air conditioners with careful adjustments to the buildings or by building new ultra-low energy buildings. These building solutions are elaborately discussed in the literature on sustainable architecture, so they are not included here.

Influencing sun and shade

One of the most influential factors of the microclimate that affect the way people experience temperature is the amount of shortwave solar radiation – so if someone is in the sun or in the shade. This radiation is much lower in a shaded spot than it is in direct sunlight. Therefore, the configuration of buildings in relation to the sun or shadow is important, as is the strategic placement of elements that provide shade, such as trees, and street or outdoor furniture. From an urban climate point of view, green elements are always preferred, as their evapotranspiration lowers the air temperature. Many cases demand a location-specific design for sun and shade, keeping in mind all continuously changing shadow patterns. That is why some design recommendations in the catalogue can be considered a 'study by design'. This means you first map the existing conditions using shadow simulations (in SketchUp, AutoCad or similar programmes, see section 5.1.1), and then testing the different alternatives on their shadow patterns in order to find the optimal place for elements. You can find the solutions to influence sun and shade on pages 119-148.

Influencing reflection

The reflection of shortwave radiation, or albedo, impacts the storage of heat in a certain material. Smooth and light materials generally have a higher albedo. Using these types of materials in many places can increase the albedo of large parts of the city. There are some issues you should consider when using materials with a higher albedo. When many reflecting materials are used in streets to keep walls (and thus indoor spaces) cool, eventually more shortwave radiation will be reflected into the street space. This shortwave radiation then hits objects again, but also people in the street who will suffer from the extra radiation during summer, as well as from glare. It is therefore best to only increase reflection in street spaces when there are no other options. In larger spaces such as squares raising the albedo can sometimes be useful. The big sky view factor allows the radiation to escape into the space above the city. You find the chart with the albedo of different materials in illustration 9 on page 32 and the overview of reflection-influencing interventions on pages 149-154.

Influencing emissivity and heat conductivity

The radiation emission characteristics of materials are also crucial for the urban energy balance. In principle, all materials store heat. They do so to different extents and emit it at different speeds. Depending on the desired effect – whether you want to create cooler or warmer places – you can use different materials. When indoor or outdoor areas have to stay cool in summer because many people use these areas, it is advisable to use building materials that store less heat, such as wood. When you want to create places that offer extra warmth in cooler seasons, you can use other suitable materials to influence this. You find the chart with the emissivity and thermal conductivity of different materials in illustration 9 on page 32 and the overview of interventions on pages 155-160.

Influencing evaporation

Evaporation is a crucial factor in tempering the air temperature (also see section 2.1.2). Evaporation occurs at the surfaces of water bodies and from water in the soil, but especially through the evapotranspiration from the stomata of plants. You can speed up the evaporation of water by spraying it as finely as possible. The enlarged surface of the fine drops strongly enhances evaporation. Still or slow-moving water bodies evaporate less water, and they also retain warmth. They can sometimes even be warmer than their surroundings. Therefore, it is very important to move the water or preferably spray it for an effective cooling of the environment, or to have water evaporate through plants' evapotranspiration. You will find the solutions for influencing evaporation on pages 161-174.

6.2 Designing for Physical Wind Experience

Wind flows in urban areas can be both a problem and a potential. At some locations and especially in the cooler seasons, people have to be protected from the wind. At other locations and especially during heat waves, sufficient ventilation is required. Therefore, you should first make a careful analysis of the location, use and period you will be designing for. Analysis and design overlap here, so make sure you have read sections 2.2.3 and 5.1.2.

Relating wind pattern analysis and design

It has to be clear from the start which human activities (such as walking or cycling) the design should serve, and at which times the locations are in use. For example: is a seating area only meant for the summer or for other seasons as well? Does an urban area need ventilation on warm nights or doesn't it, since nobody stays there at night? The design should address these exact situations, based on the site's wind analysis. But the other climate situations should not be overlooked in the analysis and the design, to prevent nuisances at other times of the year.

What is also special about designing with wind is that wind patterns are primarily determined by the combination of volumes and open spaces. It is important to keep in mind that wind does not actually 'know' if a certain volume is a building, an earthen wall or very dense planting. It is just an obstacle for the air to flow around. Thinking in terms of 'volumes' and 'open spaces' is therefore essential. In urban design, it is generally better to shape the urban tissue with the wind patterns in mind from the start. Retrofitting for these problems on the small scale is less efficient. Nonetheless, you will find extensive descriptions of these solutions in this chapter, because our cities are hardly ever designed from scratch (anymore), and a large part of the urban tissue is already there, so we'll have to work with local adjustments.

Slowing or avoiding wind

As we know from section 2.2, all objects (landscape and building volumes) and their mutual configurations create typical wind flow patterns. Some of those lead to such big wind problems that these have to be addressed in situ, or that it is better to avoid these locations for certain uses. The typical places for these problems to arise are for example the sides of larger buildings, because of the corner streams; the foot of high-rise buildings; and places where urban spaces narrow. Of course, the precise location of these places always depends on the wind. You will find the solutions for slowing the wind on pages 175-188.

Ventilation

Some outdoor places have to be ventilated well on hot days, especially in densely built-up residential areas. The slow 'large-scale' wind we experience on hot days usually is not effective and therefore we should primarily make use of local breezes. These are firstly the nocturnal valley winds we find in cities with larger differences in elevation in their relief. Another type of ventilation is the local urban wind between warmed-up and cooler areas in the city or at the city edges. When the courses of the cool airflows are identifiable, you can address those in your design by creating openings and/or guiding wind to the desired locations. You will find the solutions for channelling wind and ventilation on pages 189-191.

6.3 Designing for Protection against Precipitation

Even though the precipitation we are exposed to doesn't play a very big role in our normal experience of the microclimate, it can be a nuisance to us from time to time. Hence, it is important to create protection against precipitation, especially rain. Precipitation protection is usually only planned for bus and tram shelters or train station roofs. But people should also be better protected from rain at other places, such as shopping streets or on large squares along important pedestrian routes. This is especially important for the elderly or people with walking impairments, who need more time to cross a square for instance and who might have to rest for a little. Considering most of our societies' ageing populations, we should take this into account more often. Sidewalk cafes and such can often also be provided with better rain protection. Generally speaking, many solutions for creating shade can offer protection against precipitation as well. Many of these solutions do have a downside however: it is relatively dark underneath, and this might not be nice on rainy days. You will therefore find some alternatives on pages 193-195.

6.4 Designing for Multiple Microclimate Factors

In this book, we have seen a couple of times that certain interventions influence the microclimate in more than one way. Particularly 'green' solutions offer many advantages. But there are many more possible multifunctional combinations! You will find a number of these types of combinations in the last part of the catalogue. This entails inspirational examples that have not been realized yet, designed by me and in part together with my students. All examples are smaller installations or elements that can be placed in gardens and parks as well as in squares. They reflect how you can playfully address the microclimate in your designs. You will find these examples of multifunctional objects for influencing the microclimate on pages 197-208.

6.5 Designing for Psychological Aspects of Microclimate Experience

As we know, how people experience the microclimate does not only depend on purely physical factors such as radiation temperature, air temperature, wind and clothing. It also depends on the surroundings and what we can call 'ambiance'. As discussed in chapter 2, spaces can have a 'warm' or 'cold' ambiance with characteristics that have no thermal effect, and this ambiance influences the microclimate experience too. You can influence these factors with spatial interventions, thus manipulating the way people will experience the space. Interventions to influence the ambiance can come in so many different shapes and forms, and can be applied in so many different places, that there is no point in discussing their construction, maintenance and costs. These interventions are sketched on pages 209-212.

6.6 Implementation of Measures on the Microscale Level

You will find more elaborate descriptions of the abovementioned smaller-scale solutions in the fact-sheet catalogue. All these measures can be implemented in very different ways, by different actors and in different amounts of time.

The owners of houses, office buildings and companies, for example, can make the surroundings of their buildings 'greener' or take wind-protection measures. The owners of brownfield areas have an opportunity to improve the urban climate relatively quickly, without many procedures, by implementing temporary green measures or by allowing urban agriculture on their land. Small changes on buildings, like a different use of colour or building materials, and changing facades, can usually be implemented relatively easily by the owners. Governments could consider supporting these 'green' interventions on private properties that improve the entire urban climate with special subsidies. Some municipalities already grant such subsidies for green roofs, green facades, 'de-surfacing' gardens or planting more trees in them.

When existing public spaces have to be adapted for the microclimate, municipalities can adopt this in their plans for redevelopment, for instance for urban renewal, shopping districts, inner cities and parks. Within the framework of such plans, measures can then be implemented relatively fast. A more 'gradual' adaptation can be realized by including measures in regulations concerning the continuous adjustment of a city's public spaces. In some cities, for example, city services have 'guidelines' for public space design, and the climate adaptation measures can be incorporated in these. Many possibilities for adaptation regarding street profiles, such as materialization, planting and choice of trees and furniture in streets, can be fixed in these guidelines. It is also possible to include microclimate interventions such as placing trees in streets and on squares, green facades and such in design ordinances that address the visual quality of districts, such as the German 'Gestaltungssatzung' and the Dutch 'Beeldkwaliteitsplan'.

Other somewhat larger interventions, such as regulations for micro-climate-driven building and street configurations are generally the responsibility of municipalities. This usually concerns plans for new districts. For extensive adjustments of existing areas, municipalities have to make changes in their zoning plans. These interventions therefore take the longest to implement. The municipality should check if the zoning plan's regulations are indeed followed. That implementation through zoning plans does generally work is demonstrated by examples from the German city of Stuttgart, where measures to keep cold airflow streams clear, for example, have been taken up in the zoning plans.

Generally speaking, many changes to the urban climate can be realized with small measures that are usually rather easy to implement, provided these are consequently applied in many places. For example: if residents of a neighbourhood with many 'surfaced' gardens remove the tiles from their gardens and replace these with trees, such a neighbourhood can evolve from climatope-type 'city' to 'garden city', which has a much milder microclimate. So the sum of many small interventions can have great cumulative effects!

Influencing Sun and Shade

Covered Spaces beneath Buildings

1. **General information** If for some reason you want a location to be in the shade for a prolonged period of time, one possibility is to offer shade directly beneath a building. In principle, a building can be 'lifted', to create a columned hall underneath, a covered continuation of the outdoor space. Market halls used to be created in this way beneath town halls. In the days when there were no refrigerators and such, passive cooling through shadow was the best way to keep perishable goods fresh.
2. **Effectiveness** These spaces are cool, shaded and ventilated throughout the year. As they are shaded by a solid canopy the shading effect is maximized in the centre of the hall. During summer the incoming shortwave radiation is minimal and diffuse (max. 10% of solar radiation in open spaces) but in winter low solar angles can bring about higher incoming shortwave radiation, depending on the geometry of the openings. The UTCI can be lowered with more than 10 degrees during the summer season.
3. **Extra advantages** The advantage of these spaces is that they offer shading and protection from the weather without extra costs for cooling.
4. **Disadvantages** It can be too dark and draughty in winter. The natural cooling in these spaces is not as effective as that in a modern covered space, acclimatized with air conditioning. The allocation of private and public ground property can be a problem. Many building owners have objections when parts of their building are publicly accessible.
5. **Construction** The construction of these open, covered spaces is an integral part of the construction of the building.
6. **Maintenance** The maintenance is part of the normal maintenance of the building.
7. **Costs** € € € (depending on the size of the building)
8. **No regret:** No

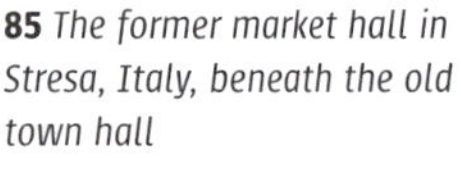

85 *The former market hall in Stresa, Italy, beneath the old town hall*

Arcades

1. **General information** When people want to be in the direct surroundings of a building or when they want to walk alongside the building while being protected – when they are shopping, for instance – arcades are a traditional option for offering shade.
2. **Effectiveness** If arcades are well adjusted to the positions of the sun, they allow the sun to come in during the winter, when it has low angles, whilst protecting people from the bright sun in the summer when it is at high angles. Shadow simulations are needed to establish the best height and width of the arcade.
3. **Extra advantages** Arcades are a robust solution to offer shelter from the sun and other weather circumstances. The arcade spaces can have several functions and enrich a city's diversity in microclimates.
4. **Disadvantages** The ground ownership conditions of arcade space can sometimes be a problem. To solve this, you need solid arrangements of whether the space is in public ownership at street level, and the building above it in private ownership; or whether it is better to have the street level area be privately owned as well, with the public having right of way.
5. **Construction** Arcades usually have to be part of the construction plans from the start. It is sometimes possible to build arcades later, but then it is often more difficult to fit the arcade into the architecture and the costs are much higher.
6. **Maintenance** The maintenance is part of the normal maintenance of the building.
7. **Costs** € € € (depending on the size and length of the arcade)
8. **No regret:** yes

86 *A classic arcade at the Plaza Mayor in Madrid, Spain*

Loggias

1. **General information** To offer a shaded, open place as part of a building that is well protected from the influences of the weather, loggias can be used. The height and depth of loggias should be well adjusted to the positions of the sun.
2. **Effectiveness** Provided the loggias have a good depth and are not facing north, they can offer protection from the bright, high-summer sun, whilst allowing the low evening and winter sun to come in. The same goes for the spaces of the building behind the loggias, where people live or work.
3. **Extra advantages** Besides effective sun protection, loggias also offer good protection from the rain and wind. Plus, they offer more privacy than balconies.
4. **Disadvantages** None
5. **Construction** Loggias have to be part of the building plans from the start.
6. **Maintenance** The maintenance is part of the normal maintenance of the building.
7. **Costs** €€
8. **No regret:** yes

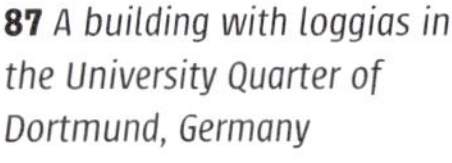

87 *A building with loggias in the University Quarter of Dortmund, Germany*

Light Roofs (preferably combined with photovoltaic systems)

1. **General information** When people want to sit on a balcony or terrace, light roofs are an option for offering shadow. Such roofs can ideally also consist of solar panels or have inbuilt photovoltaic modules to harvest solar energy at the same time.
2. **Effectiveness** The closed canopies provide effective shading, reducing solar irradiation with about 90% underneath at high sun angles. When such a roof consists of solar panels or includes photovoltaic modules the incoming solar radiation is transformed and energy is thus removed from the urban system, preventing heat accumulation.
3. **Extra advantages** Besides sun protection and generation of renewable energy, these solutions also provide some protection from the rain.
4. **Disadvantages** These roofs are fixed and the spaces beneath them might not get enough sun at certain times. This depends on the precise placement of the elements.
5. **Construction** Light (solar) roofs can be an integral part of the construction of a building, or they can be placed afterwards.
6. **Maintenance** These elements are relatively robust and low-maintenance because they are fixed to the building. Solar roofs require regular cleaning.
7. **Costs** € €
8. **No regret:** yes

88 *Glass roof with inbuilt photovoltaic modules, Piazza Gae Aulenti, Milan*

Flexible Canopies

1. **General information** If people wish to sit on a terrace right next to a building, there are several options for fixing shading objects to the building. You can open or close these to your liking. Think of classic parasols and awnings, but also less common elements such as canopies and horizontal sunscreens. You can also think of folding or sliding panel-type constructions.
2. **Effectiveness** Because of their flexibility, people can use these solutions for all kinds of weather circumstances, so they are very effective. A thick textile roof can intercept about 80% of solar irradiation.
3. **Extra advantages** The flexibility means that there are many more options than with fixed solutions. If the material is strong and impermeable, these solutions can also provide rain protection.
4. **Disadvantages** Because of their lightweight construction, flexible systems are usually more vulnerable than fixed solutions, and the lifespan of textile awnings is relatively short.
5. **Construction** Flexible awnings can be an integral part of the construction of a building, or they can be added afterwards.
6. **Maintenance** The systems need regular maintenance (for instance cleaning and oiling).
7. **Costs** € €
8. **No regret:** Yes

89 *Textile canopies covering the large courtyard of Hanul Lui Manuc in Bucharest, Romania*

Planted Pergolas

1. **General information** Attached to buildings, but also as freestanding objects, pergolas are a good option for shading. Pergolas are usually lightweight constructions with light beams or wires supporting climbing plants. These climbing plants can be deciduous (e.g. kiwi, vines, aristolochia, wisteria, climbing hydrangea and many others) or evergreen (e.g. ivy).
2. **Effectiveness** Depending on the density of the foliage, the shadow effect can be lighter or deeper. But the effect on solar radiation can easily come to a 50% reduction. The UTCI has been lowered with about 9 degrees under a pergola.
3. **Extra advantages** If deciduous plants are chosen and a pergola construction that is not too heavy, the pergola will allow sun penetration in winter. The plants offer extra cooling through evapotranspiration.
4. **Disadvantages** Pergolas are more permeable to rain than closed roofs are.
5. **Construction** Pergolas can be constructed relatively easily – also by practiced laymen. Keep in mind that the foundation has to be able to support the construction and the extra weight of the plants.
6. **Maintenance** Pergolas require regular maintenance (painting, touching up on the woodworks) and some plants require regular pruning.
7. **Costs** €€
8. **No regret:** Yes

90 *A pergola attached to an office building in Essen, Germany*

Espalier Trees at a Distance from a Building

1. **General information** To shade windows of houses in a natural way and thus prevent overheating of living spaces, you can use espalier trees. These trees are placed several metres from the buildings and are usually no taller than 5 metres. They are pruned in a candelabra-like manner. The tree types (usually lime trees) are fast-growing and must be pruned every autumn. Because of this, they hardly have any branches in winter, but when spring comes, the trees quickly grow branches and leaves for summer shading. The desired height of these branches depends on the height of the windows and the position of the sun. Espalier trees are a very classic example of influencing the microclimate, and you can sometimes still find them on old farmyards in Europe.
2. **Effectiveness** The espalier trees are reasonably effective, providing they are planted in the right spot and are maintained well, but they are less effective than flexible awnings are.
3. **Extra advantages** The trees' evapotranspiration helps temper the air temperature. In some places, these trees can also be used to demarcate owners' premises.
4. **Disadvantages** Espaliers mainly create shadow indoors and are therefore less suitable for providing shade outdoors.
5. **Construction** Young espalier trees are usually provided with a supporting construction for the branches to be trained along. If they are old enough for the branch-structure to have the desired shape, this support is no longer needed.
6. **Maintenance** The special shape of espalier trees and the need to allow for winter sun also mean they have to be expertly pruned every year.
7. **Costs** € €
8. **No regret:** Yes

91 *Espalier lime trees in front of an old house in Rotterdam, the Netherlands*

Green Facades

1. **General information** You can use very different types of facade planting to shade buildings so as to reduce the heating of walls and thus the indoor spaces. Classic green facades consist of climbers planted in the earth, but there are two different types of climbing plants. There are plants that fix themselves to the walls with small 'suckers' or root hairs (e.g. ivy, climbing hydrangea or wild vines), and there are plants that climb by curling around threads and lattices and such (most other climbing plants).

   Another classic type of green facade has fruit trees pruned in shape and guided along the walls with threads. The trees profit extra from the longwave radiation of the building, so their fruits ripen more quickly.

   New 'indirect green facade' systems have been developed over the past few decades, in which plants grow at a slight distance from the facade. Usually, plant containers are part of the facade, planted with different types of plants (including non-climbers). Often, indirect green facades also have support systems for climbing plants (lattices, wires, et cetera).

   The latest development is 'living walls', covering large parts of walls like tapestries. They consist of many separate plants, either growing in small compartments, small pots or bags, or bigger modules with various openings. These systems are directly attached to the wall and have complex irrigation systems.

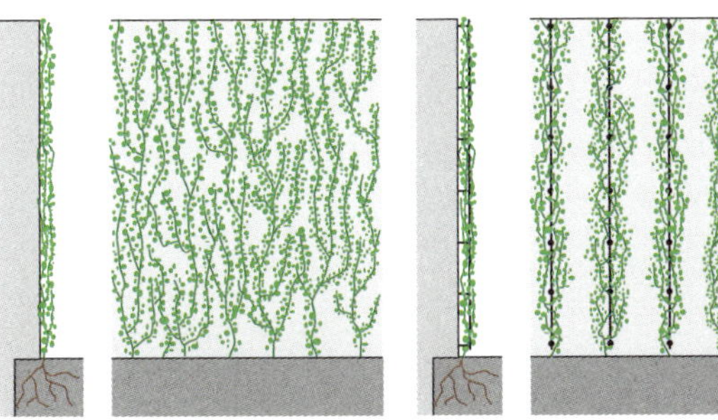

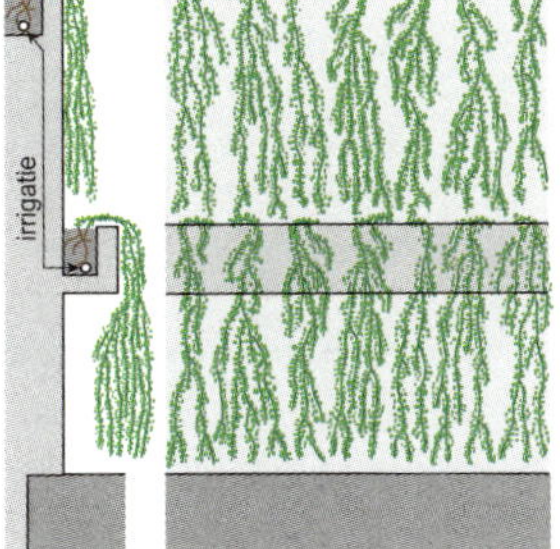

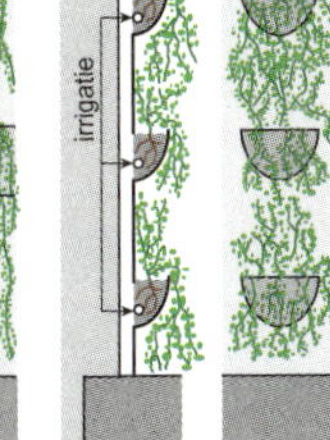

92 *Four types of green facades: self-climbing plants, supported climbers, plant containers in facades and 'living walls'*

93 *Green facade in Antwerp, Belgium*

2. **Effectiveness** The effect of plants on facades is strong when the plant cover is contiguous and dense: shading, evaporation, and protection from wind and rain are at their best then. Another positive effect is the layer of air between the planted facade and the walls of the building. This layer offers insulation in winter and can reduce heat loss by approximately 6%. The microclimatic effects vary with the different systems of green facades. Direct plant growth on walls and indirect green facade systems on walls lead to a reduction of surface temperature by 9°C, and living wall systems by about 12°C. The outdoor air temperature can be cooled up to 2°C in the vicinity of the green wall (e.g. a street canyon).
3. **Extra advantages** The evapotranspiration of the plants in green facades helps temper the air temperature, but much less effectively than trees do. The buildings behind the green facades are simultaneously protected against influences from the weather and insulated by the plants. This effect is of course stronger with evergreen plants. Direct and indirect plant growth on walls means that up to 30% less energy is needed for cooling and heating, living walls lead to reduction of up to 25% energy for cooling and 40% for heating. Green facades are often a special addition to the architecture. Some green facade plants can also contribute a little to capturing air polluting particles.

94 *Vertical garden by Patrick Blanc, Caixa Forum, Madrid, Spain*

4. **Disadvantages** The availability of water for the plants can be a bottleneck. Systems that use plant containers require irrigation and this can be a problem, especially for large 'living walls'. Some people do not like it when birds and insects live in the facade-plants. Self-climbing plants can sometimes damage the plaster or wall when they are removed.
5. **Construction** There are several ways to create a green facade. Self-climbing plants only need to be planted but systems for supported climbing plants have to be well planned and require stable constructions. Plant container systems and 'living walls' are preferably an integral part of the building's facade design. Their construction is often complicated and requires the work of professionals.
6. **Maintenance** The plant systems using planters always require irrigation systems. These must be checked and maintained on a regular basis. Especially with 'living walls', each 'planting module' in fact has to have its own irrigation. This can be problematic, and many plants die and have to be replaced. Systems with supported climbing plants have to be checked up upon once in a while. All green facades' plants need regular pruning.
7. **Costs** Self-climbing plants in deep soil €; Climbers in planters, supported climbers and trained fruit trees € €; living walls € € – € € €.
8. **No regret:** Yes

Planted Screen Elements

1. **General information** For light shadowing of a building's walls to prevent heating, you can use several types of planted screen elements. These elements are placed at least 50 centimetres from the facade and can come in the shape of panels or pillars. How much shade these elements will offer also depends on the supporting construction. Lightweight wire constructions, primarily functioning as support for climbers will not cast deep shadows themselves. Solid constructions such as plant containers will offer more shade even without the plants.
2. **Effectiveness** Planted screen elements are less effective when it comes to shading than direct greening of the walls would be. These elements do not have the advantage of an insulating layer of air and also do not provide the wall with as much protection against the weather's influences.
3. **Extra advantages** The evapotranspiration of the plants helps temper the air temperature, but less effectively than trees do. Since the green elements are not directly attached to the walls, the walls are more easily accessible, for example for maintenance.
4. **Disadvantages** The availability of water for the plants can be a bottleneck when the weather is hot. Especially plant systems using planters need irrigation and proper fertilization.
5. **Construction** These systems always have to be well planned, think of such aspects as the weight of the plant containers and the supporting construction. Professionals have to be brought in for the construction.
6. **Maintenance** When climbers root in the earth, you normally do not need an extra irrigation system and only have to take care of the upkeep of the supporting construction. Systems using plant containers always require irrigation and fertilization. You have to carefully regulate, maintain and monitor these systems.
7. **Costs** Deep soil climbing plant systems € €, Climbers in planters € € €.
8. **No regret:** Yes

95 *Planted pillars in Arnhem, the Netherlands*

Built Elements Demarcating Plots

1. **General information** Elements demarcating plots are a category of potentially shading elements that is often overlooked. These demarcations are often stone or brick walls, or wooden fences, but they can also be made of other building materials. They can provide shading for the outdoor spaces of houses.
2. **Effectiveness** The surface areas shaded by the demarcation elements are obviously smaller than those shaded by vertical sun protection, but depending on the size of the demarcations, the shaded areas can be quite large. As the materials are solid, the interception of solar radiation can easily reach 50% or more.
3. **Extra advantages** Demarcation elements provide shading and wind protection, but their main function is to protect people's property and privacy. Drywalls and gabions can also be home to plants and small animals such as lizards.
4. **Disadvantages** Demarcation elements can cast long shadows in winter. Some demarcations that retain much heat (e.g. stone constructions) can emit heat in the evening during summer, which may be an undesired side effect.
5. **Construction** The construction of demarcations can be simple (such as the wooden fences you can buy at DIY stores), but can also require real workmanship, for instance for beautifully crafted masonry.
6. **Maintenance** The maintenance depends on the type of demarcation. Walls usually require very little maintenance, whereas wooden fences should be painted regularly.
7. **Costs** Depending on the type € to € €
8. **No regret:** No

96 *A slate drywall as demarcation*

Green Demarcation Elements

1. **General information** Green demarcation elements, such as fences planted with climbers or hedges can also provide considerable shading.
2. **Effectiveness** The surface areas shaded by the green demarcation elements are obviously smaller than those shaded by horizontal sun protection, but depending on the size of the elements, the shaded areas can be quite large.
3. **Extra advantages** Demarcation elements offer shading and wind protection, but their main function is to protect people's property and privacy. Green demarcation elements also lower the air temperature through evapotranspiration. In winter, deciduous green demarcations do not cast much shadow, which can be advantageous for the sun exposure of a house.
4. **Disadvantages** Dense, evergreen demarcation elements can cast too much shadow in winter.
5. **Construction** Hedges and shrubs as green demarcation elements are relatively easy to implement. Professional work is preferred when the plants grow on grids or other construction types.
6. **Maintenance** Green demarcation elements have to be pruned on an occasional to regular basis.
7. **Costs** €
8. **No regret:** Yes

97 *Planted fences, Jardins d'Eole, Paris, France*

Park Trees and Shrubs

1. **General information** To create shading, planting more trees and shrubs is the most obvious solution. They can also significantly reduce the solar radiation on buildings. Depending on the desired shadow effect, the choice is between deciduous or evergreen trees. In more densely built surroundings, where buildings cast long shadows in winter, deciduous trees are usually preferable, to prevent too many places from being shaded. Tree types also differ considerably in the size and density of their foliage. This obviously influences the depth of the shadow (see list illustration 99) and the resulting cooling effect. Considering the effect of future circumstances (due to climate change) on the types of trees that can grow in our latitudes, we have to select suitable tree species. To this end, there are lists of trees and shrubs in temperate climate zones that are 'climate proof' and thus can stand more heat and drought (see list illustration 100).
2. **Effectiveness** The tree's shadow intercepts much of the incoming radiation. This leads to a reduction in solar radiation of up to 70% on the surfaces beneath. The shadow, however, is not as dense as that of objects that are impenetrable to solar radiation (such as walls) and strongly depends on the chosen species (see list illustration 99). Trees can lower air temperature with 1-3 °C and the UTCI with as much as 15 degrees in temperate climate zones.
3. **Extra advantages** Trees and shrubs also lower the air temperature through evapotranspiration. Besides the microclimatic effect, they have many other positive effects. They can filter air and noise; produce timber, fruit and nuts; increase biodiversity; and highlight the changing of the seasons. When buildings are surrounded by beautiful, big trees, this raises their real estate value.

98 *Large park tree in Copenhagen, Denmark*

4. **Disadvantages** Trees attract animals and insects, which might be an undesired side effect for some users or residents. Apart from this we also have to take into account that trees can emit volatile organic compounds. These are gases that can effectuate ozone production, especially isoprenes and monoterpenes play a role in this. The emission levels vary greatly between tree species. But some species are known as strong emitters, and in temperate climate zones these are for isoprenes: *Platanus, Populus, Quercus* (*pubescens* and *robur*) and for monoterpenes: coniferous tree species. These tree species should not be planted in large numbers, say as an urban forest.
5. **Construction** Planting trees and shrubs is usually quite simple, provided that the soil conditions are suitable and there is sufficient room for the roots.
6. **Maintenance** Because of their growth and their leaves, trees and shrubs do need maintenance.
7. **Costs** €
8. **No regret:** Yes

Botanical name	**Common English name**	**Transmissivity range (%)**		**a)Foliation**	**b)defoliation**
		summer	**winter**		
Acer platanoides	Norway maple	5-14	60-75	E	M
Acer rubrum	Red maple	8-22	63-82	M	E
Acer saccharinum	Silver maple	10-28	60-87	M	M
Acer saccharum	Sugar maple	16-27	60-80	M	E
Aesculus hippocastanum	Horse-chestnut	8-27	73	M	L
Amelanchier canadensis	Canadian serviceberry	20-25	57	L	M
Betula pendula	Silver birch	14-24	48-88	M	M-L
Carya ovata	Shagbark hickory	15-28	66		
Catalpa speciosa	Weatern catalpa	24-30	52-83	L	
Fagus sylvatica	European beech	7-15	83	L	L
Fraxinus pennsylvanica	Green Ash	10-29	70-71	M-L	M
Gleditsia tricanthos inermis	Honeylocust	25-50	50-85	M	E
Juglans rigra	Black walnut	9		L	E-M
Liriodendron tulipfera	Tulip tree	10	55-72	M-L	M
Picea pungens	Colorado spruce	13-28	69-78		
Pinus strobus	White pine	25-30	13-28		
Platanus acerifolia	London plane tree	11-17	25-30	L	M-L
Populus deltoidus	Cottonwood	10-20	46-64	E	M
Populus tremuloides	Trenbling aspen	20-33	68	E	M
Quercus alba	White oak	13-38			
Quercus rubra	Red oak	12-23	70-81	M	M
Tilia cordata	Littleleaf lime	7-22	46-70	L	E
Ulmus americana	American elm	13	63-89	M	M

a) E = Early = before April 30st M = Middle = May 1st-15th L = Late = after May 15st
b) E = Early = before November 1st M = Middle = November 1st-30st L = Late = after November 30st

99 *List of shadow depths of trees*

Scientific name	Synonym
Acer campestre	
Acer freemanii	
Acer monspessulanum	
Acer tataricum ginnala	Acer ginnala
Albizia julibrissin	Albizia kalkora
Alnus cordata	
Alnus incana	
Alnus rubra	Alnus oregona
Alnus spaethii	
Alnus subcordata	
Betula pendula	Betula alba; Betula verrucosa
Broussonetia papyrifera	
Carpinus betulus	Carpinus caucasica
Carpinus japonica	
Carpinus tschonoskii	
Cedrus atlantica	Cedrus libani atlantica
Cedrus deodara	
Cedrus libani	
Celtis australis	
Celtis occidentalis	
Cercis siliquastrum	
Corylus colurna	
Crataegus lavalleei	
Eucommia ulmoides	
Fraxinus angustifolia	Fraxinus angustifolia oxycarpa; Fraxinus rotundifolia; Fraxinus oxycarpa
Fraxinus biltmoreana	
Fraxinus ornus	
Fraxinus pennsylvanica	
Gleditsia triacanthos	
Gymnocladus dioica	
Hippophae salicifolia	
Juglans nigra	
Koelreuteria paniculata	
Maackia amurensis	
Maclura pomifera	
Mespilus germanica	Crataegus germanica
Metasequoia glyptostroboides	
Morus alba	Morus bombycis; Morus australis; Morus kagayamae
Morus nigra	
Ostrya carpinifolia	

Scientific name	Synonym
Picea pungens	
Pinus nigra nigra	Pinus nigra austriaca; Pinus austriaca
Pinus pinea	
Pinus sylvestris	
Pinus wallichiana	Pinus griffithii; Pinus excelsa
Platanus hispanica	Platanus acerifolia; Platanus hybrida
Platanus orientalis	
Populus tremula	
Pseudotsuga menziesii	Pseudotsuga taxifolia; Pseudotsuga douglasii
Pyrus calleryana	
Pyrus canescens	
Pyrus salicifolia	
Pyrus serrulata	
Quercus cerris	
Quercus frainetto	Quercus conferta; Quercus pannonica
Quercus ilex	
Quercus imbricaria	
Quercus macranthera	
Quercus petraea	
Quercus suber	
Quercus velutina	
Robinia ambigua	
Robinia luxurians	Robinia neomexicana HORT.
Robinia pseudoacacia	
Sophora japonica	
Sorbus arnoldiana	
Sorbus aucuparia	
Sorbus commixta	Sorbus americana HORT.; Sorbus matsumurana HORT.
Sorbus decora	
Sorbus discolor	
Sorbus domestica	
Sorbus intermedia	Sorbus scandica
Sorbus latifolia	
Sorbus thuringiaca	
Sorbus vilmorinii	
Thuja occidentalis	
Tilia cordata	Tilia parvifolia
Tilia mongolica	
Tilia tomentosa	Tilia argentea
Ziziphus jujuba	

100 *List of 'climate-proof' – mainly drought-tolerant – trees for temperate climate zones*

Perennial Plants with Very Large Leaves

1. **General information** As a green alternative to woody vegetation, you can also use perennial plants with large leaves for shading. Think of Gunnera macrophylla, tree ferns and such.
2. **Effectiveness** The effectiveness is comparable to that of trees and shrubs, so you can expect a radiation reduction of up to 50% under the leaves.
3. **Extra advantages** Such perennial plants have one big advantage: they retreat in winter. So in this period, they do not cast any shadow. Moreover, they often have a special appearance and great aesthetic value.
4. **Disadvantages** None
5. **Construction** Planting perennials is easy when the soil and growth circumstances are suitable.
6. **Maintenance** Some perennial plants require special care.
7. **Costs** €
8. **No regret:** Yes

101 *A Gunnera macrophylla can be used for shading, Dublin, Ireland*

Colonnades and Pavilions

1. **General information** If, for certain reasons, plant elements are not wanted, you can also choose built objects. The reasons for this less optimal solution may concern maintenance, aesthetics or be of a functional nature. These small buildings can be meant for people to relax in (pavilions) or move through (colonnades) while being shaded. You can provide these buildings with fixed or flexible shading elements or with solar panel roofs.
2. **Effectiveness** If the buildings do not let any sun in, the shadow effect is much stronger than it is with plants, and there is very little incoming shortwave radiation (reduction can be about 90%) and we can expect a lowering of UTCI of about 10 degrees.
3. **Extra advantages** The built elements can often add something special to a space. When you install photovoltaic systems on the roofs, they absorb extra solar energy from the environment and add to the cooling effect.
4. **Disadvantages** These built elements absorb extra heat and emit longwave radiation, so they can, to a small degree, add to a higher air temperature.
5. **Construction** Depending on the desired form, the construction can be simple or, conversely, be really specialist work.
6. **Maintenance** Wooden constructions require more maintenance than stone or metal constructions.
7. **Costs** €€
8. **No regret:** No

102 *Colonnade in Parc de la Villette, Paris, France*

Green Pavilions and Arbours

1. **General information** A good compromise neutralizing the disadvantages of built shadow elements (regarding heat absorption and radiation) are lightweight architectural objects with plants growing on them. These can be made of lightweight masonry, with slats, wires and such, along which plants can climb.
2. **Effectiveness** Like pergolas, the shadow effect can be lighter or deeper, depending on the density of growth. The deflected radiation is often a little over 50%, because the construction's shadow and that of the vegetation add up. Expected lowering of UTCI amounts to 9 degrees.
3. **Extra advantages** The positive aspects of a small building as a shadow element (e.g. a special shape) are combined with the advantages of vegetation here: the plants provide cooling and block solar radiation, which would otherwise be absorbed by the building and emitted as heat.
4. **Disadvantages** None
5. **Construction** The construction of green pavilions and arbours can be complicated, and you have to calculate for the weight of the plants.
6. **Maintenance** The construction requires upkeep, and the plants can make that difficult. The plants themselves need regular care as well.
7. **Costs** € €
8. **No regret:** Yes

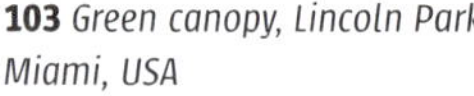

103 *Green canopy, Lincoln Park, Miami, USA*

Shadow Roofs

1. **General information** Since urban squares generally require an open visual field on eye level and space for circulation, shadow roofs resting on only a few pillars are useful here. These objects can be made with flexible textile elements or fixed roof-like constructions.
2. **Effectiveness** Because these elements are often on taller pillars and the roof isn't very large, solar radiation can enter from the sides and the shading effect is limited to smaller areas.
3. **Extra advantages** The built elements can be a special addition to a space. You can also install photovoltaic systems on or in the roofs.
4. **Disadvantages** These built elements absorb extra heat and emit longwave radiation, so they can, to a small degree, add to a higher air temperature. When these objects have flexible elements, these may be vulnerable to vandalism.
5. **Construction** Depending on the desired construction, making these objects can be relatively simple or be specialist work.
6. **Maintenance** Wooden constructions need more maintenance than metal constructions. It is not always easy to maintain constructions with flexible elements, because of the more vulnerable materials and moving parts. Fixed objects have these problems to a lesser degree.
7. **Costs** € €
8. **No regret:** No

104 *A shadow roof on a square in Barcelona, Spain*

Trees on Squares

1. **General information** Because the surrounding buildings often visually dominate urban squares, shadow trees can be used as a contrast. My research in North-Western Europe has shown that people prefer to have more green elements on squares, especially trees. The possibilities for using trees are more limited on squares than in parks, though. Squares need to be surveyed and have to provide room for markets, events and such. Trees with crown bottoms that are relatively high above the ground are therefore preferable, and you shouldn't use much or any undergrowth. Often, there are also underground constructions such as car parks to take into account that limit space for growth of roots.
2. **Effectiveness** The tree's shadow intercepts much of the incoming radiation. This leads to a reduction in solar radiation of up to 70% on the surfaces beneath. Trees also shade the paved surfaces of the squares, and as a result these absorb less energy and thus emit less heat. Trees can lower air temperature with 1-3˚C and the UTCI with as much as 15 degrees in temperate zones.
3. **Extra advantages** Trees do not only offer shade; their evapotranspiration also tempers the air temperature. In winter, many trees lose their foliage, and thus their shadow effect is reduced, allowing for extra sun penetration. Moreover, trees have an important aesthetical function: they create an attractive umbrageous ambiance. A single tree on a square can sometimes become a place for people to gather round.
4. **Disadvantages** Like all elements, trees can be obstacles, for instance on market days or when there is an event. A well-planned layout of the trees can prevent this, however, and there are ample examples where trees are not an obstacle. The available rooting space is always an issue with trees on squares, as is the availability of water and good aeration of the soil. Trees are often planted in smaller planting sites or in some cases even in containers with very limited rooting space, for instance when there is a car park beneath the square. Also, irrigation of these sites during dry summer periods has to be guaranteed. The growth conditions hence cause stress for trees and only robust species can be used in such circumstances.
5. **Construction** Specialists have to be the ones to plant trees on squares, because they often have to prepare specific planting sites with systems for aeration and irrigation.
6. **Maintenance** City trees need more care than trees in the landscape, because there are more stress factors in the city, such as heat, drought and road salt. Cleaning up the leaves and pruning are also a lot of work.
7. **Costs** €€
8. **No regret:** Yes

105 *A typical 'tree square': the Lange Voorhout in The Hague, the Netherlands*

Built Shadow Elements in Streets

1. **General information** Above the sidewalks, all kinds of shadow elements can be fixed directly onto the buildings, as discussed before in the 'Around Buildings' section (see inner back flap). When there is sufficient space in boulevard-type street profiles, other small architectural structures such as freestanding roofs and pergolas can be used for shading. You can find descriptions of these elements in the 'In Gardens and Parks' and 'On Squares' sections (see inner back flap). A special type of element is the 'shadow curtain': a flexible shadow element that can be spanned over a street.
2. **Effectiveness** If the elements block the sun entirely, the shadow effect directly under the curtains is good and there will be relatively little incoming shortwave radiation. Because these elements are often higher up in the street profile, to allow for traffic, more sun can come in from the sides. Still, the UTCI can be lowered with up to 15 degrees. The air temperature can be lowered with 1˚C.
3. **Extra advantages** The built elements can be a special aesthetic addition to a space. You can also install photovoltaic systems or sun boilers on the roofs of fixed structures.
4. **Disadvantages** Built elements can absorb extra heat and emit longwave radiation, so they can, to a small degree, add to a higher air temperature. This is not a problem with textile elements. Flexible systems are generally more vulnerable, also to vandalism, and have a shorter lifespan.
5. **Construction** Depending on the desired construction, making these objects can be relatively simple or be specialist work.
6. **Maintenance** Wooden constructions require more maintenance than stonework or metal constructions do. The moving parts of flexible systems need special attention.
7. **Costs** €€
8. **No regret:** Fixed constructions – No; Flexible constructions – Yes

106 *Shadow curtain over a street, Santa Barbara, California, USA*

Street Trees

1. General information If you want a street to have continuous shading, trees are the most obvious and efficient solution. You have to be very careful about what type of tree you choose, with regard to the desired shadow effect (also see illustration 99). Deciduous trees are generally preferable, since they allow for more sun in the winter. The trees have to be planted in such a way that they fit into the street space, keeping in mind the daylighting of the adjacent buildings. In residential streets, trees should not block the sun coming into the houses in the winter. In streets where buildings have other functions, this is not always necessary.

Each street profile with its height-width ratio is different and the orientation of streets differs as well. The path of the sun is different for each place on earth too. All of this results in very diverse shadow patterns. To address these unique situations with a design for tree

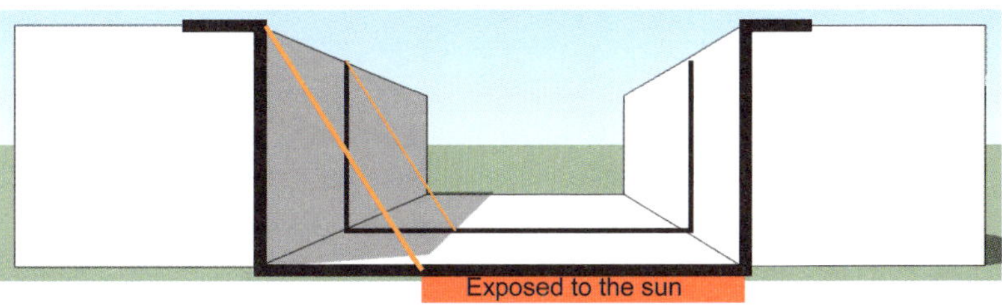

107 Simulation of the shadow in a street at 3 p.m.

a) Shopping street

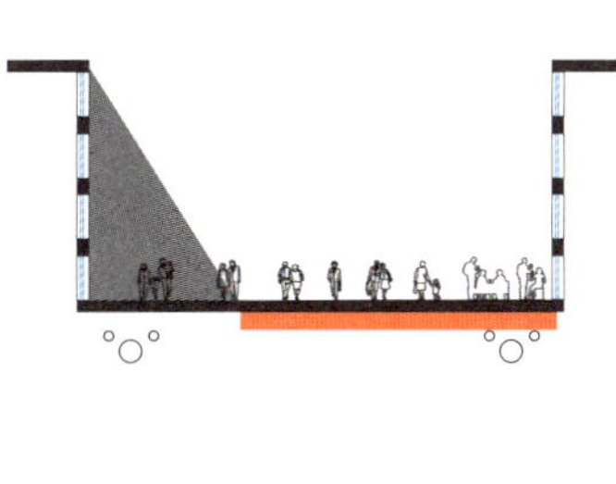

b) Street with pavement

108 Analysing places, locating people's circulation patterns, utility lines and windows of adjacent buildings

a) Shopping street

option 1

option 2

b) Street with pavement

option 1

option 2

109 Simulating different tree configuration options

rows, it is best to first make a simulation of the shadow patterns with the trees you want to plant. These shadow patterns can be visualized with 3D-software such as AutoCad, SketchUp, Rhino and others. First, you need to know which areas in the street are most impacted by solar radiation. Shadow pattern simulations depicting the situation at 3 p.m. will suffice, because at that time the heat is at its top and the heat problems are biggest (see illustration 107). Next, you have to see where in the street profile most people gather or circulate, so you know which areas need good shading. You also have to check which buildings have windows that should not be shaded, and where you can't plant trees because of underground utility lines. Illustration 108 shows what this little study can look like for a shopping street and for a street with pavements. Finally, you can project trees with different heights and properties on the street spaces, on the spots they can be planted in. The trees' shadows can then be simulated to test whether the areas with many people are shaded and the windows (if need be) are not (see illustration 109). There are usually many options here, leaving elbowroom for the designer.

2. **Effectiveness** Rows of trees in streets shade the street surface and the surrounding facades. Because of the shadow, the dark street surface is not heated up as much, so eventually there will be less longwave radiation. Planted in the right spots, trees can intercept much incoming radiation and thus heating. They intercept up to 70% of the solar radiation falling on the street surface and the facades. Trees can lower air temperature with 1-3˚C and the UTCI with as much as 15 degrees in temperate zones.
3. **Extra advantages** Street trees are valuable for reasons of aesthetics, water management and ecology as well. They can furthermore capture particulates and reduce air pollution.
4. **Disadvantages** Trees can sometimes obstruct ventilation. In streets with heavy traffic, this can slow the dispersion of air pollutants. In these cases, the trees should be planted with more space between them. This does, of course, diminish the shadow effect.
5. **Construction** Planting trees in streets is specialist work, because they often have to prepare specific planting sites with systems for aeration and irrigation. Other conditions sometimes have to considered, such as the location of underground utility lines and traffic lanes.
6. **Maintenance** Street trees need more care than trees in the countryside, because they are exposed to more stress factors in the city, such as heat, drought and road salt. Cleaning up the leaves and pruning are also a lot of work.
7. **Costs** €
8. **No regret:** Yes

Carports

1. **General information** Carports or lightweight roof constructions above parking spaces can provide the necessary shading to prevent cars from overheating in summer. Because cars have to be able to drive in and out, shadow elements should only take up limited surface space, for instance resting on just a few pillars.
2. **Effectiveness** If the elements block the sun entirely, the shadow effect is good, but because these elements are often on pillars and the roof isn't very large, more sun can come in from the sides. The cooling effect can mean a lowering of the UTCI with up to 1 degree.
3. **Extra advantages** The built elements can also block rain and other weather influences, and prevent the car from getting dirty because of pollen, leaves, bird droppings and such. It is also possible to place solar installations or photovoltaic elements on these roofs.
4. **Disadvantages** Built elements can absorb extra heat and emit longwave radiation, so they can, to a small degree, add to a higher air temperature.
5. **Construction** Building carports is usually relatively simple, but you do need professionals for large constructions.
6. **Maintenance** In general, carports are easy to maintain, but wooden constructions require more maintenance than metal constructions.
7. **Costs** €€
8. **No regret:** No

110 *Carports with a solar panel canopy*

Trees in Parking Lots

1. **General information** Trees can offer good shading for cars in outdoor parking lots. It is important for efficient shading that trees have broad crowns and are not spaced out too much. Here too, the best way to decide where to plant the trees is to use shadow simulations during the design process, taking in the potential buildings too (see 'Street Trees', page 143). For parking lots it is generally better to use evergreen trees. This way, the trees offer shade in the summer and protections against precipitation in other seasons.
2. **Effectiveness** Depending on the density of the crown and how far apart the trees are planted, these trees can block up to 70% of the solar radiation directly under the trees. Trees can lower air temperature with 1-3˚C and the UTCI with as much as 15 degrees in temperate zones.
3. **Extra advantages** Besides the cars, large surfaces of asphalt are also shaded and thus protected from strong heating. Trees also offer extra cooling through evapotranspiration. They can have aesthetical and ecological value as well.
4. **Disadvantages** Cars parked under trees can have blossoms; leaves and fruit fall on them. Animals living in the tree can be nuisances because of their droppings (e.g. birds, plant lice).
5. **Construction** Gardeners should plant trees in parking lots, because they often have to prepare specific planting sites with systems for aeration and irrigation.
6. **Maintenance** Trees in parking lots require relatively much care, because they are exposed to more stress factors in the city, such as heat, drought and road salt. The trees sometimes need extra water in hot circumstances. Cleaning up the leaves and pruning are also a lot of work.
7. **Costs** €
8. **No regret:** Yes

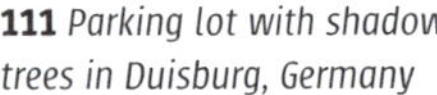

111 *Parking lot with shadow trees in Duisburg, Germany*

Planted Shadow Elements

1. **General information** Pergola-type green constructions can also provide shade in parking lots. Deciduous and evergreen plants can grow on these constructions. If you also want good rain protection in winter, evergreen vegetation is preferable.
2. **Effectiveness** Depending on the density of the foliage, the plants can shade a parking lot effectively.
3. **Extra advantages** Besides the cars, large surfaces of asphalt are also shaded and thus protected from strong heating. Plants also offer extra cooling through evapotranspiration. They can have aesthetical and ecological value as well.
4. **Disadvantages** Cars parked under pergolas can have blossoms; leaves and fruit fall on them. Animals living in the pergolas can be nuisances because of their droppings (e.g. birds, plant lice). Pergolas offer less rain protection than closed roofs do.
5. **Construction** Pergolas in car parks have to meet certain safety regulations and their foundations have to be strong enough to support the biomass. Therefore, it's best if professionals place the pergolas.
6. **Maintenance** Pergolas require regular maintenance (painting, repairing woodwork) and some plants need regular pruning.
7. **Costs** € €
8. **No regret:** Yes

112 *Green parking lot pergolas, Siedlung Schüngelberg, Gelsenkirchen, Germany*

Green Car Parks

1. **General information** The aforementioned planted shadow elements in combination with parking spaces can also be 'stacked up', thus forming a vertical 'parking park'. The walls are replaced with 'plant curtains' and, aside from the parking decks, the building itself doesn't have much thermal mass as opposed to more massive buildings. This, plus the plants' shading, ensures minimal heating. To guarantee sufficient daylight intrusion in winter as well, it is advisable to plant the structure with deciduous plants.

   Depending on the height of the building, you can use climbing plants rooting in the soil (with or without support). If the building is taller than two storeys, you have to work with plant containers planted with climbers or hanging plants. Closed 'green walls' are not a good idea, since these strongly reduce ventilation.
2. **Effectiveness** There is maximum shading on the lower levels. On the upper level, pergola constructions can offer good shading for cars as well.
3. **Extra advantages** Such constructions have a few extra advantages compared to classic car parks. The lower levels are cool and well protected against weather influences. The leaves of the plant constructions also capture some air polluting particulates. Such a vertical 'parking park' can also be a very special building, which could be used for other purposes too.
4. **Disadvantages** Trees parked under pergolas on the top floor can have blossoms; leaves and fruit fall on them. Animals living in the plants can be nuisances because of their droppings (e.g. birds, plant lice). The more open parts offer less rain protection than closed roofs do.
5. **Construction** Professionals have to plan and build such green car parks.
6. **Maintenance** The maintenance of the building is relatively intensive. Besides normal building upkeep, all climbing constructions for the plants have to be maintained. The plants have to be pruned very regularly to ensure safety.
7. **Costs** €€€€
8. **No regret:** Yes

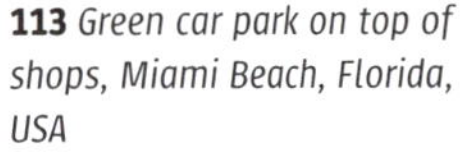

113 *Green car park on top of shops, Miami Beach, Florida, USA*

Influencing Reflection

Roofs with High Albedo

1. **General information** When heat-sensitive functions are situated right beneath the roofs (such as living or working), it is useful to apply light-coloured materials or 'cool coatings'. There are different types of reflecting roofing materials: from white glazed tiles to metal plates with special coatings. For example: a traditional tile has an albedo of around 0.10-0.35; but painted white, the albedo is 0.75. Another example: the albedo of a roof with corrugated iron sheets is around 0.10-0.15; but painted with a 'cool coating', more than twice the radiation is reflected.
2. **Effectiveness** In summer, a black roof surface can easily have a peak temperature of 80°C. A white roof, by contrast, can be 17°C cooler on average. Thanks to reflection, less heat comes into the indoor spaces and a reduction of indoor temperature of 2.5°C has been measured.
3. **Extra advantages** Because of the moderated temperature fluctuations of the reflecting roofs, the roofing materials suffer less stress. A reflecting roof will therefore have a longer lifespan than a black roof.
4. **Disadvantages** When the white roofs become dirty over time, they will be less effective.
5. **Construction** Especially if you are building a new roof or replacing an old one, it makes sense to use reflecting materials or coatings.
6. **Maintenance** For sustained reflection, white roofs have to be cleaned regularly.
7. **Costs** €€
8. **No regret:** Yes

114 *White roof on the M museum in Leuven, Belgium*

Facades with High Albedo

1. **General information** When the indoor climate of a building has to be cooled, the facades can be given a reflecting colour. This way, the wall will absorb less heat, and the rooms behind the walls will not warm up further. The albedo of a classic brick wall is 0.20-0.40 and that of a concrete wall is 0.10-0.35. White paint brings up the albedo to 0.50-0.90. Nowadays new coatings exist that have a darker colour but still have a high albedo due to special reflecting micro-particles.

   The effect of high albedo walls of buildings can help in cooling the streetscape to a small extent when only the higher parts are given a high albedo. When the entire facade has a high albedo, we see a negative effect for pedestrians due to the extra reflected solar radiation.
2. **Effectiveness** Higher albedos result in considerably lower facade surface temperatures. A dark outer wall can easily be 8 to 10°C warmer than a light one. The indoor air temperatures can be lowered with up to 3°C in badly insulated buildings. In well-insulated buildings there is no effect. When only higher parts of the wall have a higher albedo, pedestrians on street level are protected from the higher irradiation levels and are more thermally comfortable.
3. **Extra advantages** Light-coloured facades or parts of facades can sometimes form a special accentuation in the facade design.
4. **Disadvantages** Light facades can become dirty more quickly than dark facades.
5. **Construction** Replacing facade-materials can be complicated but painting them in a lighter colour is a simple, fast and cheap solution for raising a facade's albedo.
6. **Maintenance** Cleaning or painting once in a while is sufficient for keeping up the albedo.
7. **Costs** € (painting) to € € (replacing facade-material)
8. **No regret:** No

115 *White facades of apartment buildings in Salzburg, Austria*

Surfacing with High Albedo

1. **General information** When open, surfaced areas such as squares, streets and outdoor car parks absorb much heat, lighter and smoother materials can be used to reflect short-wave radiation and thus temper energy absorption of the material. For example: if black asphalt surfaces become so hot in summer that it is uncomfortable to walk on them; or if the asphalt softens and becomes a source of danger to traffic, it is advisable to use materials with a higher albedo. On low-traffic squares, light stones, concrete tiles or clinkers can be used. Asphalt is the preferred material for roads and parking lots, because it can bear heavy traffic. To make the asphalt lighter in colour, lighter types of added substances can be used. Nowadays, there are alternative new, light-coloured substances to replace the bituminous parts of asphalt, such as NaturalPAVE® or CreaPhalt®.
2. **Effectiveness** The effect of lowering the surface's temperature through higher albedos depends on the albedo's magnitude. An increase in albedo by 0.35 may lead air temperature reductions of 1°C on average and of 3°C during warm summer days. On hot days, concrete surfaces with a lighter colour, for instance, can have a surface temperature that is 20°C lower than asphalt surfaces.
3. **Extra advantages** None

116 *Light natural stone surfacing, High Tech Campus Eindhoven, the Netherlands*

4. **Disadvantages** Applying high-albedo surfacing also has a negative effect on thermal sensation levels for people walking on it due to the reflection of solar radiation onto the body. This overpowers the slight cooling effect on the air temperature. Places where people gather on warm summer days in such areas with high-albedo surfacing should hence be supplied with shading elements.

   Surfaces with a light colour become dirty more quickly and lose some of their reflectivity when they do. On sunny days, light colours can reflect the bright sun in an unpleasant way, and blinding can pose a danger to traffic.
5. **Construction** When public spaces are redeveloped, a lighter surfacing can be chosen. Or when asphalt roads need resurfacing, other additives can be used in the top layer. Specialists need to be involved in the construction.
6. **Maintenance** For sustained reflection, light-coloured surfacing must be cleaned regularly. The top layer of asphalt can be replaced with a lighter layer during regular maintenance.
7. **Costs** € €
8. **No regret:** No

Outdoor Furniture with Albedos Suitable for Seasonal Use

1. **General information** The thermal comfort of people in outdoor spaces can depend on the materials they are in direct contact with. Think especially of outdoor furniture people sit on, lean against or even lie down on. When dark surfaces become too hot in summer, for instance, people are not likely to sit on them. In spring or autumn on the other hand, it is nice to sit on a 'preheated' bench. So, if you design outdoor furniture, you have to consider when people will use it and adjust the albedo to its use.
2. **Effectiveness** Depending on the albedo, the surface temperature is clearly increased or decreased.
3. **Extra advantages** Furniture with a pleasant surface temperature also creates an inviting ambiance.
4. **Disadvantages** None
5. **Construction** Whether you need professionals to make and place the furniture depends on its size and shape.
6. **Maintenance** The maintenance is highly dependent on the used materials and the shape of the furniture.
7. **Costs** €
8. **No regret:** Yes

117 *Light mosaic bench in Barcelona, Spain*

Influencing Emissivity and Heat Conductivity

Walls with a Low Mass

1. **General information** Facade-materials with a lower mass, such as wood or aerated concrete absorb less energy and thus also emit less. They are a good solution for keeping the warm long-wave radiation in outdoor spaces of densely built-up residential areas low. To prevent the outer shell from absorbing heat because of a dark colour, lighter colours are preferable.
2. **Effectiveness** Depending on the chosen material, heat radiation is clearly reduced.
3. **Extra advantages** Porous materials always also have a good insulating effect in indoor spaces. Renewable materials such as wood or other organic materials are more sustainable than, for instance, concrete.
4. **Disadvantages** None
5. **Construction** The use of these materials is recommended for new residential areas. For existing buildings, changing the outer shell often is not an option. The building constructions often consist of materials emitting much heat, such as bricks or concrete. It is not easy to replace or cover these materials with extra materials. Sometimes the constructions are not suitable, and sometimes it is undesirable for aesthetic reasons, as in the case of historical decorative brickwork that should not be covered.
6. **Maintenance** The maintenance very much depends on the type of material and potential coatings.
7. **Costs** €
8. **No regret:** Yes

118 *Woodwork facades, Kop van Zuid, Rotterdam, the Netherlands*

‘Heat Emitting’ Walls

1. **General information** It can be useful to have some outdoor locations that offer thermal comfort in the cooler seasons. To this end, a high-mass wall that retains the scarce warmth can be an advantage. This works best with walls facing south, since these receive the strongest solar radiation for the longest time of the day. Old houses sometimes have benches in front of the facades with the best sun orientation. These benches are a nice place to sit, making use of the direct solar radiation. But even when the sun has gone, the wall’s warmth allows people to sit there a while longer. Not just the walls of buildings, but also walls demarcating plots can function as ‘heat emitting walls’.
2. **Effectiveness** On a small scale, the emitted warmth is very effective, but it depends on the material the wall is made of: very dense, dark materials work better than light and low-mass materials.
3. **Extra advantages** A wall in a special heat-storing material can also be a special touch in the architecture.
4. **Disadvantages** To prevent further warming of a city, it is not advisable to use these walls ubiquitously. It is better to place ‘heat emitting walls’ on a small number of carefully chosen spots to create a few warm outdoor public places.
5. **Construction** In principle, such wall elements should be part of the original construction of a new building or demarcation, and professionals should build them.
6. **Maintenance** These walls require rather minimal maintenance.
7. **Costs** €
8. **No regret:** No

119 *Built-in wall-seats in Madrid, Spain*

Low-Density Surfacing

1. **General information** If you want surfaces to emit as little longwave radiation as possible, it seems like a good solution to use lower-density materials conducting less heat. But because streets and roads often have to be strong enough to support heavy traffic, you can hardly ever use these lightweight and porous materials. It is, however, possible to use porous materials such as wood around houses, for terraces and garden paths and such.
2. **Effectiveness** Compared to asphalt, concrete, bricks or dense natural stone, these surfaces can have a much lower heat storage and conductivity.
3. **Extra advantages** Materials such as wood can be of special aesthetic value.
4. **Disadvantages** You can only use these materials on roads and paths with light traffic.
5. **Construction** Professionals have to plan and construct these types of surfacing. Wooden surfaces normally become slippery over time and require an extra coating in areas with much circulation.
6. **Maintenance** Porous surfaces have to be cleaned regularly, and wooden surfaces require regular damage and safety checks.
7. **Costs** €
8. **No regret:** No

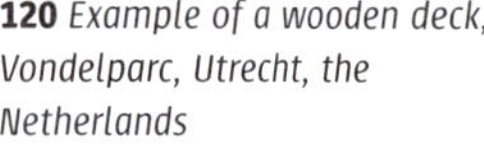

120 *Example of a wooden deck, Vondelparc, Utrecht, the Netherlands*

Low-Conductivity Outdoor Furniture

1. **General information** The materials used for outdoor furniture can have a strong influence on people's thermal comfort upon touch. In cold circumstances, fast-conducting materials such as metals can subtract heat from the body so fast that the skin can freeze on to it. In warm circumstances, they can become so hot as to cause light burns. So, it is important to select materials attuned to people's thermal sensation. In general, it is best to use materials such as wood, plastic or porous stone, because of their low conductivity.
2. **Effectiveness** The use of low-conductivity outdoor furniture has a clear effect on the people using it. The material is nice to touch, since it does not subtract extra warmth from the skin or subject it to extra heat.
3. **Extra advantages** These materials usually also give a 'warm', inviting ambiance to outdoor spaces.
4. **Disadvantages** None
5. **Construction** Depending on the type and construction, making outdoor furniture can be quite simple or require a craftsperson.
6. **Maintenance** Wooden furniture may need more upkeep (paint, stains) than plastic furniture. Porous stone has to be cleaned regularly.
7. **Costs** €
8. **No regret:** Yes

121 *Wooden bench, Parque de Manzanares, Madrid, Spain*

Influencing Evaporation

Intensive and Irrigated Green Roofs

1. **General information** There are different types of green roofs with different types of substrates, different types and densities of plants and level of irrigation. Extensive roofs with a thin, dark mineral substrate layer and sedum vegetation do not have a cooling effect and can even be warmer than reflecting roofs.

   On the other hand, intensive green roofs with a thick substrate layer and lots of vegetation can contribute to cooling their direct environment. An intensive green roof has a substrate layer of at least 25 centimetres. Perennials can grow in such a layer, shrubbery requires at least 40 centimetres and trees require a substrate layer of at least 80 centimetres.
2. **Effectiveness** Because of the plants' shadows, the lower albedo and the evaporation, the surface temperature during summer can be 18°C lower than that of black bitumen roofs. They can also cool the air in their surrounding with about 0.5°C, but that effect will not reach the lower areas in the street canyons and pedestrians there will not benefit from it.
3. **Extra advantages** If, besides cooling the roof area, you also want to efficiently lower temperatures indoors and thus be able to use less air conditioning, intensive roofs are recommended. The insulation of the substrate layer provides cooling, which can mean around 2.5°C lower indoor temperatures right beneath the roof. Eventually, this

122 *Intensive roof park, Köln Arcaden, Cologne, Germany*

can result in around 25% yearly savings on energy costs for air conditioning. Intensive roof gardens are pleasant outdoor areas, which can be seen as extra living space. When intensive green roofs are combined with photovoltaic elements, this installation works more efficiently because of the extra cooling of the plants underneath.

4. **Disadvantages** None
5. **Construction** Because of the high load, intensive green roofs need strong bearing constructions. Therefore, it usually is not possible to retrofit roofs on existing buildings. The construction of new buildings has to be designed to bear the extra weight on the roof.
6. **Maintenance** Intensive green roofs require quite a lot of maintenance (checking them about eight times a year, weeding, et cetera) and irrigation in dry periods.
7. **Costs** € € €
8. **No regret:** Yes

'Water Roofs and Walls'

1. **General information** For cooling the insides of buildings, but also for cooling closed outdoor spaces, you can consider 'water roofs and water walls'. Think of using nozzles or water films to keep roofs or other building surfaces moist; or of storing water on a flat roof with a cover over it. These techniques were already used in old Indian palaces. The cooled air from a water roof was led into the indoor spaces of these palaces. So it is an ancient technique that can still be of use today.
2. **Effectiveness** Storing water on roofs can lead to 10 to 20°C lower surface temperatures (air temperatures to a lesser degree) and indoors to around 5°C lower temperatures. On walls, surface temperature reductions up to 10°C have been measured when water films were applied.
3. **Extra advantages** Water roofs can play an important role in buffering peak rainfalls.
4. **Disadvantages** None
5. **Construction** Watering vertical building surfaces usually requires many technical installations, but storing water on flat roofs is a relatively easy thing to plan for new buildings. The building construction must be strong enough to support the extra weight of the water, though. Planning and construction have to be left to experts.
6. **Maintenance** The installations have to be cleaned and checked regularly.
7. **Costs** € € €
8. **No regret:** Yes

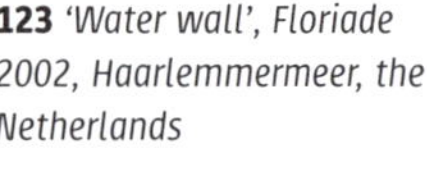

123 *'Water wall', Floriade 2002, Haarlemmermeer, the Netherlands*

Low Plants

1. **General information** Many urban areas are currently paved, ranging from public spaces such as squares, street canyons, and parking lots to front and back yards. This has many negative consequences for the radiation balance of both indoor and outdoor climate. For this reason, it is better to de-pave where possible. The use of lower plants is advisable for places where no shadows should be cast on the house or where the night temperature should be lowered (see illustration 61). Think of vegetation such as grass, perennial plants, flowers, vegetables and moss. Also, the lower plants often found in urban agriculture and gardening can contribute here. With their evapotranspiration, the plants will temper the air temperature.
2. **Effectiveness** Naturally, smaller plants have lower evapotranspiration than large plants, since they have less foliage. But because these plants usually grow in the earth, we can add the evaporation from the soil. Especially moss can evaporate much water when the water supply from the soil is continuous. Such areas can evaporate up to 80% of the rate known for water surfaces. Low vegetation also has a lower albedo than paved areas and thus reflects less short-wave radiation onto a person. Air temperature reductions in the vicinity of up to 1°C have been measured and lower PET values of up to 5°C.
3. **Extra advantages** Low vegetation is important for the biodiversity in a city, and it usually has an aesthetic effect too. Lawns can also be used for many sport, recreational and social activities. Urban agriculture falls into this category as well, and many of these areas have an educational function besides the production of food.

124 *Urban agriculture with different kinds of lower plants on a former parking lot in Overtown, Miami, USA*

4. **Disadvantages** When lawns become parched, they stop cooling and can have the opposite effect on the urban climate. Planting larger trees can partially prevent this problem, since their shadows help put a stop to yellowing.
5. **Construction** Much low vegetation in the city doesn't need to be planted. It grows on its own, for instance in brownfield areas. Planting lawns, gardens and perennial beds is easy, and only very sophisticated planting schemes require the work of professional gardeners.
6. **Maintenance** The maintenance depends on the type of low vegetation and the intensity of use. A brownfield doesn't require any maintenance and an extensive bed only a little, whereas intensive perennials, vegetables and lawns need a lot of attention (mowing, weeding et cetera).
7. **Costs** 0 – €
8. **No regret:** Yes

Waterfalls

1. **General information** On warm days, cool spots with flowing water in parks are very popular places to stay. If brooks run through these parks and the relief allows for it, waterfalls can be constructed. The falling motion spreads the water into fine drops, resulting in high evaporation and a lower local air temperature.
2. **Effectiveness** This evaporation and thus tempering of the air temperature is reasonably effective. A study at a large fountain complex with waterfalls in Japan showed that the air temperature could be lowered by 2°C.
3. **Extra advantages** A waterfall is a special addition to a park and a magnet for playing children.
4. **Disadvantages** None
5. **Construction** Professionals have to plan and construct waterfalls.
6. **Maintenance** None
7. **Costs** € €
8. **No regret:** Yes

125 *Waterfalls of the Ovato fountains in Villa d'Este, Tivoli, Italy*

Graduation Works

1. **General information** Graduation works (or thorn houses) are a special way to evaporate water. These installations were already built centuries ago to evaporate salty water and win the salt. Graduation works consist of a vertical construction with a netting of fine twigs (usually hawthorn). Salty water runs down this construction and the netting refines the water into smaller drops, so it evaporates faster. Spas also use these graduation works to seep mineral water over it, so guests can breathe in the minerals with the water vapour. The graduation works' surroundings are full of small water drops that can evaporate quickly and thus cool the air considerably. When there is sufficient natural relief, graduation works can be used without extra pumps.
2. **Effectiveness** The evaporation and thus tempering of the air temperature is very effective.
3. **Extra advantages** Graduation works are a special addition to a space and are of great experiential value.
4. **Disadvantages** None
5. **Construction** Experienced experts have to plan and construct graduation works.
6. **Maintenance** The netting has to be replaced regularly, which is very specialist work.
7. **Costs** €€
8. **No regret:** Yes

126 *Graduation works in Revierpark Mattlerbusch, Duisburg, Germany*

Swamplands

1. **General information** Water bodies generally are not very effective when it comes to lowering the air temperature, but if they are planted with dense vegetation or have a natural growth of sphagnum mosses, the plants evaporate more water. The plants' shadows also cool the water surface. Together, water and plants can control the air temperature.
2. **Effectiveness** Scientists measured the air temperature around flooded rice fields (also a kind of swampland) in Tokyo. These measurements showed that the decrease in air temperature above the fields and up to 150 metres distance on the leeward side was still 2°C; which is a considerable effect.
3. **Extra advantages** Green ponds can buffer rainwater and improve biodiversity. You can also think of a combination with helophyte-filter functions.
4. **Disadvantages** Prolonged periods of heat can cause problems with blue-green algae if the water is stagnant.
5. **Construction** Laypeople can construct small green ponds. Professionals best construct larger ponds or ponds with technically more complicated overflow systems.
6. **Maintenance** The maintenance is relatively minimal. To prevent silting, you should clear out the vegetation regularly.
7. **Costs** € – € €
8. **No regret:** Yes

127 *A pond with intensive vegetation*

Fountains

1. **General information** On paved squares without natural evaporation through the soil, evaporation of water can be increased on warm days to control the air temperature. The most obvious and traditional solution is a fountain. Fountains come in all shapes and sizes, but for effective cooling of the surroundings, a fountain ideally spreads the most possible water in the smallest possible drops over a large space. The *giochi d'aqua* (water games) in historical gardens are an early example of cooling through evaporation on a small scale.
2. **Effectiveness** A study of a larger fountain in Japan (with about 2 metres high pillars from which water flows and is finely sprayed out) showed a decrease in temperature on the leeside of the fountain of around 3°C. The cooling effect of the fountain could be felt up to 35 metres from the fountain.
3. **Extra advantages** Fountains also have an important aesthetic value and invite people to dip hands or feet into them; children love playing with water.
4. **Disadvantages** The water installations require very careful maintenance; otherwise, there can be problems with pathogens such as legionella.
5. **Construction** The planning and construction of a fountain with spray pumps for fine water drops is specialists' work.
6. **Maintenance** Fountains need to be checked-up, cleaned and maintained regularly.
7. **Costs** € €
8. **No regret:** Yes

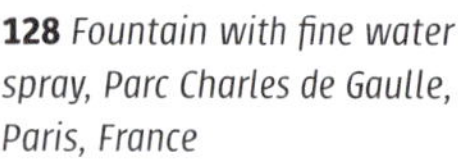

128 *Fountain with fine water spray, Parc Charles de Gaulle, Paris, France*

Misting systems

1. **General information** New techniques allow for very fine mist sprays. These mists contain such fine water particles that these are evaporated even before they precipitate as water drops on surfaces or people in the surroundings of the installations. There are several types of water mist installations. They can be mounted overhead, above seated people (e.g. under the umbrellas of café terraces). They can also be integrated in half-open spaces, for instance in so-called 'cooling towers'; where the mist is sprayed into cylinder-shaped coverings at the top, evaporates along the way down, and arrives at ground level as cool air.
2. **Effectiveness** Water mist installations are exceptionally effective when it comes to cooling the air. Measurements done at a cooling tower when it was 41°C outside, showed an air temperature of 24°C at the bottom of the tower – a huge difference in temperature! The evaporation is not the only reason for this difference, though; the tower's shadow also plays a part. Freestanding water mist installations without shading are less effective, but they are still a very good at cooling the air and showed air temperature reductions of up to 7°C.
3. **Extra advantages** With distinctive designs, these installations can be a beautiful addition to public spaces.
4. **Disadvantages** The water mist installations require very careful maintenance; otherwise, there can be problems with pathogens such as legionella.
5. **Construction** Specialists should oversee the planning and construction of water mist installations.
6. **Maintenance** Water mist installations need to be checked-up, cleaned and maintained very regularly.
7. **Costs** €€
8. **No regret:** Yes

129 *A mist shower in East River Park New York, USA*

'Greening Masts'

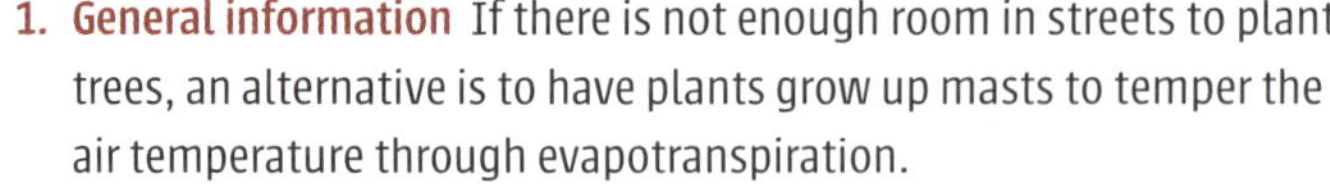

1. **General information** If there is not enough room in streets to plant trees, an alternative is to have plants grow up masts to temper the air temperature through evapotranspiration.

2. **Effectiveness** The effect is clearly much less than that of a fully-grown tree, but it can contribute a bit.
3. **Extra advantages** Birds and insects can find a home in the green masts. These masts can be a special addition to the street profile.

4. **Disadvantages** For maintenance of the masts themselves, the climbing plants have to be largely removed.
5. **Construction** Very simple: all you usually have to do is remove the hard surface around the masts and plant robust climbers.
6. **Maintenance** The maintenance is minimal, the plants might have to be pruned once in a while, especially with lampposts.
7. **Costs** €
8. **No regret:** No

130 *Green masts in Kassel, Germany*

Permeable Pavement

1. **General information** Cities have many paved surfaces that retain heat. To temper the air temperature, de-paving and using permeable surfacing instead can help. Hard surfaces should best be kept to a minimum and only be used when there is no alternative. All other places can be covered with gravel or other permeable surfacing. For example, low-traffic streets can get a minimal paving of 'cart tracks' where cars usually drive. The rest can then be covered with permeable surfacing, either with or without vegetation.
2. **Effectiveness** Removing the surfacing in itself already results in better evaporation of the soil's moisture through the capillary system of the soil. Add vegetation, and you get the shading and evapotranspiration of the plants as well, adding to the cooling effect. During the day surface temperature differences of around 6°C have been observed. The air temperature near the surface can be lowered with about 1°C.
3. **Extra advantages** Open soil is better for stormwater buffering as the soil's cavities first fill with water before excessive surface runoff starts. Minimizing hard surfacing can thus make the construction of extra water drainage systems superfluous.
4. **Disadvantages** Gravel pavement can erode with time and can get silted up with fine particles, thus reducing the water permeability.
5. **Construction** De-paving and placing gravel and grass tiles and such have to be carefully planned. In public spaces this should be done by professionals.
6. **Maintenance** To guarantee permeability, gravel has to be maintained or replaced regularly. The plants growing on or in the permeable surface have to be cut and/or weeded.
7. **Costs** € €
8. **No regret:** Yes

131 *Gravel surfacing that allows many activities*

Sprinkling Streets

1. **General information** Sprinkling is a good alternative for cooling paved traffic spaces where none of the aforementioned installations can be placed. Especially in Mediterranean countries, streets and sidewalks are often sprayed with water, and this is an old tradition in Japan as well – the *uchimizu*. During heatwaves this becomes an increasingly meaningful strategy in the temperate climate zones as well. This sprinkling can happen manually using water hoses, with special tank trucks or automatically through small, built-in nozzles in the street's curb that are connected to the water network.
2. **Effectiveness** This method seems most effective in the morning and late afternoon in direct sunlight. A maximum lowering of daytime surface temperature of 13°C has been measured and night-time lowering of 3°C in temperate climates. Air temperatures during the day at 0.5 m above the surface could be lowered by 3°C.
3. **Extra advantages** The sprinkling also suppresses dust particles. Sprinkler systems can be combined with saltwater-sprinklers against snow and ice.
4. **Disadvantages** The sprinkler systems are sensitive.
5. **Construction** Planning and constructing sprinkler systems is very specialized work.
6. **Maintenance** The sprinkler systems need regular check-ups and cleaning to prevent blockage.
7. **Costs** € for manual sprinkling to € € € for nozzle systems.
8. **No regret:** Yes

132 *Street sprinklers in Lyon, France*

Slowing or Preventing Wind

Orientation of Large Freestanding Buildings

1. **General information** For large, freestanding buildings, it is better to avoid orientations at right angles or at an angle of more than 45 degrees to the wind. An orientation parallel to the wind is preferable.
2. **Effectiveness** For the outdoor areas in front of and along the sides of the building, the effect is very clear, because corner streams and downwash effects are minimized. Also see chapter 2.2.3.
3. **Construction** You have to plan the construction of a building with a different wind orientation well, and you have to adjust the layout of the building to it, for example to guarantee optimal sunlight schemes for the rooms.
4. **Maintenance** Depends on the building.
5. **Costs** Depend on the building.

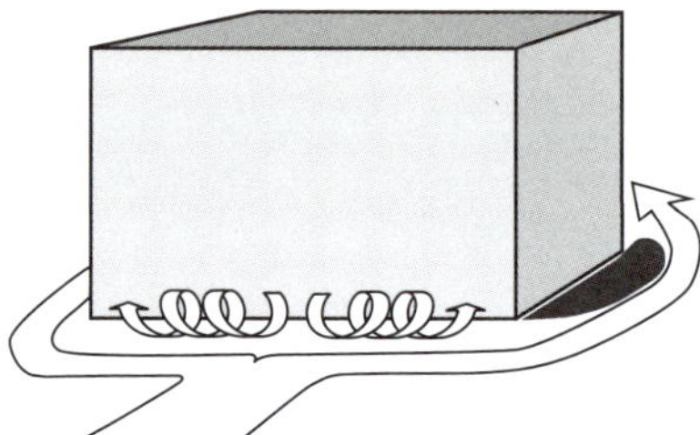

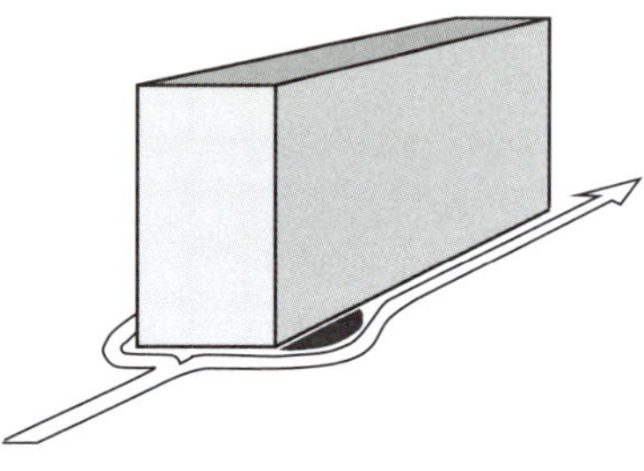

133 *Avoid orientation of large buildings at right angles to the wind and prefer orientations parallel to the wind*

Wind Protection around Tall Buildings

1. **General information** Pedestrians, cyclists and other users of areas around tall buildings (of over 20 metres) have to be protected against downwash. Wind protection should preferably be placed in or on the building itself. This can be achieved with gradually smaller building volumes, but also with elements such as awnings. These elements deflect downwash winds before they reach the pedestrian level. Alternatively, dense 'tree packages' can be planted.
2. **Effectiveness** Stepped buildings and large awnings offer good wind protection at the front and the sides of the building. Trees have a decidedly smaller wind protection effect.
3. **Construction** The construction of a stepped building or a building with awnings requires proper planning and the building's floor plan has to be adjusted to it. The 'steps' of podium-shaped buildings can be used as an extra indoor space. The precise location of tree planting has to be carefully planned, but planting them is relatively simple, providing the soil circumstances are good and there is sufficient rooting space.
4. **Maintenance** This depends on the type of wind protection and the size of the building.
5. **Costs** This depends on the type of wind protection and the size of the building.

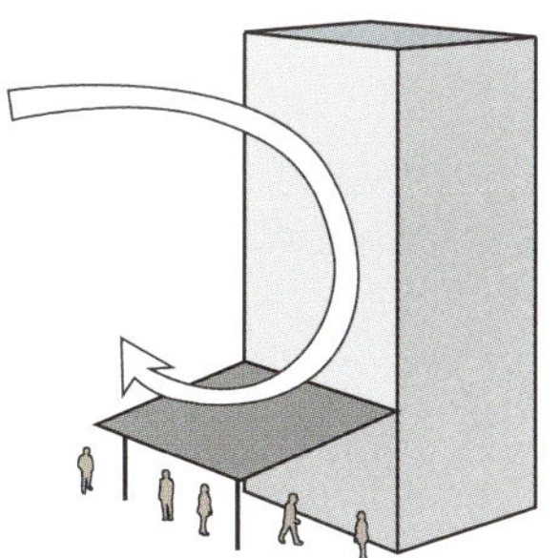

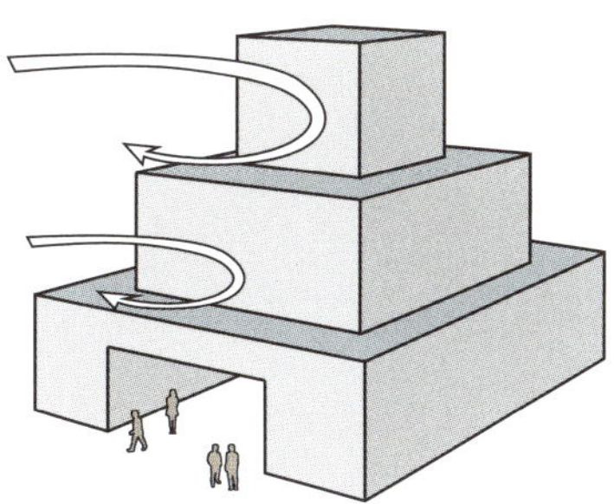

134 *Tall buildings with awnings, a stepped shape or 'tree packages' to deflect downwash*

Avoiding Outdoor Functions in Narrowed Spaces

1. **General information** When large buildings (over 20 metres tall and over 30 metres wide) are designed with underpasses or passages, or if they stand close together, these narrowed spaces suffer from draught, which makes them unsuitable as locations to stay outdoors. With very large building volumes this can even lead to wind danger, depending on the prevailing wind direction. Pedestrian and bicycle routes then have to be relocated to places without wind danger.
2. **Effectiveness** Not applicable.
3. **Construction** Not applicable.
4. **Maintenance** Not applicable.
5. **Costs** Not applicable.

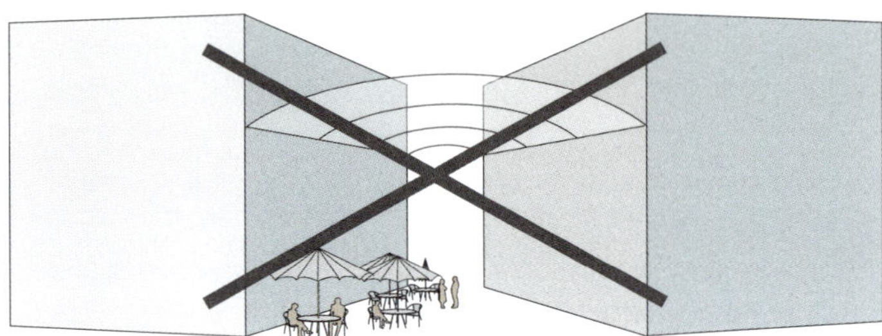

135 *Avoid outdoor functions in narrowed spaces*

Windbreaks

1. **General information** To protect gardens against wind nuisance or to protect houses from too much wind, built windbreaks, planted shelterbelts or hedgerows (or combinations of those) can deflect the wind around the buildings or the areas that are to be protected.
2. **Effectiveness** The effectiveness of windbreaks depends on their porosity. When the windbreak is impermeable, there will be a small, but very sheltered area on the leeside of it. When it is more porous, the wind protection on the leeside wake area is not as strong as it would be behind a closed obstacle, but the sheltered area behind the windbreak is much larger. The angle of the windbreak in relation to the incoming wind also influences how effective it is in creating a wake area (see illustration 137).

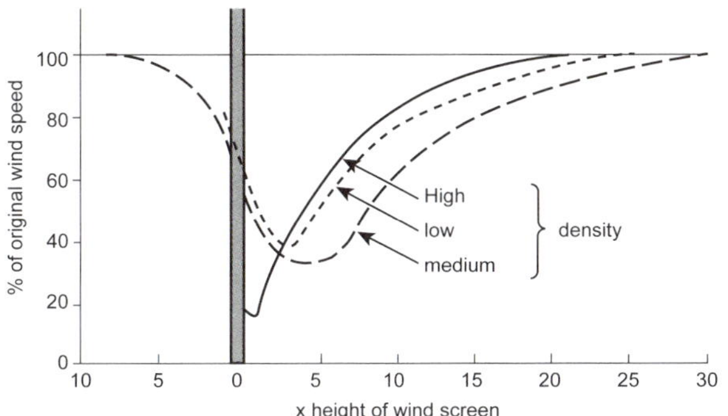

136 *Densities of windbreaks and the sheltered effect behind them*

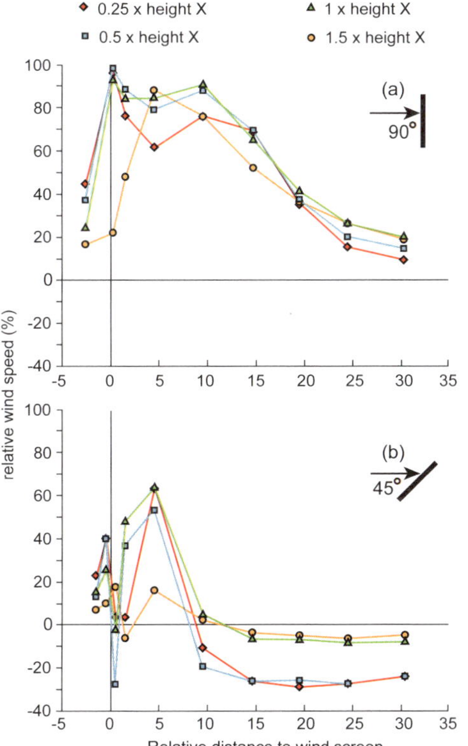

137 *Densities of shelterbelts with densities 75% and 43% and different incidence angles of wind with wind speed reduction effects behind them*

The optimal wind protection is obtained when the windbreak is at right angles to the wind direction. As soon as the orientation changes, its protection directly behind the object is reduced. With fences, the shape and direction of the boarding also plays a role (see illustration 138). The illustrations show the effect of different windbreak porosities on the wind behind it.

If you place several windbreaks at right angles to the wind direction at the end of the protected zone of the windbreak in front, an extra wind speed reduction of around 10% can be achieved.

3. **Construction** The planning of windbreaks has to be well thought out. Wind-protecting panels or fences usually must be made and placed by professionals. The planning of shelter plantings has to be well thought-out, but the planting is relatively easy.
4. **Maintenance** The maintenance depends on the type of windbreak. Wooden windbreaks have to be painted once in a while. Windbreaks made from other materials such as metal, glass or plastic require less upkeep. Shelterbelt trees do not require much maintenance. Hedges have to be pruned regularly.
5. **Costs** Depending on the type of materials or plants used, the costs vary between € and € €.

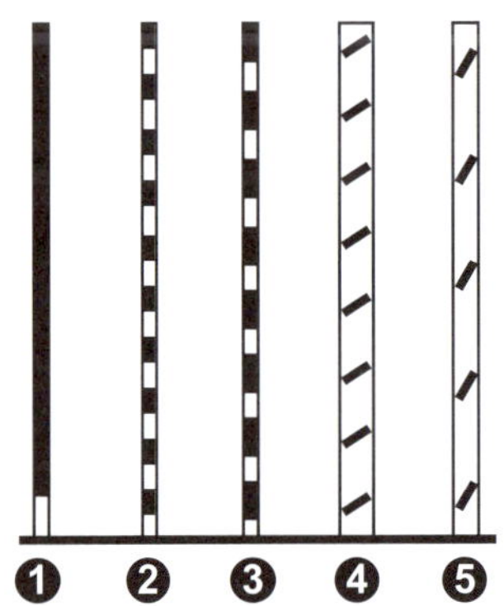

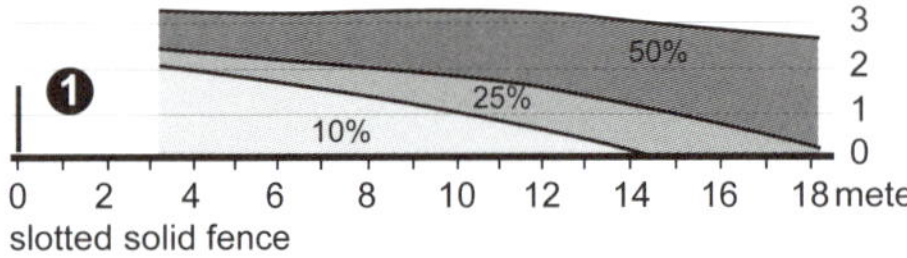

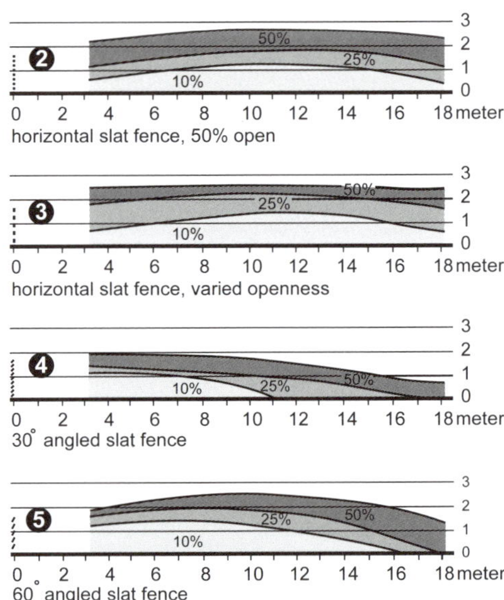

138 *Windbreaks with different boarding and their effect on the wind patterns behind them*

Changing Street Orientation

1. **General information** When streets are parallel to the direction of the most frequent and strong winds, the wind can easily be 'channelled', and you can expect problems with wind nuisance. On many days of the year, there will be too much wind for people to sit outside comfortably, and stronger winds can also be dangerous to pedestrians and cyclists. This will certainly be an issue if taller buildings flank the streets. These problems can only be solved with changes in the street orientation, especially if you want to invite people to walk or cycle through these streets.
2. **Effectiveness** For optimal countering of the wind channelling, the street's orientation should change after ten to twenty times the average building height.
3. **Construction** Changing the orientation of streets should be planned carefully, because later interventions in the urban tissue will be less effective. So, these measures are possible for new streets and mainly for streets with little traffic. These measures are less recommendable for streets with heavy and high-speed traffic, since abrupt changes of street directions hinder traffic flows.
4. **Maintenance** Not applicable.
5. **Costs** Not applicable.

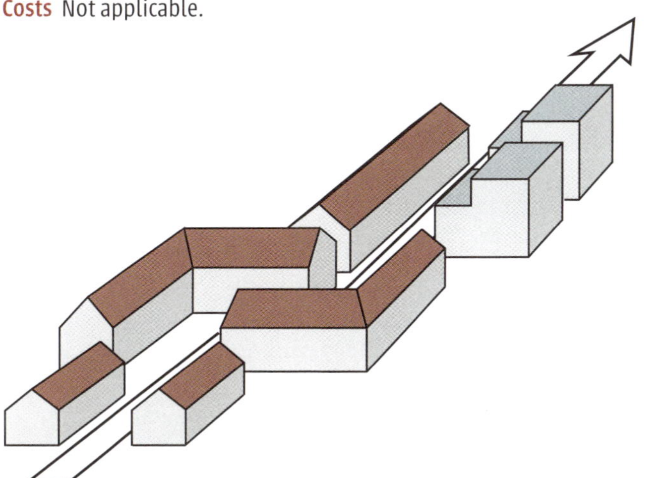

139 *Streets with alternating orientations have less wind nuisance*

Trees against Channelling in Street Canyons

1. **General information** In existing streets, wind nuisance caused by the channelling effect often needs to be overcome. But you can't simply change all the adjacent buildings. In such cases, planting street trees can help, because tree crowns softly swirl the wind and thus weaken it.
2. **Effectiveness** This measure is not as effective as the construction of streets with changing orientations is, but it is still considerable. It is important not to plant the trees too close together, because then they can form such a closed volume, that they can cause their own channelling effect. Trees planted too close together can also form a 'green tunnel', inducing accumulation of fine dust particles.
3. **Construction** Professionals should be the ones to plant trees in streets, because they often have to prepare specific planting sites with systems for aeration and irrigation.
4. **Maintenance** Street trees often need more care than trees in parks or outside cities because they are faced with more stress factors (heat, drought, road salt). They also have to be pruned and their leaves have to be cleaned up.
5. **Costs** € – € €

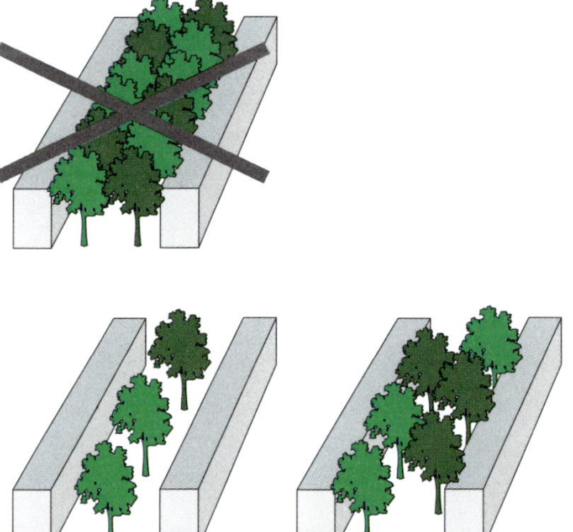

140 *Street trees reducing the channelling effect, but not yet forming a 'green tunnel'*

Building Form against Channelling in Street Canyons

1. **General information** When parts of the street pattern of a city have to be oriented parallel with the main wind direction that causes nuisance we can still prevent too much wind channelling by giving the street profile more 'roughness'. This can be achieved by creating variety in the height of buildings, roof shapes and especially by creating setbacks in the walls of the canyon.
2. **Effectiveness** This measure is not as effective as the construction of streets with changing orientations is, but it is still considerable.
3. **Construction** These measures need to be planned carefully by wind experts, urban planners and designers. They should be formulated early in the building process and can be implemented via zoning plans or similar instruments. The construction itself is part of the individual building architectures.
4. **Maintenance** Not applicable.
5. **Costs** €€–€€€

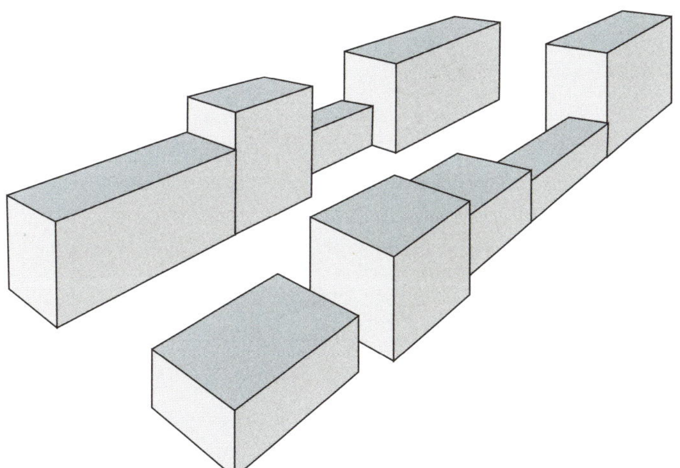

141 *Setbacks and different building types reducing the channelling effect*

'Wind-Optimized' Squares

1. **General information** For a comfortable climate on squares, controlling the wind is of the utmost importance. The proportions of the open space and the orientation to the prevailing wind have to be adapted to each other in the designs of squares. Especially in windy regions, squares should not be too wide. A rule of thumb for good square proportions regarding wind is based on the relation between square surface and the surrounding building heights. This rule has a simple formula: square surface / average height of surrounding buildings x 2 = < 6. The designers can play with the building heights and/or the size of the square surface to arrive at the right proportions.

   When a square has openings at its edges (e.g. street entrances) taking up over 25% of the square perimeter, this usually results in too high wind speeds across the square. It is therefore better not to have the openings exceed this percentage. It is also better to avoid situating large openings in the prevailing wind direction. When squares have an oblong shape parallel to the prevailing wind direction, a channelling effect will occur. Ideally, oblong squares for outdoor functions have an orientation perpendicular to the prevailing wind. If this is not an option, setting back some of the surrounding buildings can improve the situation. On oblong squares parallel to the wind direction that also taper to a narrower space, the air is compressed even more. Wind-sensitive functions should be avoided on such places in the squares.
2. **Effectiveness** We can expect improved wind climates when squares are designed with these guidelines in mind and halving wind speed reductions can easily be achieved.
3. **Construction** The opportunity to design a square from scratch does not often present itself, because the largest part of the urban tissue is already there. The shapes of the surrounding buildings of existing squares generally cannot be altered. You then have to go for smaller or less 'radical' solutions (see following solutions).
4. **Maintenance** Not applicable.
5. **Costs** Not applicable.

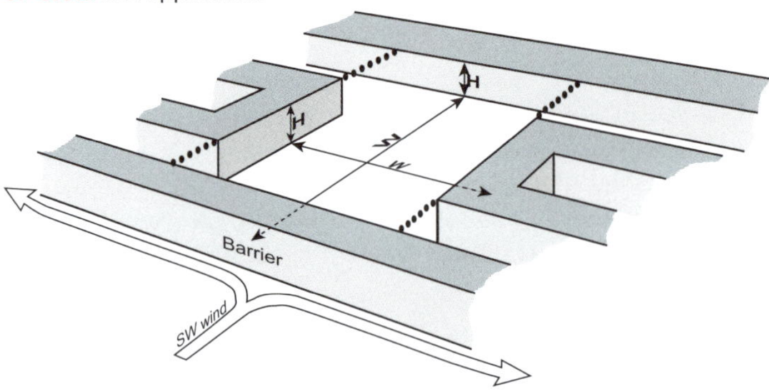

142 *Diagram of all 'ideal characteristics' of a wind-friendly square*

'Ring of Trees'

1. **General information** On squares that are too wide, a ring of trees along the edges of the square can make the open space smaller. This decreases the area for the wind to pick up speed.
2. **Effectiveness** A ring of trees is obviously less effective than improved square proportions, but trees also have many other advantages for the urban climate and biodiversity and have experiential value.
3. **Construction** Planting trees in squares should be done by professionals, because they often have to prepare specific planting sites with systems for aeration and irrigation.
4. **Maintenance** Trees on squares often need more care than trees in parks or outside cities because they are faced with more stress factors (heat, drought, road salt). They also have to be pruned and their leaves have to be cleaned up.
5. **Costs** € €

143 *Ring of trees around het Plein, The Hague, the Netherlands*

Urban Shelterbelt

1. **General information** When specific larger parts of a square have to be protected, you can think of a special kind of windbreak: a treeline with semi-permeable windscreens placed in the trunk space, a combination I call an 'urban shelterbelt'. Ideally, the windscreens are mobile, so room can be made for pedestrians, cyclists, and loading and unloading goods for markets and such.
2. **Effectiveness** The area behind an urban shelterbelt that is well protected from the wind is usually twice as long as the height of the trees. For medium-sized trees about 20 metres tall, for example, there is around 40 metres of space behind the urban shelterbelt where wind speeds are halved.
3. **Construction** Professionals have to design and place the windscreens and plant the trees on squares. For the trees, they often have to prepare specific planting sites with systems for aeration and irrigation.
4. **Maintenance** Trees on squares often need more care than trees in parks or outside of cities because they are faced with more stress factors (heat, drought, road salt). They also have to be pruned and their leaves have to be cleaned up. The windscreens need to be checked, cleaned and maintained regularly, especially if they have moving parts.
5. **Costs** €€€

144 *Diagram of an urban shelterbelt*

Windscreens on Windy Places

1. **General information** There are many places that need small-scale local wind protection because people want to stay there for a while, for instance on sidewalk cafés. These windy places can be located at the spots where streets come onto squares, on waterfronts or in open squares. These places then have to be provided with small and possibly flexible solutions for wind protection. In all cases you have to find out how the wind flows and preferably place windscreens at right angles to the wind. In many European countries, large beer breweries offer free windscreens to bar owners. Place-specific and specially designed windscreens, however, are rare. A real opportunity for designers!
2. **Effectiveness** The effectiveness of the windscreens depends on their porosity and size (see 'Windbreaks', page 179).
3. **Construction** Flexible windscreens are easy to put up. Fixed windscreens on the other hand, have to be installed by professionals.
4. **Maintenance** Occasional cleaning or painting the windscreens and oiling the moving parts are usually all the maintenance windscreens require.
5. **Costs** €

145 *Windscreen on a street corner in Salzburg, Austria*

Wind Protective Street Furniture

1. **General information** When there is no room on squares for large-scale wind protection, small wind protected places on the street level itself can be provided as an alternative. Think of furniture with integrated windscreens, as we sometimes see on coastal boulevards, or of benches combined with a hedge. We can also imagine special solutions that can address the problem when the wind comes from different directions: swivelling sheltered seats. For example: a high-backed bench, which functions as a windscreen, with a sail to turn it, so that the bench is always sheltered from the wind.
2. **Effectiveness** For people sitting on the bench, this is very effective, but beyond the seat itself, this type of street furniture has no effect.
3. **Construction** Professionals have to design and place this specially designed street furniture, especially if it is movable.
4. **Maintenance** The maintenance of these elements depends on the materials. Solutions with moving parts require much maintenance.
5. **Costs** €€

146 *Example of a 'sail-bench' that turns, so people sitting on it are always sheltered from the wind*

Ventilation

Ventilation around Houses

1. **General information** In gardens and on premises around houses, it seems like a good idea to plant as few trees as possible and place as few wind-deflecting objects as possible for ventilation, but this obviously makes no sense as we also need shade and cooling by trees in summer. So, we have to find compromises. High, closed elements around plots could, for example, only be placed where they are needed for wind protection and privacy. In other places, the plot-demarcating elements can be partially open or be made of a wide-meshed fence.
2. **Effectiveness** Ventilation options in the garden help improve the ventilation of the garden itself and indirectly of the house. Naturally, optimal placing of the windows and ventilation openings in the architecture itself guarantee good ventilation inside the house.
3. **Construction** The construction depends on the type of plot-demarcation element and the type of vegetation.
4. **Maintenance** The maintenance depends on the type of plot-demarcation element and the type of vegetation.
5. **Costs** €

147 *Diagram of a half-open plot demarcation at a house*

Channelling Cool Airflows

1. **General information** When cooling airflows have to be directed to a certain place, spatial objects such as buildings, walls, trees or hedges can be used. These must then be configured in such a way that they guide the wind to that place without staggering, because otherwise they guide the wind in undesired directions.
2. **Effectiveness** Channelling can help use the cool airflows more efficiently, but because the airflows are relatively weak, this effect is limited.
3. **Construction** The construction depends on the type of elements used to guide the wind, and these can be very different.
4. **Maintenance** The maintenance depends on the types of elements used.
5. **Costs** Depending on the type of volumes: € – € €

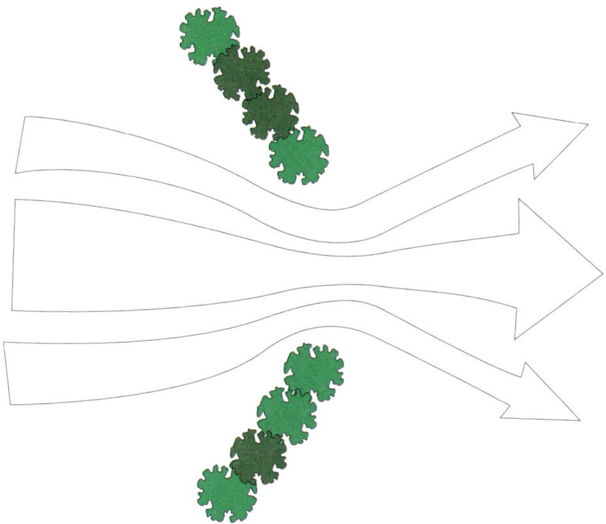

148 *Airflow-guidance by plant volumes*

Designing Protection against Precipitation

Glass Canopies

1. **General information** The designs of canopies have to ensure sufficient protection against rain. If a canopy is placed too high up, the wind often blows in the rain under it. Rain is generally paired with wind from a typical direction, which you can find out from the data of weather institutes. Canopies that are open in this direction therefore have to be sufficiently wide and not too high, so as to make sure that the rain won't fall on the people underneath.
2. **Effectiveness** With the right orientation, width and height, coverings can be very effective.
3. **Extra advantages** Many canopies can also offer shading, if so desired.
4. **Disadvantages** Glass canopies are sensitive to vandalism.
5. **Construction** The size of the construction, safety requirements and sometimes the technical finesse of the canopies require expert construction.
6. **Maintenance** For the most part, the maintenance consists of painting the supportive constructions and cleaning the glass.
7. **Costs** € – € €
8. **No regret:** Yes

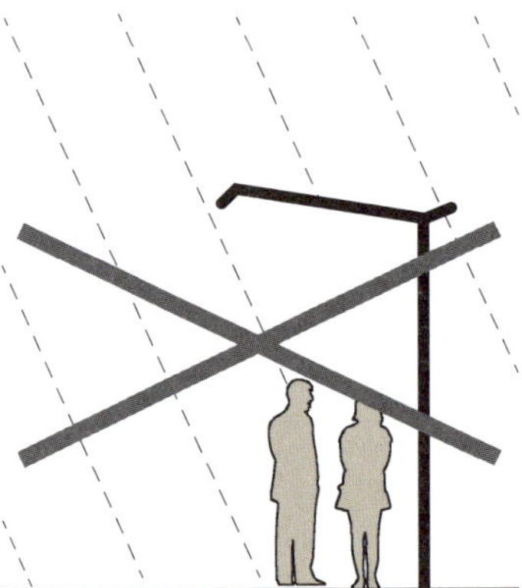

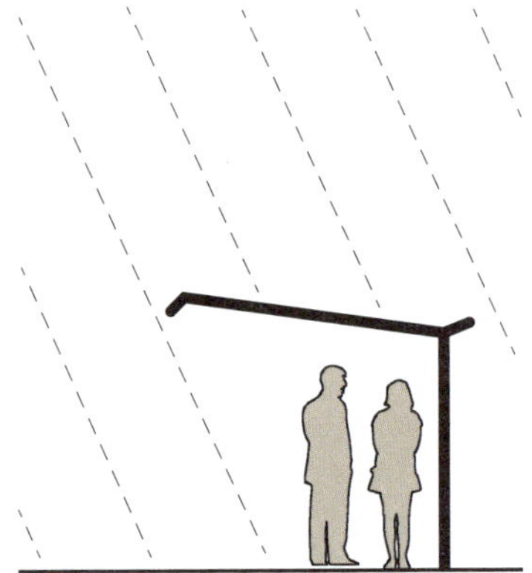

149 *Example of a bad and a good rain canopy*

Dome-Shaped Deciduous Trees

1. **General information** Many deciduous trees are also suitable for rain protection, if they have a dense and screen- or dome-shaped crown. In the dark months, the crowns allow for much light, since they have shed their leaves then.
2. **Effectiveness** In the seasons when the trees do have foliage, the leaves can offer good protection against the rain.
3. **Extra advantages** Deciduous trees have numerous other advantages for the urban climate, and also for biodiversity. They furthermore have aesthetic value.
4. **Disadvantages** You also need precipitation protection in winter, and trees are much less effective then, since they have shed their foliage.
5. **Construction** It is easy to plant trees in parks. In the paved areas of the city, planting trees requires extra facilities, such as plant holes and possible aeration and irrigation options. Generally speaking, this is work for professional gardeners.
6. **Maintenance** Trees in parks require relatively little care, but trees in paved areas often need more care because they are faced with more stress factors (heat, drought, road salt). The trees sometimes have to be irrigated in hot situations. All trees have to be pruned and their leaves have to be cleaned up.
7. **Costs** €
8. **No regret:** Yes

150 *Dome-shaped tree*

Designing for Multiple Microclimate Factors

Waterfall Pergola

1. **General information** When shadow alone does not offer sufficient cooling in hot situations, a shadow element can also be combined with a water element, which provides extra evaporation. This can be a pergola-type, green construction with water splashing down from it.
2. **Effectiveness** The combination of shadow, evaporation from the plants *and* finely sprayed water results in very effective tempering of the air temperature.
3. **Extra advantages** The advantages are a combination of those of a pergola and a fountain. When the construction of the pergola is not too heavy and it is planted with deciduous plants, it allows the sunlight to come through it in winter.
4. **Disadvantages** The water installation can become dirty and there can be problems with pathogens, such as legionella.
5. **Construction** Specialists have to do the planning, calculating and construction of these installations.
6. **Maintenance** The maintenance is intensive. The pergola has to be given a paintjob regularly and some plants have to be pruned. The waterfall-part needs to be checked and cleaned on a regular basis.
7. **Costs** € €
8. **No regret:** Yes

151 *Pergola with waterfall*

Photochromic Glass Roof

1. **General information** Sometimes places have to be protected from the rain, but also require sufficient light. On sunny days, on the other hand, the same places have to be protected from the sun. For such places, you could think of a glass roof with the same type of photochromic glass used in sunglasses. When the sun is out, the roof becomes dark so that it shades, and when it is cloudy, the roof offers rain protection.
2. **Effectiveness** This installation will be very effective.
3. **Extra advantages** Besides the combination of microclimatic advantages, this installation will let people see changes in the intensity of solar radiation in an interesting way.
4. **Disadvantages** The construction may be sensitive to vandalism.
5. **Construction** Specialists have to develop this element, and professionals have to install it.
6. **Maintenance** The glass parts have to be cleaned regularly.
7. **Costs** €€€
8. **No regret:** Yes

152 *A photochromic glass roof when it rains and when it's sunny*

‘Parasol/Umbrella’

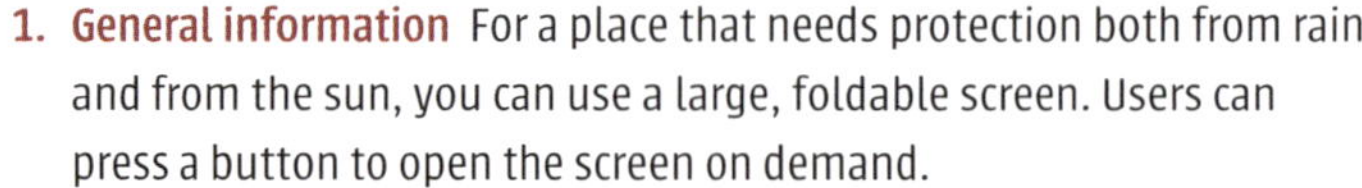

1. **General information** For a place that needs protection both from rain and from the sun, you can use a large, foldable screen. Users can press a button to open the screen on demand.

2. **Effectiveness** This is an optimal solution for sun and rain protection.
3. **Extra advantages** This installation is a playful element that people in the city can use precisely at those moments when they need it.
4. **Disadvantages** The installation, and especially the textile elements, can be sensitive to vandalism.
5. **Construction** This element should be developed and installed by professionals.
6. **Maintenance** These elements will be high-maintenance as you have to guarantee the functioning of the moving parts.
7. **Costs** € €
8. **No regret:** Yes

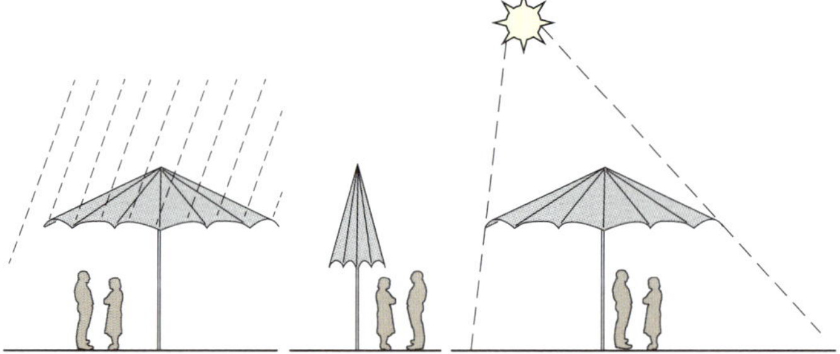

153 *Diagram of the way the ‘parasol/umbrella’ works*

'Wind plus Shadow' Element

1. **General information** For locations in need of wind *and* sun protection, you can combine these functions in one piece of outdoor furniture. For example: a higher element like a plant container or earthen wall can provide seating sheltered from the wind, and the plants in the container can provide shadow.
2. **Effectiveness** Directly behind the element, the wind speed is very effectively reduced. Depending on the density of the plants and the permeability of the foliage, a shadow depth of 50% and over can be achieved.
3. **Extra advantages** Besides having advantages for the microclimate, this option could offer possibilities for more biodiversity.
4. **Disadvantages** None
5. **Construction** In principle, you do not have to be a professional to place these elements. When these are placed in a public space, however, you may have to meet extra safety requirements, and professionals then have to install them.
6. **Maintenance** Depending on the material, the bench has to be maintained. The plants have to be weeded occasionally.
7. **Costs** €
8. **No regret:** Yes

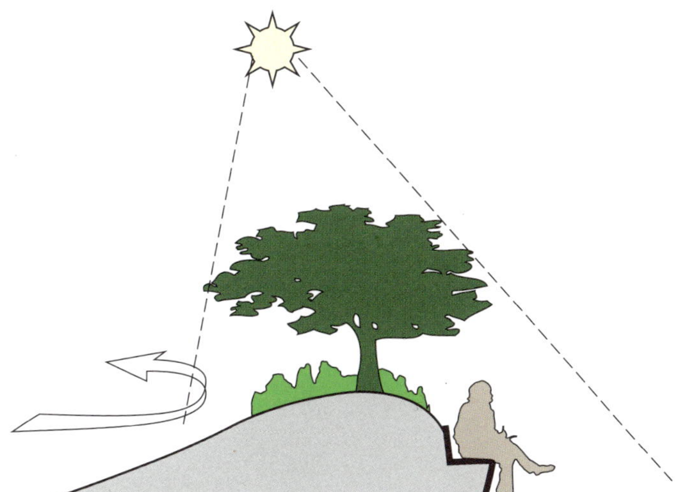

154 *'Mini-dune': a place with wind and sun protection*

'Windscreen-Tree-Bench'

1. **General information** Sometimes, you want to create a shaded spot under a tree, but because the tree is freestanding, it can be a little draughty and the wind can come from different directions. For this situation, you can think of a tree-bench with flexible windscreens. The windscreens are placed at right angles to the bench, so the person sitting on the bench is protected from wind coming in from the sides.
2. **Effectiveness** Directly behind the windscreens, the wind is blocked very effectively. Depending on the permeability of the foliage, a shadow depth of 50% can be achieved.
3. **Extra advantages** All other advantages of a tree (cooler air temperature, biodiversity and aesthetical value) hold here as well.
4. **Disadvantages** None
5. **Construction** Since the moving parts of the windscreen form a complicated construction, professionals should plan and install them. If the trees are planted on squares, specific planting sites with systems for aeration and irrigation may have to be prepared.
6. **Maintenance** Trees on squares often need more care than trees in a park because they are faced with more stress factors (heat, drought, road salt). In hot situations, the trees may require irrigation. They also have to be pruned and their leaves have to be cleaned up. The windscreens with their moving parts have to be checked, cleaned and maintained regularly.
7. **Costs** €€
8. **No regret:** Yes

155 *A 'windscreen-tree-bench'*

'Wind-or-Shadow' Screens

1. **General information** The weather circumstances in many countries with a temperate climate feature two typical situations in which protection is needed: when it is cloudy and there is a strong wind, people have to be protected from it. On hot, sunny days, on the other hand, when normally there is not much wind, people need to be shaded. Moveable screens offering protection against the wind or the sun are a simple solution. We can think of systems on various scales, from a seat for one person to protective constructions for several people.
2. **Effectiveness** Because they block wind and sun on a small scale, these elements are very effective.
3. **Extra advantages** With the options for several people, you can get continuously changing screen patterns, playfully revealing the personal comfort needs of the users.
4. **Disadvantages** If the screens are made of textile, the objects are sensitive to vandalism.
5. **Construction** These constructions have to be well planned in advance, and professionals have to build them.
6. **Maintenance** Because of their relatively complicated construction and moving parts, these objects require very regular maintenance.
7. **Costs** € – € €
8. **No regret:** Yes

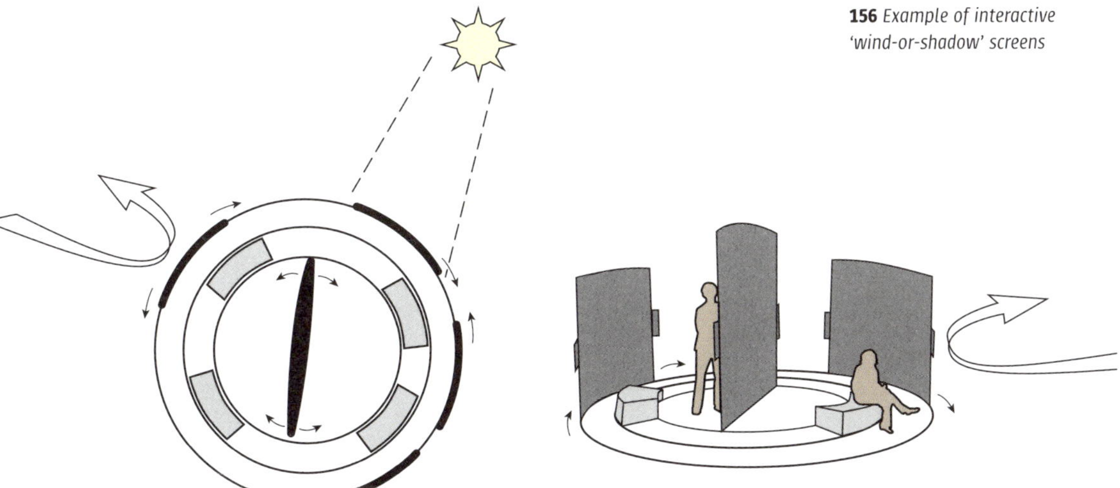

156 *Example of interactive 'wind-or-shadow' screens*

Groundwater-Driven Wind Protection

1. **General information** In areas with relatively high groundwater levels, such as river areas, you can think of a very different solution. In the cooler seasons (spring, autumn and winter), the groundwater level is often high in these areas. The wind is also stronger in these seasons. In the summer, on the other hand, the wind is weaker and the groundwater level is lower. It is possible to design a system of elements moving up and down, driven by the groundwater level and thus offering wind protection. Such a system can consist of, for instance, lightweight pillars, raised and lowered by the changing groundwater level.
2. **Effectiveness** When long rows of these pillars form a type of wall, these can offer effective wind protection.
3. **Extra advantages** Besides the windscreen function, these pillars playfully indicate the groundwater levels.
4. **Disadvantages** None
5. **Construction** This system requires specialist knowledge of hydrology and engineering, so experts have to do the work.
6. **Maintenance** This installation has to be checked regularly and the maintenance is high, because of the sliding parts and the impact of the groundwater on the construction.
7. **Costs** €€
8. **No regret:** Yes

157 *Principle of groundwater-driven windscreen pillarsdscreen*

Summer
groundwater levels 100 to 300 cm

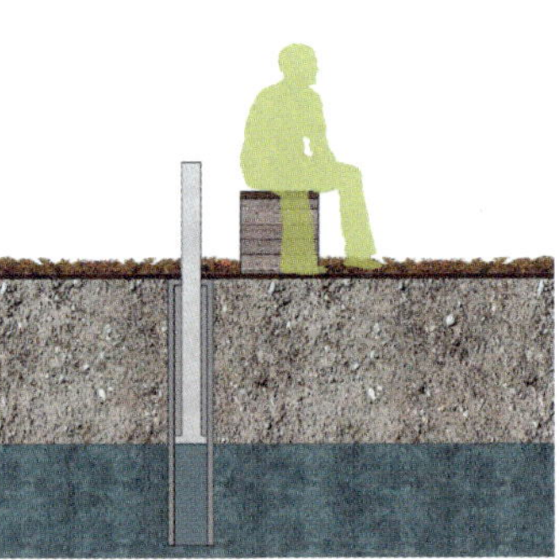

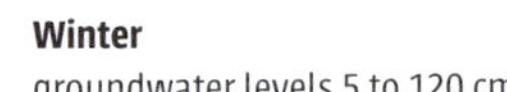

Wind Energy Bench

1. **General information** On many cool days, the wind comes from a typical direction, which can be different for different countries. This wind is uncomfortable and has to be blocked. Sitting on a bench can be much more comfortable on many days if the bench has windscreens on its sides. On cold days, however, this is not sufficient, and you have to add an extra source of warmth. Such a heat generator can be a small wind turbine at the bottom of the bench. This turbine generates electricity converted into heat to warm up the bench.
2. **Effectiveness** The combination of the heated bench and the wind protection makes this a very effective solution.
3. **Extra advantages** The small wind turbine can visualize the wind speed at street level in an interesting manner. For children, it can be an educational object that teaches them about wind in the urban environment.
4. **Disadvantages** The bench has to be placed in well-ventilated places; otherwise it won't work.
5. **Construction** The planning and construction are work for specialists, as is the installation.
6. **Maintenance** The bench itself requires normal upkeep (e.g. painting). Specialists have to maintain the wind turbine frequently.
7. **Costs** € €
8. **No regret:** Yes

158 *An example of the 'wind energy bench'*

Warm Windscreen Bench

1. **General information** Combining wind protection and warming a sitting person through longwave emission can generate an especially warm place. Think of a bench with a very large, stone back, placed at right angles to the prevailing wind, and thus offering good wind protection in many situations. The stone back receives and stores much shortwave radiation and emits it as warmth later in the afternoon and evening.
2. **Effectiveness** The back offers very good wind protection. If the sun does not shine, the bench absorbs less radiation and also emits less longwave radiation. So the effectiveness of the longwave radiation depends on the incoming radiation that was absorbed earlier.
3. **Extra advantages** Besides improving the microclimate, the large back can also be specially designed as public art and have aesthetic value.
4. **Disadvantages** The bench is less effective when the wind comes from a different direction and on cloudy days.
5. **Construction** The construction is not too complicated. Professionals can do it, but experienced laypeople can do it as well.
6. **Maintenance** The maintenance is minimal.
7. **Costs** €
8. **No regret:** No

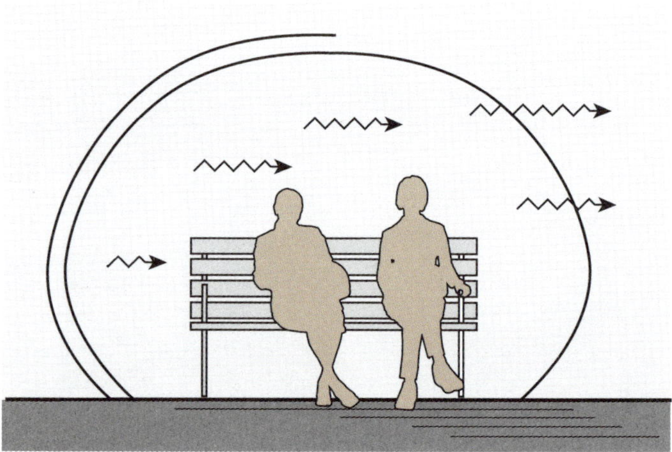

159 *Diagram of a warm windscreen bench*

Wind Energy/Cooling tower

1. **General information** In Middle Eastern countries wind towers that tower high above the urban fabric and have a very large opening to the main wind direction have been used for centuries. These towers guide wind that blows above the roofs down into houses where it exits via another opening, thus cooling the interior. This principle can also be used in outdoor spaces. The 'extended' version of this wind tower system has a revolving opening that turns towards the different wind directions in summer and in cool seasons. In summer it guides the wind down into the urban fabric for ventilation. The cooling effect can even be enhanced by adding water-evaporating elements at the bottom, creating extra cool air leaving the tower. In the colder and windier seasons, the evaporating elements are replaced with a wind turbine and via this turbine the wind's energy is transformed into renewable electrical energy.
2. **Effectiveness** Only a low amount of wind is needed at the inlet to reach a comfortable breeze on the street level during summer. A wind speed of 1.7 m/s at the inlet can generate up to 8 m/s at the outlet. A tower of about 20 m height might be able to produce about 100.000 kWh/year.
3. **Extra advantages** Besides cooling and generating energy, these towers can house other functions such as residences, offices, or car parking. Apart from that, they form true landmarks in the urban fabric.
4. **Disadvantages** None.
5. **Construction** The construction is complicated and has to be done by experts.
6. **Maintenance** The maintenance is minimal.
7. **Costs** €€€
8. **No regret:** Yes

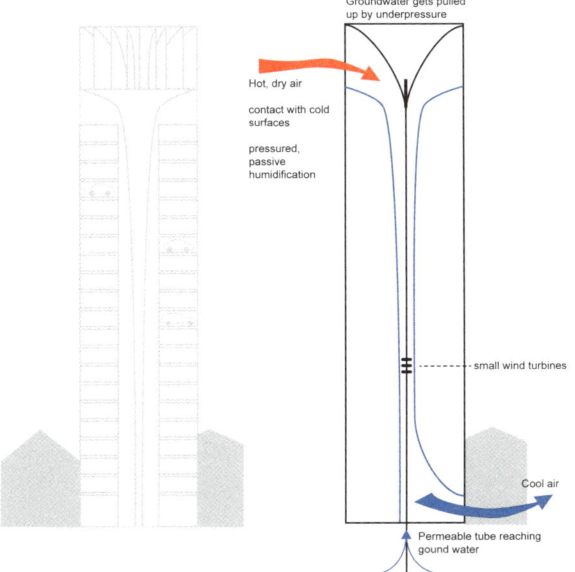

160 *Example of a wind energy/ cooling tower*

Photovoltaic Shading Roof

1. **General information** To create shaded spots, we can use photovoltaic shading panels instead of a 'normal' roof. The photovoltaic panels create renewable solar energy and also absorb energy from the urban system.
2. **Effectiveness** Standard photovoltaic panels have an input rate of around 1000 W/m^2, with an efficiency of around 15-20%. A photovoltaic panel of 1 m^2 would produce around 150-200W under good sunlight conditions (which are at about 1000 W/m^2).
3. **Extra advantages** Besides casting shade and generating energy, these 'roofs' look interesting and can also create special spaces for people to gather underneath.
4. **Disadvantages** None.
5. **Construction** The construction is not that difficult but should be done by professionals.
6. **Maintenance** The maintenance entails regular cleaning of the photovoltaic surface.
7. **Costs** € €
8. **No regret:** Yes

161 *Example of a photovoltaic shading roof*

Designing for Psychological Aspects of Microclimate Experience

Influencing 'Ambiance' through Spatial Configuration

The fact that people perceive wide, open spaces as uncomfortable (and thus try to avoid these), plus the fact that the microclimate often is indeed problematic, means that interventions are in order. When urban outdoor spaces have to be made more suitable for people to spend time there, you have to adjust the spatial proportions and openness. This can be done by placing buildings in different configurations, but also by adding larger vegetation elements such as trees (also see section 6.2). The openness of large spaces can be broken with many of the different elements discussed before to manipulate shadow and wind. This is not to say that a space should be filled with these elements. A few 'comfort islands' often do the trick. These can add to the required diversification of the microclimate. People often do have a clear preference for green elements. When you make spaces smaller or place elements that change the microclimate, your design obviously has to factor in other functions. On market squares, for example, there has to be sufficient room for the stalls and logistics. Terrains for events require open spaces for attractions and tents and such; and parks have to provide room for people to play and exercise.

162 *'Comfort island' with a large solitary tree on a square in Munich*

Influencing 'Ambiance' through Materials

The materials used in urban spaces also influence the temperature experience – partly in line with the measurable facts and partly less so (also see section 2.3). In this context, especially the use of 'warm' materials such as bricks, sandstone, or wood is recommended. We do have to keep in mind that many of these materials store quite a lot of heat and increase the urban heat island effect (see section 2.1.1). It is therefore better to make well-balanced use of these materials and apply them in strategically important places, for instance places where many people see the materials. It is also better to avoid using materials with a cold appearance (steel, glass, concrete, marble, enamel, tiles) in outdoor spaces. These materials have a rather 'cold touch' in the temperate climate zones most times of the year. Yet, this last recommendation does not apply to areas with many people originating from for instance the Middle East or Southern Europe gather. They have a different perception of these materials, probably originating from the thermal behaviour of these materials in their warm home regions, and where these materials thus invoke a 'feeling' of thermal comfort.

163 *A 'warm', light combination of materials in Rotterdam, the Netherlands*

Influencing 'Ambiance' through Colours

Colours also have a big influence on the experience of 'cold' and 'warm' spaces. As indicated before, colour only has a limited physical effect on the temperature. That is why applying colours is a suitable way to invoke cool or warm microclimate associations. Changing the colours, for example by painting facades in a different colour, is often a relatively easy and inexpensive intervention to change the ambiance. You have to keep in mind, though, that manipulative use of colour is a very simple solution. Because the actual physical problem (like heat or wind) is not addressed, we have to see this as treatment of the symptoms, not as a structural solution. We also have to keep in mind that people from different cultural backgrounds have different associations with colours. The use of colours could address these associations.

164 *Light and 'warm' colour combination in apartment facades in Vienna, Austria*

7
The Future of Urban Climate Responsive Design

In this book, I've written about how special the weather in the city is and that cities have their own climates. Climate change will add to the warming of the urban climate in our cities in the temperate zone. This will intensify the problems with urban heat we already have. The climate affects the lives of many people living in cities. I have therefore described the influence the urban climate directly has on people. For this, I have used the concept of 'microclimate experience'. The microclimate experience primarily entails the experience of temperature, wind and ambiance. Urban design can be of influence on all these factors.

But before people start implementing design interventions, the urban climate has to be analysed at the scale of those interventions. This is very important, because the urban climate is different everywhere, depending on the city's location, the configuration of districts and open areas, of streets and buildings. The analyses and design interventions can be made for different scale levels. Generally speaking, air temperature and ventilation can be influenced on the larger scale; whereas sun and shadow, wind protection and ambiance can be influenced on a small-scale level. For all scale levels, this book offers many different solutions for influencing the urban climate. As you can see, many of these interventions aren't only good for the microclimate, but also for other important themes such as biodiversity, rainwater storage, energy conservation and aesthetic value. Therefore, integral designs are needed with climatological *and* other themes in mind.

I hope this book has shown that the urban climate is a fascinating combination of invisible processes around us, characterized by radiation, heat and dynamics. You will look at the city with new eyes! All these volatile and invisible processes are clear to you now. You don't only feel them but can 'see' them as well. With this knowledge, you can analyse many aspects of the urban climate yourself, without having to involve experts such as meteorologists. Making these analyses isn't just necessary, but exciting too, since it brings new insights and interesting challenges to address with innovative solutions. And finally, you can also start influencing the urban climate with the knowledge you've gained from this book. You have seen that we can design the urban climate to a great extent, and that there are numerous possibilities to do so. Because the interactions within the urban climate are unique for each location, every design for the urban climate is unique for each location as well. Even though there are many 'ephemeral' interactions in the urban climate, using urban climate responsive design can offer a 'common thread' in design processes. As the landscape architect Mathieu Derckx once said during a workshop on urban climate responsive design: 'The theme urban climate gives you something to hold on to. You can base designs on it and rationalize them with it.'

We are already facing problems with the urban climate now and these will only get worse in the future due to climate change. So, we should act now and adapt our cities to these problems. And everyone can contribute.

The government sector has much influence. Policymakers and cities can incorporate urban climate adaptation in their decision-making and make it part of their urban master plans or other large-scale plans. Municipal civil servants that co-design the structure of the city can incorporate urban climate adaptation in zoning schemes, embed it in design ordinances or building regulations, take it up in guidelines for public space planning or design competition briefs. In countries where the planning system does not offer such tools, they can still do a lot. This entails raising public awareness, stimulating bottom-up initiatives and creating incentives for homeowners, and housing and retail corporations.

Landscape architects, urban designers and designers of public space working for design agencies can also do much to foster implementation of adaptation measures. If the urban climate is a constant theme in their designs, it will naturally become part of the design of the city. Designing for the urban climate forms a new specialism for this group, which can bring in new commissions. Designers can also have a very important role as 'visualizers'. They can show how different our cities would look if they were adapted to the circumstances of the urban climate. Over the past few years, I have experienced the power of visualizations through my consulting work. I have worked often and intensively with municipalities and citizens on urban climate adaptation and have used visualizations frequently. Our designs and visualizations were always met with much enthusiasm, because they made the

165 *The world's first 'urban climate tree' was inaugurated in Arnhem in 2014*

166 *Professionals enthusiastically designing for the urban climate at a workshop*

'invisible' theme of the urban climate tangible. So, there is a potentially new field of work for many spatial designers here. And in economically uncertain times it can be a good investment to specialize yourself in this future-oriented theme of urban climate adaptation.

All the other people who also 'make the city', such as retail managers, shopkeepers' associations, the catering industry, neighbourhood councils and other civic interest groups, can also contribute by demanding urban climate adaptation measures from municipalities, designers and private owners. But these private owners can also start with urban climate adaptation in their own houses and gardens or their immediate urban environment. For instance, residents of the city of Arnhem and I have planted the world's first 'urban climate tree' – a tree on a bare square in their 'overheated' urban district. This tree has an ornate ring that indicates the role of trees in improving the urban climate. This way, the residents have not only improved the urban climate in their own neighbourhood, but they have also made a statement to raise awareness for it. And recently the entire square around the tree has been de-paved to make it even more microclimate responsive.

Last but not least, all future 'makers' of the city should of course also know something about the urban climate and its adaptation. All students in landscape architecture, urban design, public space design, city management and planning should be educated in this. To this end, the urban climate theme should be part of the curricula of many universities and universities of applied sciences. I am in the lucky position to have participated – and continue to do so – in the development of urban climate design courses for students and professionals for such institutions. We need to train more 'educators' in this topic in order to meet the growing interest in courses on urban climate adaptation.

It is my hope that this book helps all these people and institutions involved to make concrete steps in urban climate adaptation. To share all this knowledge about the urban climate in a practical and personal way, my team and I will happily keep giving lectures, seminars and design workshops. My dream is to form a *community of practice* with you, dear readers, in which we can work on improving the urban climate together and thus create comfortable cities!

Index

Recommended Literature

Bottema, M., *Wind climate and urban geometry*, Doctoral Thesis University of Eindhoven (Helmond: Wibro, 1993).

Boutet, T., *Controlling Air Movement: A Manual for Architects and Builders* (New York: McGraw-Hill ,1987).

Brown, R.D., *Design with Microclimate-The Secret to Comfortable Outdoor Space* (Washington D.C.: Island Press, 2010).

Brown, R.D. and Gillespie, T.J., *Microclimatic Landscape Design: Creating Thermal Comfort and Energy Efficiency* (New York: Wiley, 1995).

Erell, E., Pearlmutter, D., Williamson, T. J., *Urban Microclimate: Designing the Spaces Between Buildings* (Routledge, 2011).

Krautheim, M., Pasel, R., Pfeiffer, S., Schultz-Granberg, J., *City and Wind- Climate as an Architectural Instrument* (DOM, 2014).

Ng, E, Ren, C. (eds.) *The Urban Climatic Map- A Methodology for Sustainable Urban Planning* (Routledge, 2015).

Oke, T. R., Mills, G., Christen, A., & Voogt, J. A. *Urban climates* (Cambridge University Press, 2017).

Santamouris, M., *Energy And Climate in the Urban Built Environment* (Routledge, 2013).

Photographs and Figures Used in this Book

Illustration 7 Different angles of the sun in different parts of the world
(adapted from: Kunne, D., Floors, R., Meijer, L., Wolters, H.J., Sijbers, J., Elberse, J., Hageman, S., Linssen, G., Drummen, M., Vries, A. de, Klok, L., Brandsma, T. *Summer in the City : weersverschijnselen en luchtkwaliteit in de stad,* Wageningen 2010, 16)

Illustration 9 List of albedo, heat capacity and thermal conductivity of different materials (compiled from: Brown, R. D., Gillespie, T. J., *Microclimatic Landscape Design: Creating Thermal Comfort and Energy Efficiency,* New York: Wiley, 1995; Littlefair, P. J., *Environmental Site Layout Planning: Solar Access, Microclimate and Passive Cooling in Urban Areas*, London: CRC BRE Publications, 2000, pp. VIII; Oke, T. R., Mills, G., Christen, A., & Voogt, J. A. *Urban climates* , Cambridge University Press, 2017)

Illustration 11 Tropical night temperatures in The Hague, clearly showing the heat archipelago
(Koopmans, S., Ronda, R. J., Steeneveld, G. J., Holtslag, A. A. M., & Klein Tank, A. M. G. (2018). *Quantifying the effect of different urban planning strategies on heat stress for current and future climates in the agglomeration of The Hague (the Netherlands)*, Atmosphere, 9(9), 353. doi:10.3390/atmos9090353)

Illustration 12 Wind rose for Detroit City Airport during the autumn 2010 period
(Snyder, M., Arunachalam, S., , Isakov, V., Talgo K., Naess B, Valencia A, Omary M., Davis N., Cook R., Hanna, A., 2014, 'Creating Locally-Resolved Mobile-Source Emissions Inputs for Air Quality Modeling in Support of an Exposure Study in Detroit', in *Int. J. Environ. Res. Public Health* 2014, 11 (12), Figure 4)

Illustration 14 Valley wind systems during the day and at night
(adapted from: Liljequist, G.H., *Allgemeine Meteorologie*, Braunschweig: Friedrich Vieweg Verlag,1994)

Illustration 16 Profile of large-scale wind over open landscapes, woods or sparsely built-up areas and densely built-up cities
(adapted from: Bjerregaard, E. , Nielsen, F., 'Vindmiljø omkring bygninger', *SBI Anvisning* 128, Statens Byggeforskningsinstitut, 1981)

Illustration 17 In a wind tunnel, fine dust is blown around a building volume to see how the wind flows
(source unknown)

Illustration 18 Wind flows around a shelterbelt
(adapted from: Oke, T. R., *Boundary Layer Climates*, London: Methuen, 1987, p. 435, p. 245)

Illustration 19 Wind profiles for different types of groves
(adapted from: Robinette, G. O., MacClennon, C., *Landscape Planning for Energy Conservation*, New York: Van Nostrand Reinhold, 1983, p. 224, p. 35)

Illustrations 20-24 Wind flows around buildings
(adapted from: Blocken, B., Carmeliet, J., 2004, 'Pedestrian Wind Environment Around Buildings: Literature Review and Practical Examples', in *Journal of Thermal Envelope and Building Science* 28(2), 107-159)

Illustration 25 Diagram with different building depths and the expected sheltered areas at their leeside
(adapted from: Boutet, T., *Controlling Air Movement*, New York: Mc Graw Hill, 1987, figure 6.5/6.7)

Illustration 29 Wind flows in a building configuration
(Peutz Nederland, 2023)

Illustration 30 Profiles of the three wind regimes: skimming flow, wake interference and isolated roughness flow
(adapted from: Oke, T. R., *Boundary Layer Climates*, London: Methuen, 1987, 267)

Illustration 47 Climatope map of Piacenza, Italy
(student work by Francesca Ferrara, Diego Antonio Fuentes Solis, Rosaria Thea Cali, Virginia Delia Cornejo Díaz, Politecnico di Milano, 2022)

Illustration 48 Infrared photograph showing the surface temperatures in Arnhem, the Netherlands
(Municipality of Arnhem, 2009)

Illustration 49 Simulations for nighttime temperature differences
(MSc thesis Hao Yan, 2020)

Illustration 50 Example of a wind map
(student work by Francesca Ferrara, Diego Antonio Fuentes Solis, Rosaria Thea Cali, Virginia Delia Cornejo Díaz, Politecnico di Milano, 2022)

Illustration 51 Example of simulations of valley winds in Freiburg, Germany
(source unknown)

Illustration 52 Example of a local climate zone map generated with WUDAPT for Amsterdam
(Theeuwes, N., Steeneveld G.J., Sterenborg, G., Lenzholzer, S., Wageningen University, 2017)

Illustration 53 PET map for a part of the city of Arnhem
(Koopmans, S., Vreugdenhil, C. Steeneveld G.J., Lenzholzer, S., 2022)

Illustration 54 shadow map for a part of the city of Arnhem
(Koopmans, S., Vreugdenhil, C. Steeneveld G.J., Lenzholzer, S., 2022)

Illustration 55 Nocturnal valley wind map for a part of the city of Arnhem
(Koopmans, S., Vreugdenhil, C. Steeneveld G.J., Lenzholzer, S., 2022)

Illustration 57 Example of a vulnerability map: Piacenza, Italy
(student work by Francesca Ferrara, Diego Antonio Fuentes Solis, Rosaria Thea Cali, Virginia Delia Cornejo Díaz, Politecnico di Milano, 2022)

Illustration 66 Planning recommendations map Arnhem, the Netherlands
(Municipality of Arnhem)

Illustration 67 Analysis and recommendation maps for valley winds, forming a basis for zoning plans, Stuttgart, Germany
(Landeshauptstadt Stuttgart, Referat Städtebau und Umwelt, Amt für Stadtplanung und Stadterneuerung, Abteilung Städtebauliche Planung Mitte, *Rahmenplan Halbhöhenlagen*
2008, figures 5.02 and 10.06)

Illustration 74 Experimenting with kitchen salt in scale models
(Gert-Jan Steeneveld)

Illustration 75 A model of a city in the wind tunnel
(Peutz associés, Mook)

Illustration 76 Smoke simulations in the wind tunnel
(Peutz associés, Mook)

Illustration 77 CFD-wind simulations for a project in The Hague, the Netherlands
(Peutz associés, Mook)

Illustration 78 Envi-met®-simulation for the Nieuwe Mark, Breda
(UIA Green Quays project, Sytse Koopmans,)

Illustration 80 Measurement transects in Toronto with differences in air temperature (red) and solar radiation (blue)
(Graham Slater)

Illustration 84 Crowd state parameters map derived from mobile phone location data (from: Franke, T., Lukowicz, P. & Blanke, U. Smart crowds in smart cities: real life, city scale deployments of a smartphone based participatory crowd management platform. J Internet Serv Appl 6, 27 (2015). https://doi.org/10.1186/s13174-015-0040-6

Illustration 99 List of shadow depths of trees
(Brown, R.D. and Gillespie, T.J., *Microclimatic Landscape Design: Creating Thermal Comfort and Energy Efficiency*, New York: Wiley, 1995, 116)

Illustration 100 List of 'climate-proof' – mainly drought-tolerant – trees (Ravesloot et al. 2024, based on literature reviews, expert observations of morpho-physiological properties and their experiential knowledge)

Illustration 132 Street sprinklers in Lyon, France
(http://blogs.grandlyon.com/plan-climat/2012/12/19/ilots-de-chaleur-la-buire-teste-le-rafraichissement-urbain/)

Illustration 136 Densities of windbreaks and the sheltered effect behind them
(adapted from: Oke, T. R., *Boundary Layer Climates*, London: Methuen, 1987, 244)

Illustration 137 Windbreaks with different boarding and their effect on the wind patterns behind them
(adapted from: Boutet, T., *Controlling Air Movement*, New York: Mc Graw Hill, 1987, 79-81)

Illustration 138 Windbreaks of different heights, and angles and their wind speed reductions
(Dierickx, W., Gabriels, D., Cornelis, W. M., 2002, 'Wind Tunnel Study on Oblique Windscreens', in *Biosystems Engineering* 82(1), 87-95)

Illustration 151 Pergola with waterfall
(Yi Shan)

Illustration 157 Principle of groundwater-driven windscreen pillars
(Darius Reznek)

Illustration 158 An example of the wind energy bench
(Josje Hoefsloot)

Illustration 160 Example of a wind energy/cooling tower
(Niki Kampen, Anna Leiknes, Emmelie van Ommen, Jing Peng, Frank Wortelboer)

Illustration 161 Example of a photovoltaic shading roof
(David de Boer, Angeles Casares, Jian Long, Ulrika Palola, Juni Teigene)

Illustration 165 The alderman unveils the world's first 'urban climate tree' in Arnhem (Courtesy of Han Koppers)

Photos on introduction pages of chapters
Opening photo, Unsplash
2 Ryoji Iwata, Unsplash
3 Stock Exchange
4 Jorg Hackemann, Shutterstock.com
5 Shutterstock.com

All other photographs and illustrations: Sanda Lenzholzer and Landscape Architecture group, Wageningen University

Credits

Texts: Sanda Lenzholzer
Copy editing: Jean Tee, Leo Reijnen
Design: Ad van der Kouwe (Manifesta)
Printing: Veldhuis Media, Meppel
Lithography: PRDigitaal, Meppel
Publisher: Marcel Witvoet, nai010 publishers
Production: Sara Duisters, nai010 publishers

This publication was made possible by financial support from Wageningen University

nai010 publishers is an internationally orientated publisher specialized in developing, producing and distributing books in the fields of architecture, urbanism, art and design. www.nai010.com
nai010 books are available internationally at selected bookstores and from the following distribution partners:

North, Central and South America – Artbook | D.A.P., New York, USA, dap@dapinc.com

Rest of the world – Idea Books, Amsterdam, the Netherlands, idea@ideabooks.nl

For general questions, please contact nai010 publishers directly at sales@nai010.com or visit our website www.nai010.com for further information.

Printed and bound in The Netherlands

ISBN 978-94-6208-914-3
NUR 648, 950
BISAC ARC018000
THEMA AMV

Title (book) also available as e-book:
ISBN 978-94-6208-917-4 (e-book)